The Growing Trend of Living Small

This book examines the growing trend for housing models that shrink private living space and seeks to understand the implications of these shrinking domestic worlds. Small spaces have become big business. Reducing the size of our homes, and the amount of stuff within them, is increasingly sold as a catch-all solution to the stresses of modern life and the need to reduce our carbon footprint. Shrinking living space is being repackaged in a neoliberal capitalist context as a lifestyle choice rather than the consequence of diminishing choice in the face of what has become a long-term housing 'crisis'. What does this mean for how we live in the long term, and is there a dark side to the promise of a simpler, more sustainable home life? *Shrinking Domesticities* brings together research from across the social sciences, planning and architecture to explore these issues. From co-living developments to the Tiny House Movement, self storage units to practices of 'de-stuffification', and drawing on examples from across Europe, North America and Australasia, the authors of this volume seek to understand both what micro-living is bringing to our societies, and what it may be eroding.

Ella Harris is Leverhulme Early Career Fellow in Urban/Cultural Geography at Birkbeck, University of London, UK.

Mel Nowicki is a Reader in Urban Geography at Oxford Brookes University, UK.

Tim White is undertaking a PhD in Cities at the London School of Economics and Political Science, UK.

HOME
Series editors: Rosie Cox and Victor Buchli

This interdisciplinary series responds to the growing interest in the home as an area of research and teaching. The titles feature contributions from across the social sciences, including anthropology, material culture studies, architecture and design, sociology, gender studies, migration studies, and environmental studies. Relevant to students as well as researchers, the series consolidates the home as a field of study.

Food Identities at Home and on the Move
Explorations at the Intersection of Food, Belonging and Dwelling
Edited by Raúl Matta, Charles-Édouard de Suremain and Chantal Crenn

Ethnographies of Home and Mobility
Shifing Roofs
Alejandro Miranda Nieto, Aurora Massa and Sara Bonfanti

Globalising Housework
Domestic Labour in Middle-class London Homes, 1850–1914
Laura Humphreys

Home Improvement in Aotearoa New Zealand and the UK
Rosie Cox

Reading Home Cultures Through Books
Edited by Kirsti Salmi-Niklander and Marija Dalbello

The Growing Trend of Living Small
A Critical Approach to Shrinking Domesticities
Edited by Ella Harris, Mel Nowicki and Tim White

For more information about this series, please visit: www.routledge.com/Home/book-series/BLANTHOME

The Growing Trend of Living Small

A Critical Approach to Shrinking Domesticities

Edited by Ella Harris, Mel Nowicki and Tim White

Routledge
Taylor & Francis Group
LONDON AND NEW YORK

First published 2023
by Routledge
4 Park Square, Milton Park, Abingdon, Oxon OX14 4RN

and by Routledge
605 Third Avenue, New York, NY 10158

Routledge is an imprint of the Taylor & Francis Group, an informa business

British Library Cataloguing-in-Publication Data
A catalogue record for this book is available from the British Library

ISBN: 9780367764463 (hbk)
ISBN: 9781032001692 (pbk)
ISBN: 9781003173052 (ebk)

DOI: 10.4324/9781003173052

Typeset in Sabon
by Newgen Publishing UK

Contents

Contributors

Samuel Alexander is Director of the Simplicity Institute and the author of 20 books, including *Entropia: Life Beyond Industrial Civilisation* (2013), *Art Against Empire* (2017), *Degrowth in the Suburbs* (2019), and *Beyond Capitalist Realism* (2021). Most of his writing is available at samuelalexander.info.

Adam J. Barker is a Settler Canadian originally from the overlapping territories of the Haudenosaunee and Anishinaabe, near Hamilton, Ontario. He is currently a research assistant in the Department of Geography, University of Sheffield, UK. His work focuses on the production of settler colonial space and identity, processes of social change, and contemporary decolonization activism. Adam holds a PhD in Human Geography from the University of Leicester and an MA in Indigenous Governance from the University of Victoria (Canada). He is the author of *Making and Breaking Settler Space: Five Centuries of Colonization in North America* (Vancouver: University of British Columbia Press, 2021).

Tegan Bergan is a PhD candidate in the School of Social Sciences at Western Sydney University.

Frances Brill is Margaret Tyler Research Fellow in Geography, Girton College, University of Cambridge.

Clemens Driessen is Assistant Professor at the Cultural Geography Group of Wageningen University, the Netherlands, where he works with robots, pigs, cows, and ducks.

Rae Dufty-Jones is Associate Professor, Western Sydney University, Australia.

Daniel Durrant is a lecturer in Infrastructure Planning at UCL's Bartlett School of Planning and Alexander von Humboldt Fellow at Humboldt Universität zu Berlin's Integrative Research Institute on Transformations of Human-Environment Systems (IRI THESys).

Louisa Elbracht is Research Assistant, Department of Geography, University of Münster, Germany.

Megan Carras is Director of Institutional Giving.

Michael Friesenecker is a PhD researcher in Geography and a research assistant in Sociology at the University of Vienna.

Maximilian Krankl is an architect, currently working for Jadric Architects, Vienna.

Jeffrey Kruth is an urbanist and Assistant Professor at Miami University in Oxford, Ohio, USA. At Miami, he teaches courses on urban design history and theory and works closely with the Miami University Center for Community Engagement in Over-the-Rhine.

Johanna Lilius is Senior Scientist, Department of Architecture, Aalto University.

Petra Lütke is Substitute Professor, Department of Geography, University of Münster, Germany.

Manuel Lutz is a planner and political scientist interested in the transformations of housing and urban life. He works as a postdoc at The Institute for Urban Futures at the University of Applied Sciences Potsdam, Germany.

Pauline McGuirk is Senior Professor, School of Geography and Sustainable Communities, University of Wollongong. She is also Director, Australian Centre for Culture, Environment, Society and Space (ACCESS).

Miriam Meissner is Assistant Professor in Urban Studies, Faculty of Arts and Social Sciences, Maastricht University.

Jennifer Owen is Research Associate in King's College London.

Hilton Penfold is a PhD candidate, School of Geography and Sustainable Communities, University of Wollongong, Australian Centre for Culture, Environment, Society and Space (ACCESS).

Jenny Pickerill is Professor of Environmental Geography at the University of Sheffield, UK.

Heather Shearer is a Research Fellow at the Cities Research Institute, Griffith University, Queensland Australia.

Lauren Wagner is Associate Professor of Diasporic Mobilities in the Department of Society Studies at Maastricht University, the Netherlands, where, for research, she follows people on their holidays.

Gordon Waitt is Senior Professor, School of Geography and Sustainable Communities, University of Wollongong, Australian Centre for Culture, Environment, Society and Space (ACCESS).

Amy Jingjing Wang is currently a Teaching Associate at the University of Sheffield, School of Architecture. She completed and was awarded a PhD at the University of Sheffield. Her cross-disciplinary doctoral research is focusing on cohousing, community research and sustainability. She also had more than 5 years practice in international aging studies and interior design.

Alice Wilson is an ESRC-funded PhD researcher at the University of York.

Anne Hedegaard Winther is Process Advisor at Henning Larsen Architects.

Introduction

Over recent years in Western countries, there has been a growing trend for housing models that shrink private living space. This trend includes Tiny Housing – small, freestanding and often mobile structures, micro apartments – multi-unit developments where homes fall below minimum space standards, and co-living – for-profit, privately delivered and managed shared housing aimed at young professionals. These emerging typologies have been the subject of intense debate across academic, journalistic and policy circles. But the minimalisation of domestic life is not in and of itself new. For example, mobile homes have been a prominent feature of the residential landscape, particularly in the United States, for many years, while small living space has long been commonplace in East Asian megacities such as Tokyo and Hong Kong. Indeed, historically small and shared living is associated with anti-capitalist movements (e.g. Chatterton, 2016; Kamola & Meyerhoff, 2009), with, for example, the likes of Israel's Kibbutz movement and the 1960s and 70s squatting movements in Berlin and London based on non-hierarchical structures and principles of collective stewardship (Vasudevan, 2017).

Particularly over the past decade or so, however, the shrinking of domestic space has been increasingly tied to the housing crisis conditions emerging under neoliberalism. While set in train long before, the rise of small living arrangements has accelerated in the wake of the 2008 global financial crash and subsequent long-term austerity measures, collapse of the subprime mortgage market, escalating role of finance in housing and the growing disconnect between house prices and earnings. This has curtailed access to affordable, high-quality and secure housing – forcing ever more people to live in ever smaller residential units. The rise and normalisation of small housing has gone hand in hand with the rise of so-called 'Generation Rent' (Blunt & Dowling, 2006), referring to the growing proportion of young people excluded from homeownership and therefore spending increasing amounts of their lives in what is often an unregulated and precarious private rental sector. Within this sector, itself also prohibitively expensive, many have been pushed into shared living arrangements. While conventionally associated with those in search of short-term, cheap accommodation, transitioning between the parental home and independent housing, or seeking alternative

DOI: 10.4324/9781003173052-1

living models for political reasons, scholars have noted that sharing is now becoming a dominant housing form for urban singles in general, regardless of age, income or ideology (Druta et al., 2021; Heath et al., 2017). Whatever form it takes, this new surge in the shrinking of private domestic space raises profound questions about the role of housing in contemporary society – what it does, who it's for, how it's produced and experienced.

These transformations have not been equally distributed. The shrinking of domestic space has been felt most acutely by those already marginalised and excluded from housing markets – differentially experienced along the lines of class, race and gender. Whilst for the majority domestic space has shrunk, wealthy individuals and corporate interests have amassed ever more. The commodification of housing has been a key driver of this, enabling residential real estate to become a primary object of financial investment and speculation – a principle frontier for global finance capital perpetually on the hunt for yield (Aalbers, 2017; Madden & Marcuse, 2016; Rolnik, 2019). The increasing entry of finance into the housing sector has driven units ever smaller – as investors look to squeeze more value out of every inch. In this context, market actors, governments and individuals have sought housing 'solutions' that embrace the reduction of domestic space as an inevitable and desirable choice rather than the consequence of diminishing possibilities.

Increasingly entrepreneurial governments in Europe and North America, particularly at the city level, are complicit with this trend – with many now embracing and encouraging small housing models. This is because they align with a range of pressing agendas – not least the desperate need for (often cash-strapped) cities to increase housing supply – in addition to bolstering talent attraction and retention efforts, and even offering emergency housing solutions. Many authorities are therefore beginning to relax minimum space requirements, creating new zoning categories and entering into direct partnerships with micro-housing companies. In New York, for example, the Department of Housing Preservation and Development has partnered with co-living companies to produce 'affordable' housing (Plitt, 2019). The city of Los Angeles is developing tiny house 'villages' for the homeless (Walker, 2021). In London (UK), the mayor's office recently launched a major initiative with micro-living company Pocket Living (Mayor of London, 2017). So shrinking domesticities are gaining traction and support at an institutional and legislative level.

Shrinking domesticities are also being attached to new imaginaries and ideals within popular culture. Housing models like micro apartments, Tiny Housing and co-living have emerged alongside television shows like *Tidying Up with Marie Kondo*, spearheading the promotion of 'de-stuffification', or the prioritisation of experiences over material goods. The Tiny House movement has itself quickly become a media sensation, with HGTV's Tiny House programming reaching an average of 5 million viewers per week in 2016 (Shafrir, 2016), while The Minimalists have built something of a cultural empire through their website, podcast, book deals and Netflix films. Global brands like Ikea now offer a range of products specifically for small living spaces, and a brief browse on online marketplaces such as Etsy reveals a myriad of tiny living merchandise, including T-shirts celebrating freedom from materialism. Tiny home cultures are therein subsumed into, while ostensibly being pitched against, consumerism. The shrinking of domestic space is now beginning to establish mainstream ideological legitimacy – framed as offering a host of individual and society-level benefits, from affordability and sustainability to freedom and flexibility. Meanwhile, while across popular culture, media and politics, these new forms of domesticity are celebrated, others are stigmatised as problematic and regressive. In opposition to small housing like the UK's 'beds-in-sheds' or mobile homes in the United States – presented as unequivocally problematic (Harris & Nowicki, 2020) – new forms of small housing are positioned as a solution to, rather than symbol of, urban inequalities. But the promises of these emerging sectors are dubious even for wealthy consumers of micro-living, arguably representing a middle class forced to reimagine what constitutes aspirational housing.

Shrinking domesticities can, however, represent genuinely progressive, emancipatory and even subversive modes of dwelling. The role of housing in climate change – from material construction, to day-to-day energy consumption, to broader questions of urban morphology – is now widely recognised. There is an urgent need for housing models that allow for a more balanced relationship between humans and the environment, and smaller units could play a key role in this. Some tiny house variations (e.g. eco-cabins) are indeed explicitly designed with ecological impact in mind – promoting the minimisation of material consumption and resource usage through, for example, adaption, recycling and reuse. Collective housing models like cooperatives and co-housing – citizen-led initiatives geared around co-responsibility, co-production, reciprocity and stewardship – can represent genuine alternatives to the residential status quo beyond market logic. Such forms of dwelling can also offer alternatives to the heteronormativity and mononormativity associated with homeownership and the nuclear family. Tiny homes have even been directly used as strategies for political protest. In British Columbia, for example, the activist group Tiny House Warriors constructed tiny homes in an effort to strategically block the expansion of a pipeline running from Alberta's oil sands to the Pacific coast (Kassam, 2020). As this book seeks to demonstrate, the issue of shrinking domesticities is therefore not solely one of size, but of power, choice and agency.

The Book's Conceptual Contribution

Whilst there is increasing interest in the implications of shrinking domesticities among academics, particularly in the social sciences, architecture and planning, there are to date no publications that bring together debates regarding this emerging phenomenon. This book seeks to plug this gap, serving as the first edited collection to collate a substantial set of critiques and analyses of shrinking domestic space from a wide range of geographical contexts and disciplinary perspectives. Together the collection examines a spectrum of manifestations of shrinking domesticities and the politics they engender, from London, to New York, to Helsinki – with contributions across sociology, urban studies, geography and cultural studies. In addition to its scholarly and disciplinary breadth, the book also covers a wide array of methodologies for examining shrinking domestic space – from auto-ethnography to policy analysis. In so doing, it crucially brings into dialogue lived experience and political economy approaches to this phenomenon.

Moreover, as small living spaces become a growing feature of urban landscapes and housing systems, the task of this book is to take a critical lens to them. Through in-depth examinations of their causes, consequences and potentials, the book seeks to demonstrate how shrinking domesticities are politically mediated and produced with implications for inequality and injustice. In particular, the contributions confront the contradictory and ambivalent nature of shrinking domesticities. They demonstrate how, in some ways, these housing models can empower communities, providing alternatives to rigid housing structures and the privileging of the family home, while also in places promoting mutual support and civic engagement. Shrinking domesticities can enable subversive and radical ways of living – encouraging environmental consciousness, challenging normative housing trajectories and alleviating individuals from wage labour. But they also show how, in other ways, beneath the guise of virtuous environmentalism and sociability, they can legitimise squeezing profit out of ever-smaller units and extract market opportunities from – while reinforcing – precaritisation, gentrification and dispossession. These contradictions show how the phenomenon of shrinking domestic space is not a clearly delineated, singular process, but is enrolled in, and inseparable from, all sorts of contexts, politics and understandings.

The issue of shrinking domestic space is of heightened importance in the context of COVID-19. It is now well established that substandard and cramped living conditions substantially increase the risk of transmission, and we have seen some of the highest infection rates among disadvantaged communities for whom overcrowding is known to be an issue (see, for example, Butler, 2020). The size of living space and comfort of possessions have also attained new value in lives led largely at home. People have been forced to add unexpected dimensions to their homes – transforming them into offices and schools, entertainment venues and gyms. Lacking space in this context has been shown to have detrimental impacts on people's mental and physical health. Meanwhile, the economic aftermath of the pandemic may ensure that for all but the most privileged, domestic space will continue to shrink. While COVID-19 may entrench and reinforce the injustices associated with shrinking domesticities, it can also be used as an opportunity to contest, rethink and reset these structural flaws. It is therefore a pertinent time to bring scholars across the world together to understand the implications of shrinking domesticities.

The shrinking of domestic space is most explicit in its urban manifestations – a product of intersecting processes such as financialisation, flexibilisation, precaritisation and densification. For this reason, the vast majority of contributions in this collection focus on the phenomenon as it is emerging in cities. However, as several chapters show, the shrinking of domestic space is also occurring – albeit in different ways and driven by different social and cultural factors – in rural contexts. The Tiny House movement, for example, is largely speaking positioned as a rural phenomenon – associated with Thoreauvian images of living simply and in sync with nature, away from the stresses of urban environments (Harris & Nowicki, 2020).

In sum, the aim of this collection is to understand the implications of our shrinking domestic worlds, with specific focus on the following:

1 The political economic context giving rise to shrinking domesticities;
2 How shrinking living space is narrativised and marketed by developers, governments and other stakeholders;
3 The everyday experiences of life in shrinking domestic space;
4 The intersections between shrinking domestic space and environmental sustainability;
5 Alternative, anti-capitalist housing models centred around living small.

In addressing these issues, the book provides new insights in terms of how we might research and conceptualise this increasingly prominent feature of our housing systems – grappling with its complexities and developing analytical frames to engage with its futures. It prompts us to consider how the destructive impacts of this phenomenon can be minimised and its progressive potential realised. In the remainder of the introduction, we highlight the key themes and discussions running through the book.

Overview of Sections

The chapters in Part I, *Politicising Shrinking Domesticities*, dissect the political economy of micro-dwelling, linking it to neoliberal policy priorities and considering how companies pushing these new models navigate housing systems. First, Bergan and Dufty-Jones' chapter examines the 'servitisation' of domestic space in the co-living sector. They consider how this has enabled providers in New York City to thrive under the institutionally precarious circumstances catalysed by the COVID-19 pandemic. In so doing, they reveal shifting power relations between cities and market actors in the production of shrinking domesticities. Second, Kruth situates micro-dwelling within the politics of regeneration in downtown Cincinnati, making links between real estate development and the displacement of African American and low-income residents. Finally, Lilius, Friesenecker and Krankl's chapter examines the production of shrinking domesticities in Helsinki and Vienna – cities associated with highly interventionist approaches to housing – arguing that current policies do little to prevent developers from building smaller units in order to increase profits.

Together these contributions shed light on the relationship between shrinking domesticities and political structures and processes. They not only show how cities are often key agents in producing and facilitating shrinking domesticities– but also reveal the limits of government power in the present context of economic transformation. In so doing, they help us consider how authorities can redirect focus in order to provide more socially just, inclusive forms of domestic space.

Part II, *Narrativising Shrinking Domesticities*, deconstructs the discourses and imaginaries being used to justify and promote shrinking domesticities – the reframing of small housing as positive and inevitable. First, Durrant and Brill consider the form of domesticity offered by London's new Build-to-Rent market – arguing that such housing models are shrinking the domestic aspirations of tenants. Their findings challenge industry narratives (e.g. flexibility, empowerment) that often accompany developments. Second, Owen examines the material movements, services and aesthetics being used to rebrand micro-living as a lifestyle choice rather than a limitation of choice, arguing that these obscure the structural causes and unequal realities of shrinking domestic space. Finally, the editors' contribution analyses the film *Nomadland* to consider how freedom is construed in relation to small, mobile domestic space. Discussing representations of labour, mobility and 'stuff' in the film, we argue that while life on the road brings with it possibilities for individual liberation, it can just as easily represent dispossession and constraint.

Through the contributions in this section, we can see how housing conditions previously deemed unacceptable are reconstrued under present political economic conditions. New ideologies are being born for small living space – from the ability to follow a passion or hobby, to living affordably or flexibly, to living in common with others – pushed by states, private actors and participants. The sharer or micro-liver is reimagined in parallel with new market and spatial reconfigurations, producing alternative residential ideals. But, as these chapters demonstrate, it's important to look beyond the seductive appeal of these narratives and remain attentive to what such housing models restrict and foreclose, and what conditions they exploit and perpetuate.

Part III, *Experiencing Shrinking Domesticities*, departs from examining the rise of micro-dwelling – problematising its politics and imaginaries – to exploring shrinking domesticities 'on the ground': the experiences and rationales of those inhabiting the spaces. First, Winther's study of people living in compact spaces in Denmark reveals that, when spatially restricted in this way, households seek to realise residential ideals that compensate for the size of their homes: comfort, functionality and aesthetics. Second, drawing on governmentality theory, Carras makes parallels between motivations for adopting the Tiny Home Lifestyle in the United States and a wider climate of economic uncertainty. Third, Penfold, Waitt and McGuirk use an urban political ecology framework to understand how flows of water, energy and food are integrated into everyday domestic practices in order to sustain tiny house domesticities in Australia – arguing that governments need to take a more active role in enabling their sustainability. Finally, drawing on ethnographic research in shared Airbnb properties – observing the mundane negotiations of occupying such spaces – Wagner and Clemens explore how contemporary practices of home sharing are reformulating the ways in which we consider homes to be our own.

The chapters in this section highlight the implications of small and shared domestic space as lived and embodied – who is opting into these housing models, why, and how the spaces are experienced on a day-to-day basis. In so doing, they offer insights into the ways in which homes are made and unmade at these diminished scales – from trust, belonging, negotiation and conflict to identity formation and sociality – while crucially drawing parallels between these experiences and broader political economic circumstance. We see how, at times, shrinking domesticities challenge established meanings of home (e.g. long-term, fixed, stable) and homemaking, for example, blurring the lines between private and common, work and leisure – potentially resulting in the construction of new domestic identities and materialities.

Part IV, *Sustainable Shrinking Domesticities*, turns towards the potential of shrinking domesticities in driving and supporting ecological change. First, Meissner asks whether the minimalist lifestyles associated with micro-dwelling have the potential to act as a cultural stepping-stone towards a post-growth politics. She argues that minimalists should join degrowthers in the collective struggle for social institutions that overcome reification and extractivism. Second, Shearer and Alexander consider how the tiny house movement may encourage a progressive 'expanded domesticity' through an economics of sufficiency as more households seek to escape the market and build new autonomous household and community economies. However, they argue this is constrained by the fact that, for many, this way of living is a response to harsh socio-economic circumstances rather than an active choice. Finally, Lütke and Elbracht confront the tension between an accelerating per capita consumption of living space on the one hand, and the growing popularity of tiny houses on the other. In this context, they consider the potential of tiny housing as a 'sufficient everyday practice', reshaping consumption practices and changing how households perceive sustainability in relation to the domestic.

The contributions in this section shine a more optimistic light on the possibilities of shrinking domesticities – making the case that reducing the size of living space is an important social and material practice towards environmental sustainability. They demonstrate the desperate need for housing models that significantly reduce consumption. At the same time, however, they suggest that this cannot be done in isolation, and we must push for a political environment in which such every day, small-scale sustainability practices are met with broader changes in social and environmental relations.

Finally, Part V, *Alternative Shrinking Domesticities*, considers the radical potential of alternative micro-dwelling arrangements within housing systems. First, Pickerill, Barker and Wang examine a spectrum of tiny homes, from hyper-neoliberal 'jewel box' homes at one end, to eco-homes at the other, to consider which are effective at promoting social justice and which are not. They conclude by arguing that the community must drive the appropriate use of tiny homes if they are to be successful in this aim. Second, Lutz interrogates the transformative potential of cluster apartments in German-speaking countries – asking whether this genre of shared housing will become just another elite subsector, or could in fact enable a form of lived solidarity while fulfilling the need for affordable, ecological, diverse and accessible housing. Finally, Wilson uses the concept of heterotopia to examine the case of female-led tiny house developments, arguing that expanding the legal availability of tiny houses could support a number of important social justice and human rights matters – especially women's health, safety, wealth and education.

This closing section demonstrates how small homes, both in their physical structure and the residential practices they encourage, could and should be part of the quest for housing justice – used to enact social, economic, political and environmental change. Crucially, however, they argue that this can only happen under the right structural conditions. They therein push for a politicised understanding of shrinking domesticities that champions its radical potential while pushing back against its exploitative, extractive, regressive and normative tendencies under neoliberal capitalism. This captures the ethos and purpose of the collection as a whole.

References

Aalbers, M. (2017). The variegated financialization of housing. *International Journal of Urban and Regional Research*, 41(4), 542–554. doi:10.1111/1468-2427.12522

Blunt, A. & Dowling, R. (2006). *Home*. London: Routledge.

Butler, P. (2020). Poor housing linked to high Covid-19 death rate in London borough. *The Guardian*. Retrieved from: www.theguardian.com/world/2020/aug/17/poor-housing-linked-high-covid-19-death-rate-london-borough-brent

Chatterton, P. (2016). Building transitions to post-capitalist urban commons. *Transactions of the Institute of British Geographers*, 41, 403–415. https://doi.org/10.1111/tran.12139

Druta, O., Ronald, R. & Heath, S. (2021). Urban singles and shared housing. *Social & Cultural Geography*, 22(9), 1195–1203, doi:10.1080/14649365.2021.1987507

Harris, E. & Nowicki, M. (2020). "GET SMALLER"? Emerging geographies of micro-living. *Area*, 52(3), 591–599.

Heath, S., Davies, K., Edwards, G., & Scicluna, R. (2017). *Shared housing, shared lives: Everyday experiences across the lifecourse*. London: Routledge.

Kamola, I. & Meyerhoff, E. (2009). Creating commons: Divided governance, participatory management, and struggles against enclosure in the university. *Polygraph*, 21, 5–27.

Kassam, A. (2020). 'Our land is our home': Canadians build tiny homes in bid to thwart pipeline. *The Guardian*. Retrieved from: www.theguardian.com/world/2018/may/08/canadian-activists-pipeline-tiny-homes-british-columbia

Madden, D. & Marcuse, P. (2016). *In defense of housing*. New York, NY: Verso.

Mayor of London. (2017). *Mayor invests in more than 1,000 'Pocket homes' for first-time buyers*. Retrieved from: www.london.gov.uk/press-releases/mayoral/sadiq-invests-25m-in-pocket-homes

Plitt, A. (2019). NYC to partner with co-living start-ups to create affordable housing. *Curbed New York*. Retrieved from: https://ny.curbed.com/2019/10/9/20906545/nyc-affordable-apartments-co-living-common

Rolnik, R. (2019). *Housing under the empire of finance: Urban warfare*. London: Verso Books.

Shafrir, D. (2016). Who benefits from the tiny house revolution? *Buzzfeed*. Retrieved from: www.buzzfeednews.com/article/doree/who-is-the-tiny-house-revolution-for

Vasudevan, A. (2017). *The autonomous city: A history of urban squatting*. London: Verso.

Walker, A. (2021). L.A. Built a Tiny-House Village for Homeless Residents, and Some Aren't So Sure About It. *Curbed*. Retrieved from: https://www.curbed.com/2021/04/tiny-home-village-homeless-los-angeles.html

Part I

Politicising Shrinking Domesticities

1 Co-living Housing-as-a-Service and COVID-19

Micro-housing and Institutional Precarity

Tegan Bergan & Rae Dufty-Jones

Introduction

Emerging during the late-2000s in response to technological, economic, socio-cultural and demographic changes, co-living housing is a 'commodified form of shared housing catering to knowledge economy labourers' (Bergan et al., 2021, p.1205). While the physical structures of co-living vary, there are key characteristics that define this type of micro-housing. First, co-living is generally run by commercial operators. Second, co-living tends to be concentrated in downtown areas of global cities,[1] and is predominantly marketed to 'digital nomads' (von Zumbusch & Lalicic, 2020). Last, common across the housing type is reduced private space. Significantly, the shrinking of private domestic space provided is marketed to residents as being compensated by the provision of 'all-inclusive' services. The services provided typically include fully furnished living spaces in a central location (to reduce the burdens of moving); flexible subscription-style access; a community of like minded roommates (screened and managed by the organisation); networking and social events; internet access; cleaning and maintenance etc. Exemplifying the success of the co-living 'Housing-as-a-Service' (HaaS) business model has been the sector's rapid development over the past decade into a multi-billion-dollar industry (Serbaniewicz, 2018).

In this chapter, we contend co-living housing – and, more broadly, the international trend of shrinking domesticities – should be understood as part of the wider trend of servitisation in the platform-sharing economy particularly, the rise of 'Everything-as-a-Service' (XaaS) business models (Richardson, 2021; Dishotsky, 2016). We advance this argument through our analysis of how the range of regulatory constraints introduced at the national, state, and municipal levels of New York City (NYC) in response to the COVID-19 pandemic created an environment of institutional precarity for the city's co-living sector. We find that, despite the uncertainty created by COVID-19 pandemic, NYC's co-living HaaS model enabled these businesses to not only survive but also consolidate their position within the city's real estate industry and housing market.

DOI: 10.4324/9781003173052-3

New York City, Co-living Housing, and COVID-19

From a market perspective, co-living is routinely presented as an 'innovative' or 'disruptive' housing product. For consumers/tenants, co-living is argued to provide a comparatively affordable form of housing (Pepper & Manji, 2019). Because of this, co-living has been promoted as a solution to housing affordability (for a critique of see Bergan et al., 2021 and Harris & Nowicki, 2020). Despite the premium fit-outs synonymous with co-living housing, when compared to traditional types of multi-dwelling housing, co-living is also argued to reduce overall construction costs (Cleaver & Frearson, 2021; Pepper & Manji, 2019). The commercial viability for co-living businesses is increased by offsetting the reduced physical space with access to bespoke in-house services that are included in a flexible daily, weekly, or monthly subscription-fee. The business model of bundling services and subscription-style access is commonly known as 'Everything-as-a-Service' (we will return to the XaaS business model in the next section of this chapter).

Initial investment in co-living housing was driven by the ready supply of vacant office spaces in downtown districts in global cities immediately after the Great Recession, low global interest rates, high-levels of available capital, and the idea that co-living could offer a solution to housing affordability crises. Despite the headline-making investments and rapid expansion of co-living businesses (or perhaps because of these), by 2019 questions were being raised about the sustainability of the housing type. As Pepper and Manji (2019, p. 3) argued, co-living was a 'nascent' real estate type yet to prove its long-term sustainability.

In 2020, the sector was put to the test by the SARS-CoV-2 virus. The World Health Organisation's March 11, 2020, declaration that COVID-19 had reached 'pandemic' proportions catalysed the introduction of wide-reaching institutional responses. To control the spread of the virus, governments around the world introduced a range of regulatory measures including 'stay-at/work-from-home' orders, social distancing mandates, travel bans, and quarantine requirements. The raft of COVID-19-related restrictions created unforeseen and unprecedented risks to the commercial viability of the co-living industry (Coliving Hub, 2020). Indeed, in the first year of the pandemic, some co-living businesses closed down.[2] However, the speculative fears that the entire industry would fold never materialised. By the end of 2020, media outlets were again reporting that the industry in North American cities was *booming* (Hirschfeld, 2021; Lia, 2020; Park, 2020; Purdon, 2020; Velsey, 2021; Magistretti, 2020; Zaleski, 2020; Tjarksen et al., 2020).

However, the question of how the sector not only *survived* the catastrophic impacts of the COVID-19 pandemic but seemingly *thrived* in these conditions remains unanswered. To investigate this, we conducted a thematic analysis of the web-based communications (websites and blogs) from ten co-living businesses with operations in NYC from March 11 to July 11,

2020. NYC was selected as a case study site because it has been a key location for the establishment of co-living dwellings since the industry's inception (see Bergan., 2021 for more detail on the history of co-living in NYC). Furthermore, during the pandemic, NYC – usually an epicentre of economic and cultural activity – became an epicentre of COVID-19 infections and deaths. These circumstances placed extreme pressure on governments and co-living housing providers to respond, which they did with alacrity and success. Integral to the successful adaptation of NYC's co-living housing sector to the challenges of the COVID-19 pandemic was the industry's HaaS business model.

Co-living 'Housing-as-a-Service'

Led by technology-based companies such Amazon, IBM, and Microsoft, XaaS businesses – as we know them today – emerged around 20 years ago, providing subscription-style access to a product *and* associated services. However, the XaaS business model has a longer history. Offering subscription-style access to services provided by large infrastructures emerged during the 19th and 20th centuries. Principally, this was used as a way of recouping some of the significant costs associated with the development and maintenance of public urban infrastructures (e.g. water, gas, electricity) required to facilitate processes of urbanisation and industrialisation during this time (O'Neill, 2010). The revival of the XaaS business model has been facilitated in part through the development of ubiquitous and faster internet connections and other technologies. According to Kalagas (2019),

> The 'as-a-service' terminology has since evolved into generalised shorthand for moves away from simply selling products to providing bundled services (and locking in recurring revenue). Increasingly, this means combining physical and digital systems, developing integrated platforms to support two-way engagement, and leveraging data to understand how products and services are consumed, to continually improve and personalise customer experience.

The rise of aftermarkets as a way of securing ongoing revenues for products after consumption (Warren & Gibson, 2021), and the range of digital technologies and platforms that have enabled the shift to 'servitisation' as a business model (Vandermerwe & Rada, 1988), have provided fertile ground for the (re)development of XaaS businesses. Co-living is one example of the ever-expanding range of XaaS businesses. More specifically, co-living is part of a range of 'Space-as-a-Service' (SPaaS) businesses – such as WeWork, AirBnB, etc. – that developed after the Great Recession (Marom, 2019; Richardson, 2021; Dishotsky, 2016). Part of the value in XaaS businesses is the 'convenience of frictionless access to services, versus the burden of owning and maintaining tangible property' that it offers customers (Kalagas, 2019; c.f. Schaefers et al., 2016). Pepper and Manji (2019, p.34) observed that it was the ability of co-living 'Space[/Housing]-as-a-Service' businesses in alleviating the 'burden of ownership' associated with housing as being pivotal to the success of the sector:

> Co-living builds on ... [the] convenience [of traditional renting] ... by offering features like lumping the rent, internet, and utility bills into one monthly payment. Most also offer weekly or bi-weekly cleaning, provide furniture for the units, and supply certain other household items. These make the move-in and move-out process simple, reduce potential friction between residents, and further reduces the number of household chores residents need to do themselves.

Drawing on Bergan et al. (2021), we identify three main housing 'services' that co-living operators offer: mobility, workplace, and community. Co-living businesses provide *mobility* as-a-service by offering subscription-style access to 'move-in-ready', fully furnished accommodation on flexible, short-term leases, with dwellings in multiple locations. By constructing co-living housing 'as-a-mobility-service', operators coordinate the provision of physical elements of housing (furniture, location) in a way that smooths the mobilities of digital nomads. Co-living also provides *workspace* as-a-service, marketing a range of tangible and intangible business services to residents. Tangible workspace services include high-speed Wi-Fi, Skype/Zoom spaces, podcast studios, etc. Intangible business services marketed include inspiration, success, and 'boundless' opportunities (Bergan et al., 2020). Last, co-living housing providers advertise *community* as-a-service to residents. Related to the mobility of its target market, providers promote these services in terms of screening, curating, and managing subscribers' roommates/community. Operators promote 'community' services as a way for subscriber-tenants to address issues of 'loneliness' and 'isolation' that come with frequent moves. Co-living providers do this by creating conditions for social connection to be formed between subscriber-tenants through a range of services including organising social events, providing networking opportunities, developing 'house rules' to smooth roommate relations and reduce subscriber-tenant conflicts, and in the purposeful design of co-living communal spaces, constructed to facilitate 'incidental' social interactions.

As outlined earlier, NYC co-living housing business were significantly disrupted through the introduction of regulatory measures by various levels of government in response to COVID-19. The restrictions imposed on NYC co-living providers created an unprecedented institutionally precarious environment for these businesses. We use the term institutional precarity to explore how contemporary issues of precarity are not only a product of market-based interactions. For instance, as Bergan et al. (2021) identified, co-living housing emerged out of the precarious economic conditions created by the Great Recession in the late 2000s. Notably, co-living housing provided a solution for the real estate industry and the state to develop a spatial fix around the twin issues of empty commercial spaces and housing supply. Extending this work, we show that co-living housing can also be understood as a product of institutional precarity. That is, precarity is also a product of the regulatory environments that seek to govern individuals, communities, and markets. The concept of institutional precarity helps demonstrate how the governance of housing is relational, uneven, and contingent. Institutions (which can include state or private entities or individuals involved in the governance of housing) can mediate, entrench, and diffract precarity through, for example, expanding or rescinding regulatory measures and/or funding, enforcing or failing to enforce legislation.

Significantly, while some co-living businesses closed because of these institutionally precarious conditions, other NYC co-living operators strategically used the COVID-19 regulations to adapt their bundle of housing services. In the sections that follow, we examine the specific ways in which the HaaS business model enabled NYC co-living providers to rapidly adjust to this institutionally precarious environment. Enabling operators to repurpose their bundle of core housing 'services' – mobility, workspace, and community – consolidated this nascent sector within the wider real estate industry.

Co-living Housing-as-a-Mobility-Service under COVID-19

The capacity of NYC co-living operators to sell mobility as part of their HaaS business model was undermined by a range of travel restrictions and quarantine requirements introduced to reduce the spread of COVID-19. The COVID-19 pandemic exposed the fragility and contingency of co-living as a mobility infrastructure – disrupting the sector's ability to 'smooth' international labour mobilities through domestic services (see Cresswell & Martin, 2012 for a theoretical framing of mobility infrastructures as always-contingent). While international travellers had been restricted since January 31, 2020, on June 25, 2020, New York introduced a complex set of reporting, testing, and quarantine requirements for domestic travellers entering the state (Cuomo, 2020). Anyone entering New York State who had been in a state with high infection rates for over 24 hours were required to self-quarantine for 14 days. This essentially meant that anyone entering from 'any state that doesn't border New Jersey or Connecticut [was] subject to quarantine' (Whitmore, 2020). Those required to quarantine needed to do so in accommodation that adhered to strict standards to minimise the risk of spreading the virus to other household members and the wider community (New York State Department of Health, 2020). For instance, quarantine accommodation needed to provide each individual the capacity to self-quarantine from household members if symptoms developed, meaning a separate room with a separate door and a separate bathroom. Further, quarantine accommodation needed to provide a range of additional services such as food delivery, hygiene and cleaning supplies, and systems for monitoring quarantining individuals for symptoms.

The combined effects of travel restrictions and quarantine accommodation requirements challenged the HaaS business model by undermining the value of the mobility services operators sold. Housing that facilitated mobility for digital nomads was no longer needed as people were not travelling in the same ways. As Naito (2021), CEO of Anyplace, observed '... the impact of the coronavirus was such that people stopped traveling and, instead, moved out of the cities, which greatly reduced revenues.' Furthermore, the high ratio of shared space relative to personal space that made co-living housing so profitable before 2020 meant that co-living housing operators had to reduce their tenant numbers to meet higher requirements around quarantine accommodation, or simply not offer quarantine accommodation. Both options posed a risk to profit and demand for co-living businesses (Zaleski, 2020).

Despite these challenges, co-living providers in NYC responded to these institutionally precarious circumstances by deftly turning their HaaS business model to accommodate these new conditions. One way this was achieved was by pivoting away from the digital nomad as its primary target market towards healthcare workers who, because of COVID-19, emerged as a new cohort of short-term mobile labourers in need of flexible housing services. At the height of the pandemic, healthcare workers were mobilised from all over the United States and sent to New York (OECD, 2020). In response, NYC co-living providers adapted their HaaS to accommodate the specific needs of healthcare workers – targeting this cohort in their advertising (Common, 2020a, 2020b; Outpost Club, 2020b). For example, Common (2020a) sought to attract transient health workers by providing them a $500 Uber voucher to cover their transport to and from work, incorporating the advice from the NYC Mayor for healthcare workers to avoid public transport. Similarly, Outpost Club (2020b) dedicated an entire co-living dwelling to travelling healthcare workers:

> If you're a traveling nurse or other healthcare worker, we've set aside dedicated housing for you...We take care of everything you need as a traveling nurse or healthcare professional. You're providing a vital service to our city and we want to make it as easy as possible to get here and get started without having to worry about navigating Airbnb or complicated lease terms.

Outpost also offered reduced costs for this cohort. However, this was really just providing 'HaaS-lite' as some usual services were excluded to keep the cost down. NYC co-living providers therefore nimbly responded to COVID-19 travel restrictions and quarantine accommodation requirements, adapting to the reduced digital nomad demand for their HaaS products by offering a new version of co-living targeted at healthcare workers. Meanwhile, other co-living providers have predicted that a long-term impact of the pandemic will be an increase in digital nomads, and an overall increase in the demand for co-living housing in locations beyond traditional global cities (Naito, 2021). This essentially points to a re-energising of the conditions that gave rise to the industry; increasing prevalence of digital communication technologies, a growing cohort of mobile gig-economy labourers, and high levels of available stock – such as underutilised hostels and office spaces in downtown, regional, and remote areas.

Co-living Housing-as-a-Workspace-Service under COVID-19

The COVID-19 pandemic saw many co-living providers rework their existing housing-as-a-workspace services. On March 22, 2020, New York enacted a 'stay-at-home[3]' order, known as 'New York State on PAUSE'. Overnight, residents were instructed to work from home, and permitted to leave their dwellings only for 'essential' activities. The stay-at-home orders and social distancing guidelines introduced a type of institutional precarity that challenged providers' all-inclusive business model of offering a workspace. With tenants residing in co-living spaces 24/7, the increased risks of infection and disharmony between residents were heightened. However, the co-living housing sector used the institutional precarity of COVID-19 and the risks these regulations posed to the sector's workspace services by adapting its HaaS in response to these circumstances.

Despite COVID-19, the sector retained its focus on offering productive workspaces to its subscriber-tenants, albeit with new spatial, social, and temporal arrangements that responded to the unique pressures of working from home during the pandemic. For example, in their promotional materials, NYC co-living provider Cohabs (2020a) stated that

> ... whether you're working from home or are simply germophobic our new homes are made for you.

Cohabs (2020b) also advertised that, in response to COVID-19 restrictions, they had 'tweaked' their spaces – such as having larger communal areas, and configuring lounge rooms into work spaces – to offer 'a more comfortable connected-workspace'. In addition to reconfiguring their shared spaces to accommodate residents working from their co-living homes, NYC providers also responded to the 'working-from-home' impacts by digitising their career workshops mentoring services (Ollie, 2020a, 2020b; OpenDoor, 2020; Outsite, 2020b; Starcity, 2020; The Collective, 2020c; WeLive, 2020). For example, The Collective (2020b) ran an online workshop for maximising the impact of Instagram stories for businesses with 'future females'.

Last, providers responded to the potential negative impacts of working from home on their co-living businesses by developing new housing cultures around 'considerate' working from home practices. Subjectivities around considerate working from home practices were introduced and developed through a range of guides designed and distributed by co-living providers. For example, Outpost (2020c) published its guide on 'Tips for working from home with roommates', and Common (2020d) created, 'The ultimate guide to social distancing with roommates'. Guidance on considerate working from home practices included advising tenants to take their zoom calls in bedrooms to minimise disruptions to roommates working in communal areas.

The rapid reconfiguration of co-living HaaS workspace services during COVID-19 supports Richardson's (2021) work on the 'platformisation' of office spaces. Platformisation aims to facilitate work 'through spaces of co-ordination that can adjust the definition of purposeful activity' (Richardson, 2021, p. 359). Prior to March 2020, the co-living housing sector co-ordinated productive work by delivering shared workspaces (Bergan et al., 2020). However, when the pandemic redefined the spatialities of productive work, and intensified challenges related to working from home, the sector adapted its workspace HaaS to accommodate these new definitions.

Co-living Housing-as-a-Community-Service under COVID-19

As 2020 progressed, both the national Centers for Disease Control and Prevention (CDC) and New York State provided extensive advice on how businesses and individuals should practice hygiene, clean and disinfect spaces, use personal protective equipment (PPE), and practice social distancing to help prevent the spread of COVID-19 (CDC, 2020b). As the CDC (2020a) noted, the challenge of implementing this advice around hygiene, cleaning, and social distancing were heightened in shared housing. Restrictions effectively shifted the community services (and associated high levels of face-to-face contact) of co-living housing from being a valuable amenity for subscriber-tenants to one that posed a significant health risk. In response to these institutionally precarious circumstances, NYC co-living operators redefined their community HaaS in terms of providing a solution for their subscriber-tenants to manage the physical and mental health challenges and risks associated with the COVID-19 pandemic and concomitant public health measures.

Adhering to CDC advice regarding group isolation, providers used the lockdown circumstances to emphasise the value that co-living housing provided in terms of enabling tenants to access a supportive community within the dwellings. Many operators identified how the circumstances of the COVID-19 pandemic had made the need for community more important than ever (Cohabs, 2020a, 2020b; Common, 2020c; Mauldwin, 2020a, 2020b; Ollie, 2020b; Outpost Club, 2020a; The Collective, 2020a, 2020c). One industry advisory stakeholder Mauldwin (2020b) even argued that the community services provided by co-living housing prevented the spread of the COVID-19 virus:

> As the novel coronavirus continues to call for increased preventative measures, we know it's not always easy to practise social distancing in shared living spaces.... [but] think of it this way: if someone is sick right now and they're all by themselves, it's much harder to completely self-quarantine because they need to get things like food, medicine, and other essentials... On the other hand, if someone is sick and has a nearby tribe [i.e., a co-living housing community], they can self-quarantine in their own space without going out as much because the tribe[/co-living housing community] can safely send them what they need and leave things at their door.

Similarly, NYC co-living operator Outsite (2020b) argued that

> In a time where our members are feeling nervous, or they're in a place where they don't speak the local language, it seems to us that the real irresponsible thing to do would be to remove them from the place they're considering to be home for a crisis.

NYC co-living businesses essentially reframed their community services in terms of how they introduced measures to protect residents from the virus. For instance, all providers introduced new protocols and policed who could access the dwellings and how, limiting access to only residents and workers (Common, 2020a, 2020c; Outsite, 2020a). Similarly, many operators increased supplies and deliveries of groceries and cleaning products to minimise the need for residents to leave their accommodation. Cohabs (2020b) even provided quarantine packs for those needing to self-isolate. Meanwhile, co-living businesses advertised they provided residents with access to medical services (e.g. telehealth, rapid antigen testing, etc.), further restricting the need for residents to leave the residence and put the co-living community at risk (Cohabs, 2020a, 2020b; Common, 2020c; Outpost Club, 2020a; Outsite, 2020a; The Collective, 2020c; WeLive, 2020). In further limiting the need for members to leave their co-living dwellings, providers also modified the role of the community manager to include greater wellbeing and care services during the pandemic.

The community managers employed in dwellings are central to fostering community during COVID-19. Community managers are frequently enrolled in SPaaS businesses to deliver cultures of hospitality (Richardson, 2021). The role of a community manager sits somewhere between a college dorm residential advisor, concierge, professional mentor, building manager, and event planner. Before the pandemic, they were often tasked with smoothing the transition of tenants in and out of the dwelling, ameliorating frictions between tenants, organising household logistics, running events, and helping tenants socially integrate into the community. During the pandemic, this role shifted to being a crucial point of information about the COVID-19 regulations and restrictions. Community managers were advertised as information repositories on COVID-19 – regularly communicating to residents the latest health announcements and what this meant for them. For example, Outsite (2020a) advised customers that their community managers were available:

> ... if [tenants had] questions about how things work, which has been hugely beneficial for those travelling in this period.

The 'community service' that co-living managers provided expanded during COVID-19 to incorporate greater care for the physical and mental well-being of residents. 'Care' was featured as an additional service across all the providers we analysed and included access to mental health supports, check-in calls, establishing digital communication systems, etc. Community managers were also used to police tenant behaviour and monitor residents' adherence to the new health and hygiene rules. Many operators made it clear that tenants were expected to adopt behaviours in line with expert advice to reduce the risk of COVID-19 transmission. WeLive (2020) required tenants to wear a mask in common spaces and introduced new house rules limiting the amount of people allowed to occupy a shared space at any one time. Some highlighted expectations that tenants should clean up after themselves, or not enter shared spaces if they were unwell (Cohabs, 2020b). Tenants were even encouraged to report other tenants to the community manager for breaches of the new rules.

As 2020 progressed, many NYC co-living housing providers began to advertise their community services as a solution to the loneliness and isolation many people were experiencing during the lockdown periods of the pandemic (Lia, 2020). The Collective (2020a) reassured subscribers that tenants could 'still find togetherness in our spaces'. Co-living operators marketed themselves as solving the absence of familial and friendship care networks by setting up systems between roommates. Before the pandemic community, events were a central aspect of the community services sold to tenants. During the pandemic, community events moved online. Cohabs (2020a) digitised their events rather than cancel them as they felt it was vital they kept 'community central to what [they] do'. Other co-living operators used the move of community events online as an opportunity to expand their customer base. For example, Ollie (2020a) sold access to their digital community events to those who did not live in their co-living dwellings. Similarly, The Collective (2020b) announced that

> ... our Virtual Experiences are now open to all. For years we've been bringing the best performers, speakers, and creatives into our co-living spaces for a cutting-edge cultural events programme, exclusive to our

> members. Now, due to COVID-19, we've taken these events online, making them available to all — live to your laptop, tablet or smartphone. Why? Because we wouldn't want anyone to feel disconnected now, when community is more important than ever.

Essentially, co-living business began selling access to the community element of communal living, displacing the spatial situatedness that had been so intrinsic to the pre-COVID-19 iteration of this service. This speaks to the radical implications that HaaS models like co-living have in mediating institutional precarity through incredibly agile (and arguably fragile) services that extend beyond the physical structures of housing.

Conclusion

In this chapter, we have charted how NYC co-living businesses repurposed their core housing services – mobility, workspace, and community –in response to the rapidly changing regulatory environment that characterised 2020. In so doing, co-living housing providers not only survived the institutionally precarious circumstances catalysed by the COVID-19 pandemic but thrived under these conditions (Velsey, 2021). Using this analysis, we argue that co-living (and more broadly micro-living) housing should be understood as not only an infrastructure that facilitates precarity but also an outcome or product of a range of precarious (in this case, institutionally precarious) conditions. Previous work on the emergence of co-living housing found that the economic precarity of the Great Recession in the late 2000s accelerated the development of this type of micro-housing (Bergan et al., 2021). During 2020, co-living was once again a mediator and product of the precarious conditions created by the COVID-19 pandemic. Furthermore, we contend that co-living operators were able to consolidate this type of micro-living housing development within the wider real estate industry because of their HaaS business model. Specifically, co-living housing providers were able to quickly adjust to new regulatory – institutionally precarious conditions by adapting their core housing services of mobility, workspace, and community.

Beyond the example of co-living, our findings demonstrate that the political-economic potency of the domestic is not spatially contained or fixed within physical housing structures. Rather, we need to recognise the aftermarket or servitisation of housing and how agile services are used to rapidly reframe and support precarious conditions of life and labour, including the shrinking of domestic spaces. That is, the servitisation of housing is used to justify the reduced physical size or 'micro' scale of housing. Furthermore, our study shows how regulatory frameworks introduced to (directly or indirectly) govern how housing is produced and consumed are variously engaged with and diffracted by housing market actors leading to unintended and/or unforeseen consequences. By adopting and adapting the

XaaS business model to real estate commodities, stakeholders in the co-living housing sector have also acquired a capacity to deftly respond to the institutional precarity that comes with regulatory changes. Maalsen's (2021) application of 'hacking' as an urban concept is useful to understand the significance of the agility of co-living in response to changing regulatory, social, and economic conditions. Co-living operators optimised their businesses, by working 'around and within existing constraints...[this] allows systems to continue working without necessarily changing them' (Maalsen, 2021, p. 3).

Significantly, this means that these entities are not as vulnerable to regulatory disruption as they would lead public policy makers to believe. The trends of micro-housing and shrinking domesticities should not be underestimated as passing fads that will be rapidly embraced and just as quickly dispensed with by millennial cohorts often satirised as mercurial. Rather, how new iterations of this growing housing typology are built, regulated, and governed needs to be taken seriously by both housing scholars and practitioners. When it comes to the regulation of housing, such as co-living, our work points to the urgent need to ensure that any regulatory changes are fundamentally assessed in terms of their capacity to reduce, rather than entrench, precarity into urban landscapes.

Notes

1 This type of housing has also emerged in cheaper disused or underutilised warehouse spaces in the peripheries of global cities. There are also locations in the Global South – particularly around South-East Asia – that market a more tourist style 'retreat' type of co-living housing.

2 We note that although some organisations closed, this was possibly in part due to larger organisations buying out and amalgamating with smaller operations (Velsey, 2021). It is not uncommon to see companies engage in predatory property-led accumulation strategies as a response to financial crises.

3 This legislated order closed all nonessential businesses; prohibited nonessential gatherings; introduced social distancing regulations; and limited outdoor activities. New Yorkers were allowed leave their homes only for essential activities (e.g. medical care, purchasing household groceries).

References

Bergan, T. L., Gorman-Murray, A., & Power, E. R. (2021). Coliving housing: Home cultures of precarity for the new creative class. *Social & Cultural Geography, 22*(9), 1204–1222. https://doi.org/10.1080/14649365.2020.1734230

Centers for Disease Control and Prevention. (2020a). COVID-19 guidance for shared or congregate housing. *COVID-19*. www.cdc.gov/coronavirus/2019-ncov/community/shared-congregate-house/guidance-shared-congregate-housing.html

Centers for Disease Control and Prevention. (2020b). How to protect yourself and others. *COVID-19*. www.cdc.gov/coronavirus/2019-ncov/prevent-getting-sick/prevention.html?CDC_AA_refVal=https%3A%2F%2Fwww.cdc.gov%2Fcoronavirus%2F2019-ncov%2Fdaily-life-coping%2Fshared-housing%2Findex.html

Cleaver, N., & Frearson, A. (2021). *All together now: The co-living and co-working revolution*. RIBA Publishing. https://doi.org/10.4324/9781003164777

Cohabs. (2020a). *COVID-19: Your safety is our priority*. Retrieved July 10 from www.cohabs.com/covid-19-coliving

Cohabs. (2020b). *FAQs: What measures has Cohabs taken to protect its members?* Retrieved July 10 from www.cohabs.com/faq#faq-32

Coliving Hub. (2020). *An open letter to coliving space landlords*. https://coliving hub.medium.com/an-open-letter-to-coliving-space-landlords-faf55ab770bf

Common. (2020a). *Common is helping public health professionals with temporary housing in NYC*. Retrieved July 10 from www.common.com/blog/2020/04/temporary-housing-healthcare-professionals-common/

Common. (2020b). *How Chicago's medical students can find flexible summer housing*. Retrieved July 10 from www.common.com/blog/2020/05/how-chica gos-medical-students-can-find-flexible-summer-housing/

Common. (2020c). *How we're keeping our field employees and members safe during an outbreak*. Retrieved July 10 from www.common.com/blog/2020/04/how-were-keeping-our-field-employees-safe-during-an-outbreak/

Common. (2020d). *The ultimate social distancing guide for roommates*. Retrieved July 10 from www.common.com/blog/2020/03/the-ultimate-social-distancing-guide-for-roommates/

Cresswell, T., & Martin, C. (2012). On turbulence: Entanglements of disorder and order on a Devon beach. *Tijdschrift voor economische en sociale geografie, 103*(5), 516–529. https://doi.org/https://doi.org/10.1111/j.1467-9663.2012.00734.x

Cuomo, A. (2020). *Executive Order: No.205.2: Quarantine restrictions on travelers arriving in New York*. New York State. www.governor.ny.gov/news/no-2052-qua rantine-restrictions-travelers-arriving-new-york

Dishotsky, J. (2016). The housing as a service revolution has begun .... *Medium*. https://medium.com/@jondishotsky/the-housing-as-a-service-haas-revolution-has-begun-fcec08a7562d

Harris, E., & Nowicki, M. (2020). "GET SMALLER"? Emerging geographies of micro-living. *Area, 52*(3), 591–599. https://doi.org/10.1111/area.12625

Hirschfeld, A. (2021). Why co-living is booming despite the pandemic. *The Business of Business*. www.businessofbusiness.com/articles/co-living-industry-common-pandemic-roommates/

Kalagas, A. (2019). Redesigning renting: Housing as a service. *Assemble Papers*. https://assemblepapers.com.au/2019/05/20/redesigning-renting-housing-as-a-service/

Lia, G. (2020). To share or not to share? *National Post*. www.pressreader.com/can ada/national-post-latest-edition/20200711/282608855109525

Maalsen, S. (2021). The hack: What it is and why it matters to urban studies. *Urban Studies*, Advanced Online Publication. https://doi.org/10.1177/004209802 0986300

Magistretti, B. (2020). Starcity raises $30 million in a post-wework, COVID crisis to scale its affordable co-living spaces. *Forbes*. www.forbes.com/sites/berenicemagi stretti/2020/04/27/starcity-raises-30-million-in-a-post-wework-covid-crisis-to-scale-its-affordable-co-living-spaces/#7c28b9f048f7

Marom, L. (2019). *What 'Space-as-a-Service' could mean for the future of real estate*. www.forbes.com/sites/forbescoachescouncil/2019/01/30/what-space-as-a-serv ice-could-mean-for-the-future-of-real-estate/?sh=1fff9115db4b

Mauldwin, L. (2020a). Best practices to avoid the coronavirus in coliving & shared living communal environments. *Kndrd*. https://kndrd.io/coliving-community/best-practices-to-avoid-the-coronavirus-in-coliving-shared-living-communal-environments

Mauldwin, L. (2020b). Tribe survival vs. being alone in the midst of COVID-19: Things to do in social distancing and coliving. *Kndrd*. https://kndrd.io/coliving-community/tribe-survival-vs-being-alone-in-the-midst-of-covid-19-things-to-do-in-social-distancing-and-coliving

Naito, S. (2021). Co-living will sustain itself in the postpandemic world. *Forbes*. www.forbes.com/sites/forbesrealestatecouncil/2021/03/04/co-living-will-sustain-itself-in-the-post-pandemic-world/?sh=7b74172679da

New York State Department of Health. (2020). *Interim containment guidance: Precautionary quarantine*. https://coronavirus.health.ny.gov/system/files/documents/2020/03/quarantine_guidance_0.pdf

OECD. (2020). *Contribution of migrant doctors and nurses to tackling COVID-19 crisis in OECD countries*. https://read.oecd-ilibrary.org/view/?ref=132_132856-kmg6jh3kvd&title=Contribution-of-migrant-doctors-and-nurses-to-tackling-COVID-19-crisis-in-OECD-countries&_ga=2.197214383.1443811647.1624076158-786616249.1624076158

Ollie. (2020a). All our events are going virtual. *LinkedIn*. www.linkedin.com/posts/ollie-ollie.co-_olliesocial-coliving-community-activity-6647851765221871616-NKgQ/

Ollie. (2020b). *Ollie social: Lets get together*. Retrieved July 10 from https://olliesocial.co/

O'Neill, P. (2010). Infrastructure financing and operation in the contemporary city. *Geographical Research, 48*(1), 3–12. https://doi.org/https://doi.org/10.1111/j.1745-5871.2009.00606.x

OpenDoor. (2020). *COVID-19 response*. Retrieved July 10 from https://opendoor.io/properties/workshop/

Outpost Club. (2020a). *COVID-19: All updates from the Outpost Club in one place*. Retrieved July 10 from https://outpost-club.com/covid-19

Outpost Club. (2020b). *Private rooms for travelling nurses*. Retrieved July 10 from https://outpost-club.com/travel-nurse-housing

Outpost Club. (2020c). *Tips for working from home productivity*. Retrieved July 10 from https://outpost-club.com/blog/tips-for-working-from-home-productively-

Outsite. (2020a). *Outsite COVID-19 response & guest guidelines*. Retrieved July 10 from www.outsite.co/faq/corona-virus

Outsite. (2020b). *Why we'll keep our co-living spaces open during Covid-19*. Retrieved July 10 from www.outsite.co/blog/covid-outsite-still-open

Park, S. (2020). Coronavirus pandemic leads to increased demand for co-living spaces: Co-living has proven to be a resilient asset class during most recent economic downturn. *Fox Business*. www.foxbusiness.com/lifestyle/co-living-students-university-coronavirus-pandemic

Pepper, S., & Manji, A. (2019). *Co-Living as an emerging market: An assessment of co-living's long-term resiliency* [Thesis, MIT]. https://dspace.mit.edu/bitstream/handle/1721.1/123605/1135867129-MIT.pdf?sequence=3&isAllowed=y

Purdon, A. (2020). Will co-living survive the pandemic? *CBRE*. www.cbre.com.au/united%20kingdom/services/business-lines/valuation-and-advisory/valued-insights/articles/will-co-living-survive-the-pandemic

Richardson, L. (2021). Coordinating office space: Digital technologies and the platformization of work. *Environment and Planning D: Society and Space, 39*(2), 347–365. https://doi.org/10.1177/0263775820959677

Schaefers, T., Lawson, S. J., & Kukar-Kinney, M. (2016). How the burdens of ownership promote consumer usage of access-based services. *Marketing Letters, 27*(3), 569–577.

Serbaniewicz, L. (2018). Global co-living company with U.S. holdings raises €1bn for European expansion in sector's largest-ever single investment. *Business Wire.* www.businesswire.com/news/home/20181212005478/en/Global-Co-Living-Company-with-U.S.-Holdings-Raises-%E2%82%AC1Bn-for-European-Expansion-in-Sector%E2%80%99s-Largest-Ever-Single-Investment

Starcity. (2020). *Starcity's measures for coliving during COVID-19.* Retrieved July 10 from https://blog.starcity.com/starcitys-measures-for-coliving-during-covid-19

The Collective. (2020a). *Finding connection in isolation.* Retrieved July 10 from www.thecollective.com/the-journal/finding-connection-in-isolation

The Collective. (2020b). *Join The Collective from anywhere with our virtual experiences.* Retrieved July 10 from www.thecollective.com/the-journal/join-the-collective-from-anywhere-with-our-virtual-experiences

The Collective. (2020c). *What we're doing about COVID-19.*

Tjarksen, S., Albers, J., Bitner, D., & Garcia, K. (2020). *Coliving during COVID-19: How communal living has adapted to the new normal.* www.cushmanwakefield.com/en/insights/covid-19/coliving-during-covid-19

Vandermerwe, S., and Rada, J. (1988). Servitization of business: Adding value by adding services. *European Management Journal,* 6(4), 314–324.

Velsey, K. (2021). The co-living start-ups that survived the pandemic are merging – and flourishing. *Curbed* www.curbed.com/2021/06/co-living-common-quarters-consolidation-utopian-marketing.html

von Zumbusch, J. S. H., & Lalicic, L. (2020). The role of co-living spaces in digital nomads' well-being. *Information Technology & Tourism, 22*(3), 439–453. https://doi.org/10.1007/s40558-020-00182-2

Warren, A., & Gibson, C. (2021). The commodity and its aftermarkets: Products as unfinished business. *Economic Geography*, 1–28. https://doi.org/10.1080/00130095.2021.1939007

WeLive. (2020). *WeLive response to COVID-19 (Coronavirus).* Retrieved July 10 from www.welive.com/covid-19/

Whitmore, G. (2020, 13 November). What's open? The latest November 2020 travel restrictions. *Forbes.* www.forbes.com/sites/geoffwhitmore/2020/11/13/whats-open-the-latest-november-2020-travel-restrictions/?sh=6121da774146

Zaleski, A. (2020). Yes, adults are still renting $2,000 co-living dorm rooms during the pandemic. *Medium.* https://onezero.medium.com/yes-adults-are-still-renting-2-000-co-living-dorm-rooms-during-the-pandemic-9b6213794eb1

2 Shifting Domesticities in the Metropole Hotel

Jeffrey Kruth

Introduction

"They put us on the inside and they surrounded us," (The Metropole is Our Home, 2009) recounts a former resident of the Metropole affordable housing complex in downtown Cincinnati, Ohio, describing the experience of a tenant meeting with developers, police, and other officials notifying them of the building's sale in 2009. The building's federally subsidized efficiency apartments of 300 square feet (27.8 m^2) would be converted to a luxury "museum hotel." Opposition from local groups and a tenant organization failed to prevent the displacement of more than 200 individuals, mostly African American, and many of them elderly.

Just north of the downtown, Black Lives Matter banners fly from row houses built on the violent displacement of those same Black bodies from the neighborhood partially enacted through a "highly visible" and "zero tolerance" policing campaign called Operation Vortex (Schell, 2007). Operation Vortex was part of a coordinated gentrification effort in the early and mid-2000s focused specifically in the Over-the-Rhine neighborhood—a historic neighborhood often seen by US media as a bellwether for broader urban redevelopment strategies and trends. Political will for restructuring the neighborhood in the early 2000s emerged after multi-day civil unrest caused by years of racial profiling and tensions, culminating in the police shooting death of Timothy Thomas, a young African American male, after a string of police shootings and police brutalities.

This influx of development over the past two decades stands in contrast to the work of the Over-the-Rhine People's Movement—a decades-old organization of housing rights activists, institutions, and residents at the forefront of preserving affordable housing, access to public space, and broad issues related to the idea of the right to the city. With origins in 1960s counterculture, the People's Movement continually works as a poor people's movement to ensure racial and economic justice. Over-the-Rhine was predominantly built up in the second half of the 19th century by German immigrants, and the neighborhood is seen as one of the finest collections of Italianate architecture in the country. Decades of preservation by neglect during the era of

DOI: 10.4324/9781003173052-4

Figure 2.1 Police patrol during the civil unrest of 2001 in Over-the-Rhine. Photos by Jimmy Heath. Courtesy of The Greater Cincinnati Homeless Coalition.

federal Urban Renewal programs in the 1950s and 1960s left a surprisingly intact neighborhood fabric, now seen as an opportunity for development activities due to its high degree of walkability, access to city amenities, and historic architecture.

On the one hand, the case of Over-the-Rhine stands as a familiar, if somewhat intensified case study of gentrification, privatization, and securitization of urban environments. The case echoes Mike Davis' studies of Los Angeles or Lieven de Cauter's studies of capsularization in cities, both of which suggest an intensifying of accumulation through privatized enclaves, resulting in the dispossession of marginalized populations and a shrinking sense of agency for many (de Cauter, 2005). However, of particular interest in this chapter is how domestic space is constructed, both by the expansion of capital and, conversely, through grassroots efforts by the People's Movement attempting to assuage the impacts of gentrification and dispossession. Both dismantle conceptions of the domestic, albeit in very different ways. I argue that the domestic sphere, as shaped by contemporary forms of capital, is tied to platforms shaping the agency of individuals. Those who dwell in such spaces are shaped as "users" as opposed to tenants, residents, or citizens. This interplay between ownership and the role of the user shapes new subjectivities, unique to the early 21st century. Together, the overlapping of data-driven housing platforms, finance capital, and local austerity reconfigures both notions of the local and the domestic. In such a model, local notions of sovereignty and ownership are destabilized as ownership models shift to more invisible and diffuse structures of power. I argue that, in contrast, the domestic sphere as shaped specifically by the People's Movement reimagines the role of private and public through relationships between community, family, and self. Both sides of this framework ultimately shrink the footprint of the domestic as it is understood today, reshaping our lifestyles and our cities. Ultimately, I suggest that to de-domesticate space is to shape new social realities within housing as a political project.

To investigate this, first, I will look at the conversion of the Metropole building in downtown Cincinnati from a site of single-room-occupancy transitional housing to a luxury boutique art hotel as an example of how domestic models and their intended occupants shift in the early 21st century city. Second, I will show how large-scale redevelopment presents itself as small-scale and pluralistic, while exercising large amounts of control and consolidation as a way for capital to de-domesticate space in the interests of further accumulation as a platform. Finally, by looking at the practices of the People's Movement, I examine the notion of kinship as a grounds for considering 21st-century housing relationships—contrasting this with notions of the user.

Domestication, Movement, and Use in the Urban Interior

How is it that precarity has come to represent something of an urban ideal in urban housing, particularly in American cities? Certainly precarity, transience, movement, and the itinerant are common features of cities across the modern era. In the example of the Metropole above, transitional housing was seen by residents as a means towards stabilization and permanence in the city. Today, precarity as the absence of economic stability is now framed as a choice marketed towards those traditionally included in the middle-class workforce with entire industries spawning around them. Of course, traditionally marginalized communities in urban space have long known precarity as a condition. For those who might be considered part of the creative class, van life, tiny houses, and experiments in housing platforms like WeLive are promoted as novel solutions to persistent housing crises.

Typically, these lifestyles are marketed towards creative class individuals as offering freedom of choice through digital platforms like WeLive and AirBnB. Theorist Benjamin Bratton describes the subjectivities constructed through such digital platforms and identities as users, shaped by the cultures emerging from algorithmic and software logic (Bratton, 2014). Users as subjects in the early 21st century also emerge from Gilles Deleuze's notion of the control society where individuals' agency and power is increasingly shaped by a set of individual spending patterns and financial incentives. In such a framework, the "platform" as a set of relationships between individuals and networked institutional forms begins to replace traditional notions of the public sphere. Here, I contrast the user as Bratton and Deleuze define it with Henri Lefebvre's concept of use and use value. Lefebvre suggests that users of space should regain the means to appropriate space and make it their own. Lefebvre (1991) says, "*For* appropriation and for use … and *against* exchange and domination" (p. 368).

Both the public sphere and the private sphere are increasingly reliant on the smooth circulation of data and financial transactions. The private sphere of domestic space is increasingly mediated by technologies of the "cloud." In the 1970s, Raymond Williams considered the conflicting relationship between movement in the outside world and the domestic sphere as mediated by the technology of the television. Williams echoes Walter Benjamin's exploration of interior space and its relationship to capital. Benjamin suggests that the individual's relationship to the interior world of the domestic is shaped by external forces of capital—acting as both a refuge from the external world, while at the same time bringing the external world to the interior through collections of images and objects. Benjamin (1999) says:

> The private individual, who in the office has to deal with realities, needs the domestic interior to sustain him in his illusions. This necessity is all the more pressing since he has no intention of grafting onto his business interests a clear perception of his social function. In the arrangement of his private surroundings, he suppresses both of these concerns. From this derive the phantasmagorias of the interior – which, for the private individual, represents the universe. In the interior, he brings together remote locales and memories of the past. His living room is a box in the theater of the world.
>
> (p. 19)

Beyond Benjamin's "box in the theater of the world," or the inherent consumerism tied to Williams' dissection of the television, the house itself has become a site of capital extraction. The domestic is no longer only living in Benjamin's "box in the theater of the world," but the theater box is itself a site of extraction. Boundaries between inside and outside and private and public are blurred. Property and land have long been emphasized as commodities, preferencing their exchange value for their use value. However, what is new within the neoliberal period is the idea that land and property can be used as financial instruments themselves. Land is not only a commodity in this situation, but also the debt on the property can be resold to other creditors. Therefore, movement, flow, and constant turnover ultimately help drive prices upwards as they are exchanged on debt and credit markets.

Physically, units shrink, as space is divided into smaller micro-units or temporary rentals. For high-end real estate, financialization results in what architectural historian Mabel Wilson refers to as "space-deposit boxes" (Wilson, 2017). These are typically high-end apartments that may be intentionally held as vacant for an indefinite period of time to be later sold and leveraged as a financial instrument. No human occupancy may ever be anticipated in such units. Many new high rises in New York suffer from such a phenomenon. Taken to its extreme, this logic suggests that the city may evolve to hold no use value at all, and may simply emerge as a series of exchangeable financial units.

In this situation, not only does the interior domestic space maintain a representation of the exterior world, as Benjamin might suggest, but the exterior world is now also the interior making it a space of economic exchange. This ultimately reshapes notions of the domestic. The domestic, broadly understood, suggests a continuation of the project of domestication. Emerging from the Imperial Roman concept of the upper-class housing typology of the *Domus*, the domestic implies a continuity of patriarchal relationships and a centering of familial relationships as a primary source of social life. To domesticate space, then, is to tame it as a site and reproduce hierarchical power structures. While capital breaks these boundaries, it does so for its own purposes of capital accumulation, not for any inherent social benefit. This ultimately furthers space as a site of extraction where the constant shifts in tenancy, smaller spaces, and more frequent transactions accelerate wealth accumulation.

Dominion as a form of absolute ownership also takes its roots from the Roman concept of the *Domus*. Emerging forms of ownership are tied more closely to usufruct relationships, granting access to spaces, without explicit ownership. Much like the automobile platform Uber, where access to a car is granted to a user for a short period of time without explicit ownership, we see an expansion of usufruct models tied to domestic space through platforms like AirBnb and WeLive. While serving tourist markets, they also cater to the mobility and transience of much of today's workforce. While WeLive ultimately failed as an experiment, it is not alone in its desires to use big data and shifting demographics to try and accumulate property for rental purposes. While traditional landlord-tenant relationships may have depended on 12-month leases, such platforms accelerate the rate of turnover in domestic space. Many wealthy individuals purchase homes in the urban core explicitly for AirBnB rentals. Cumulatively, this breaks down ideas of the local in favor of quick capital accumulation through a usufruct relationship. Twelve-month rentals shift to more lucrative short-term rentals, limiting opportunities for engagement with local politics.

The Metropole as a Domestic Public

Such productions of space further accelerate the notion of the city as a collection of transient users as opposed to citizens or residents. The introduction of precarity and transience as a cultural ideal coincides with shifts in regional and even global market flows. Spaces are made to be moved through, not for long-term dwelling. The hotel and transient living models echo this urban ideal, built upon the fragments of the welfare state. Economic instability and the gig economy also encourage this transience, as captured in recent popular culture through films such as *Nomadland* (Zhao, 2020), and documentary journalism like "Home is where the Parking Lot

Is" (Oppenheim, 2016), which highlight the precarious living situations of a multitude of workers engaged in 21st century gig economy work.

This precarious lifestyle is juxtaposed against the petit bourgeoisie lifestyles of choice represented through the expansion of AirBnB, WeLive, and tiny house asceticism. In this sense, the hotel acts as something of a model for the city. In Michel Foucault's famous description of heterotopias, he describes the hotel as a place of nowhere, without geographical markers, a place where otherwise culturally unacceptable events might take place (Foucault, 1984). The hotel, for Foucault, was an important model in his disciplinary society; a social structure in which power and knowledge are embodied in designed relationships between individuals in space or in the spatialization of surveillance, observation, and transience. Indeed, the Metropole's conversion to the 21C luxury boutique hotel suggests consistent transience. Populations and ideas move through the space without ever being grounded to any specific geographical context. The transformation from a space of low-income organizing and social life to one of global anonymity ultimately flattens localized culture and politics.

The ten-story brick-clad Metropole Hotel in Cincinnati was completed in 1912 at the height of Cincinnati's industrial prowess as a midwestern city. Strong connections to the Great Lakes cities, as well as river access to the Mississippi River, fostered decades of competition with cities like Chicago as a midwestern US industrial hub. As its industrial power waned, and suburbanization shifted local wealth beyond the city's core beginning in the 1950s, the Metropole came to serve the needs of those whose access to suburban wealth-building was limited. With fewer sites to contest with wealthier classes, opportunities for low-income populations to access social services, downtown amenities, and public transit sites meant multiple downtown and Over-the-Rhine sites opened for occupation. The People's Movement occupied buildings, sometimes illegally, to serve the needs of homeless individuals, eventually leading to the establishment of core neighborhood housing institutions still in operation today.

The Metropole came to serve low-income residents, a majority of whom were seniors, and a large proportion African American, amid austerity measures and deinstitutionalization. This conversion emerged as federally subsidized affordable rental housing in 1971, supporting 230 efficiency units sized at approximately 300 square feet (27.8 m^2) in size. These small units, however, fostered various types of community and organizing. Although federally operated, the Metropole Tenants Association emerged in the building's dayroom to advocate for their needs, coordinating regularly with other institutions of the People's Movement. This organizing spread to challenge the building's sale, with contested meetings with federal housing officials from Housing and Urban Development as it looked to offload the property to lighten its portfolio amidst broader austerity measures, but ultimately they lost their case (Cincinnati Business Courier, 2009).

The Metropole as a site of low-income organizing for the city's precarious population suggests a kind of de-domestication of space. In thinking about

Figure 2.2 The 21C Museum Hotel adjacent to the Zaha Hadid designed by Contemporary Arts Center (CAC). Photo by Author.

public matters versus private matters, Nancy Fraser distinguishes privacy in one's personal life with the domestic as a site of gendered and hierarchical relationships. For example, she refers to the topic of domestic violence as one often removed from public discourse, as it is often relegated to a matter of personal issues to be resolved within the household. Additionally, the privatization of space removes economic matters from public debate. Fraser (1990, p. 73) offers that

> ... the result is to enclave certain matters in specialized discursive arenas and thereby to shield them from general public debate and contestation. This usually works to the advantage of dominant groups and individuals and to the disadvantage of their subordinates.

Alternatively, this kind of domestication disappears in the Metropole, as social life with neighbors emerges as a primary form of interaction. Large spacious dayrooms, a lobby, and a downstairs cafe served as primary sites of gathering outside their relatively small living conditions in their single room occupancy spaces. Given that many residents transitioned from conditions of homelessness, many partook in treatment programs, job training, and recreational activities within the building, or in close proximity to it. From these relations, the Metropole Tenants Association formed as an advocacy group in coordination with the Greater Cincinnati Homeless Coalition. Social life was primarily organized around other tenants in the building, and a formative relationship to the broader aspects of public life and the city foregrounded one's experience.

The Metropole as Domestic Capital

De-domestication through the lens of capital emerged as the Metropole was sold and rebranded as the 21C Museum Hotel, purchased by the corporate-led nonprofit Cincinnati Center City Development Corporation (3CDC). Pressures from local development forces to sell the building emerged in the early 2000s after civil unrest rippled through the city after the police murder of Timothy Thomas. This unrest was the culmination of years of community-police tensions, prompting further securitization of the city through initiatives such as Operation Vortex and intentional gentrification.

Born out of the unrest in the city, 3CDC was concocted as a neoliberal solution. Lauded by the business press and urban consultants, 3CDC is often promoted as a market-based solution to urban deterioration and referred to as "the Cincinnati model" (Sheridan, 2011). The privatization echoed other shifts, including Mayor Charles Luken's abolition of the city's planning commission and economic development department. This was part of an effort to make the city more "developer-friendly," effectively limiting public input and democratic processes on projects and transferring those powers to private developers like 3CDC (Knight, 2017). 3CDC exists without the pressures of bureaucratic or political accountability, as might be found in planning departments or the halls of local governance. 3CDC engages a multitude of financial tools to achieve its goals. Primarily, it relies on private investment dollars and public grants, meaning that public dollars are leveraged for private benefits. Together, it owns or has developed hundreds of properties within a compact geographic footprint of Over- the-Rhine and key projects in the downtown area, including the Metropole.

In many respects, the redevelopment of the Metropole is a familiar case of neoliberalization in the city. Public amenities like social housing are underfunded and then told they are failing. They are privatized in order to attract capital to an otherwise struggling city. Subsidies are shifted to support these public interests in the form of tax breaks and tax credits for preserving the building. Often, this is exercised through intimidation, surveillance, and force, as was the case at the Metropole. The welfare state that emerged from President Johnson's Great Society of the 1960s is replaced with private interests and the attraction of outside capital, privatization, and broad securitization.

As a territorial occupation, the 21C hotel is more complex. 21C is currently owned by Accor Hotels, a French multinational hospitality company

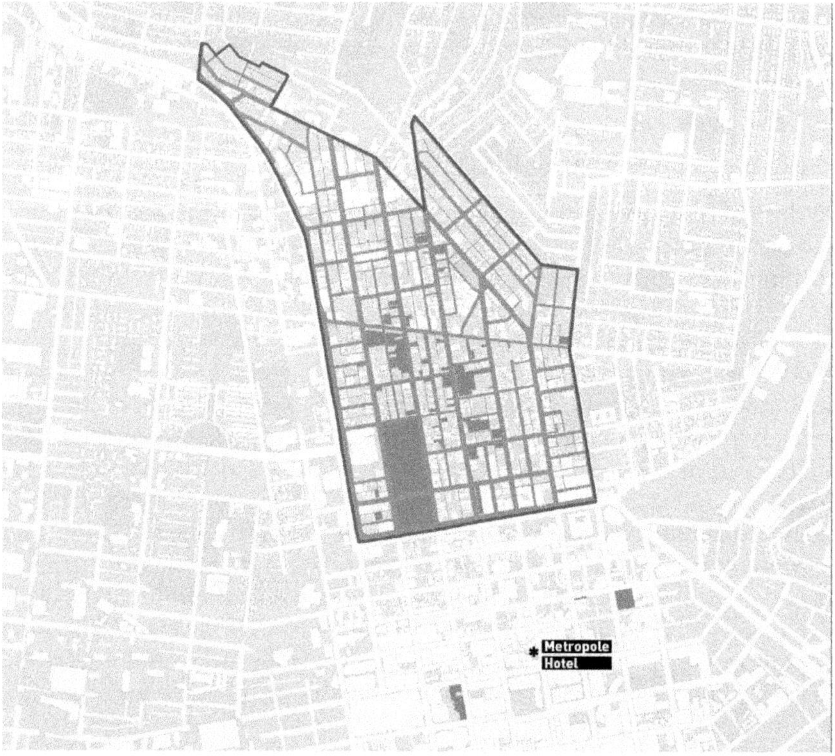

Figure 2.3 3CDC redevelopment projects and properties with the Metropole to the south of Over-the-Rhine. Map by Author. Created using data from the Hamilton County Auditor. 2021.

whose portfolio includes more than 700,000 hotel rooms across the globe (Fox, 2018). While the 21C works closely with a curator to bring in specific art pieces, other aspects of visual culture from Accor influence the overall experience of the 21C hotel. Similarly, user testing and design research from 21C-specific branding campaigns emphasize a digital presence that "drives revenue" (Accor Hotels, 2015). The 21C social media presence suggests similar affects. The city is presented as an accumulation of experiences, disconnected from its material and social histories, and replaced with an abstracted and placeless nod to progressivism. The Black bodies represented on the gallery walls act as a consumable experience for largely white audiences, replacing actual resistant bodies who once occupied, dwelled, and organized in the space.

What to make of such a contrast? The gallery is filled with politically charged rhetoric of resistance by internationally acclaimed artists of color, like Kehinde Wiley. The progressivism evinced by the gallery installations is, however, sparsely realized in the actual hotel environs. Hotel and gallery guests are almost exclusively white. Maintenance and hotel workers are, by contrast, largely people of color. The solidarity and radicalism suggested in the galleries is part of an abstracted heterotopic experience. To walk into the 21C Hotel and experience its public gallery is itself an exercise of dissociation. The interiors create an aura of international spatial neutrality, a turn of the 20th-century building that might exist anywhere. While certain intentional nods to the building's historical architecture are retained and even emphasized in certain areas, other areas suggest the building as backdrop to the gallery activities it now hosts. A space of former community meetings and informal daily activities is whitewashed and left empty in anticipation of larger scheduled events. The building's own local history of dispossession is hidden under a veil of abstracted progressive social values, while the 21C benefits from the dispossession of low-income people of color.

Figure 2.4 Top images: Photos of Metropole Tenants Association Organizational Meeting. Film still from "The Metropole is Our Home." Courtesy of Barbara Wolf. Bottom images: The converted Metropole as 21C Museum Hotel and gallery. Photos by Author.

The de-domestication of space by capital suggests something akin to Marx's notion of creative destruction. Capital through 3CDC and Accor is not simply breaking down traditional notions of domesticity to seek an altruistic new social reality. Rather, they restructure domesticity to more efficiently extract value. Domesticity is further removed from notions of the social, the commons, or associations with the public. While more traditional housing developments might reproduce expected social relationships surrounding the nuclear family and gendered relationships, the 21C and similar developments operate at two scales—a phenomenon we might refer to as both shrinkage and bloating. First, domestic space is effectively diminished across the neighborhood in favor of temporary rentals and quick infusions of cash. Smaller units occupied for less time accelerate capital accumulation for fewer people. Second, domestic space in housing is simultaneously aggregated into the hands of fewer and fewer owners like 3CDC and Accor.

Individual owners of buildings also benefit from an expansion of the domestic footprint. For example, former multi-unit rentals bought by 3CDC for less than $30,000 were converted into a single luxury unit and sold for more than $1 million. The aggregate result of such conversions across the neighborhood makes the city less dense and more expensive. Recent US Census data from 2020 suggest that Over-the-Rhine lost population over the past ten years, despite an investment of more than $1.4 billion for 3CDC properties on more than 166 buildings (Wetterich, 2021).

This shrinkage in terms of the number of overall units also correlates to an increase in the number of short-term rentals. More than 1,100 short-term rentals appeared across the city in recent years through platforms such as AirBnB and Vrbo, mostly concentrated in the downtown and Over-the-Rhine areas (AirDNA, 2021). In such a model of what David Harvey refers to as accumulation by dispossession, ownership as a form of dominion is concentrated into fewer hands, while usufruct relationships grow.

From Domestic Platform to Kinship

Taken together, what does it mean to a city to dissolve ideas of the domestic as a social model and dominion as an ownership model? Certainly, civic and tech boosterism suggests that the promise of platforms like AirBnB and developers like 3CDC offer fluidity, dynamism, and choice. Boundaries blur between global traveler, urban explorer, and local expert. Interior spaces like those of the converted Metropole announce both their attempts to globally showcase the city as a world-class art destination, while promoting ideas of the quantified self through social media postings. The domain of such spaces is consolidated into ownership using 3CDC as a vehicle for accumulating properties. This has the cumulative effect of transferring wealth from a variety of owners from the middle or upper middle class to the super wealthy.

Those traditionally excluded from home ownership are further dispossessed. Where they previously may have been able to rent is no longer affordable, and so they are pushed to the fringes of the city where their participation in city life is highly policed and economically limited.

The restructuring of ownership in such ways also reshapes subjectivities. If the domestic as we understand it largely emerges from the 19th-century bourgeois framework investigated by Walter Benjamin and others, then new shifts in ownership, digital platforms suggest an altered framework for understanding the domestic. If the domestic was largely seen as a differentiation between private life and public activities, and between the interior and the exterior, then how might we understand the restructuring of power and culture today? Indeed both capital and the People's Movement de-domesticate space as it is traditionally understood. What to make of the new reality posed by such shifts?

Architectural and social theorist Benjamin Bratton attempts to understand such phenomena through what he refers to as "the Stack." Bratton (2014) believes our traditional subjectivities and agency should be considered, "less as citizens of a *polis* or as *homo economicus* within a market, but rather as users of a platform." In considering platforms, he suggests that they are not merely individual software companies or technical infrastructures, but also institutional forms. Bratton (2014) goes on: "They centralize (like states), scaffolding the terms of participation according to rigid but universal protocols, even as they decentralize (like markets)." Together, they constitute noncontiguous geographies, while very much influencing local geographies on a larger scale. Metropole's owner Accor, or the banks that fund 3CDC who sell mortgages on credit markets as mortgage-backed securities suggest such a platforming. This geographically spreads financial risk for banks, while at the same time making it more difficult to trace as a local condition. Aesthetically, this plays out as the abstract and generic yet familiar aesthetics of the interior spaces like the Metropole hotel. Socially, this reshapes the domestic participant into a user. The *Domus* for the user holds no interior or exterior, as their economic participation in broader platforms is linked to their standing in society. The user in relation to the domestic is a set of spending patterns that enable banks to extend credit, and users' social value emerges less through familial or civic relations than through things like social media "likes."

If the primary domestic condition driven by capital in the examples cited above is to foster a subjectivity of the user, then the primary domestic condition driven by the People's Movement might be that of kinship. Kinship, as described by Donna Haraway, Lauren Berlant, Octavia Butler, and others, suggests a kind of ethically necessary relationship between people of different backgrounds, linked to each other in a way that holds consequences. These are relationships not inherently tied to being biologically related, as in a family. As Haraway (in Paulson, 2019) offers in regards to a kinship relationship, "I have accountabilities and obligations and pleasures that are different than if I cared about another place. Nobody can be kin to everything, but our kin networks can be full of attachment sites." While Haraway is largely talking about commitments to ecology and climate change, the insistence on the specificity of location and commitment to relationship structures beyond family, work, marriage, or even friends suggests grounds for a different kind of politics and housing.

Certainly, many chosen families, nontraditional families, partnerships, and networks of care have emerged from the People's Movement housing efforts. Resistance at the Metropole through the Metropole Tenant's Association is one example of advocacy through kinship. Other campaigns through the years by the People's Movement include examples like the occupation of city-owned buildings for affordable housing, or gathering a network of 664 low-income people to purchase a single building to thwart gentrification. Kinship as a form of responsibility offers new potentials for thinking about housing as a social relationship. The People's Movement commits to offering multiple forms of alternative housing. From informal occupations to transitional housing, to more permanent forms, their "people first" mission to providing housing drives alternative forms of sociability. While many of the decisions made for the housing conditions they create are mandated through various grant structures, or out of economic necessity, they are fundamentally committed to housing as a social, political, and cultural project. They also commit to cultural production and civic participation through programs like their "Agents of Change" program for youth, and "Homeless Speaker's Bureau." Emphasizing housing as a process of social production drives residents' participation in advocacy, activism, and kinship. As resident and People's Movement representative Ms. Dorothy Darden offered in a recent art installation in reference to the recent gentrification in the neighborhood, "When I lost my neighbors, I lost my wealth!" Such a position suggests that values of fulfillment rooted in social production are possible in cities, while also emphasizing loss as a potential condition of kinship. The rootedness of those who co-produce the city and ties to location foster networks of care.

Figure 2.5 People's Movement "Take off the Boards" housing campaign (left). Courtesy of Bonnie Neumeier. Ms. Dorthy Darden in the *Vigil* art performance (right). Courtesy of Mary Clare Reitz.

As concepts of the domestic progress through the first half of this century, the prevailing tendency to shape these spaces around subjectivities of the user as defined by finance capital is by no means inevitable. Use value and kinship are terms that contrast with these new forms of domestication and extraction of value from space. Kinship as a framework for housing suggests affinities across boundaries that traditionally shape the domestic sphere. As domestic spaces physically shrink and access to those who hold dominion over them shrinks, new opportunities to define housing emerge.

The Metropole offers a prescient local example to understand the nuances of these dynamics, while broader neighborhood shifts highlight the overwhelming scale and pace at which change occurs. Traditional notions of public space and private space collapse into a platformed network that encourages transience and individual digital participation as users. Ownership consolidates further into a usufruct model encouraging short-term rentals as opposed to longer term neighborhood tenancy. Such a model thwarts efforts at local organizing in favor of shaping neighborhood identities that cater to tourists and platforms. Further, while networked platforms rely on more participation from individual users, the power structure they enable tends towards further consolidation of power as a form of sovereignty. In the case of the Metropole, this can be seen in the transfer from publicly supported affordable housing to 3CDC, and then to the global corporation Accor Hotels. Previously, the Metropole Tenants Association could advocate for their own desires as citizens, while building kinship through an alternative form of domesticity in the Metropole. However, through their displacement, they are further marginalized as economic "others" into other precarious spaces away from core amenities of the city, shrinking their impact and participation in the city. The replacement of Metropole residents as citizens with users linked to the logics of the platform obscures agency and ownership. Today, the rebranding of the Metropole as the 21C Museum Hotel is advertised as a bespoke way to locally experience the city. It works to abstractly advocate for seemingly progressive agendas through the promotion of Black artists, while at the same time profiting from the displacement and erasure of the narratives of those same populations.

When these processes take place across multiple sites in the city, they have broader impacts on domestic and public space. Interior-exterior conditions and public-private boundaries dissolve in platformed domestic spaces. This suggests a shift away from the US postwar model of domestication, predicated on suburbanization, sprawl, and reinforcing gender hierarchies with a preference for the nuclear family. Today, private and domestic life is platformed in two key ways, both of which make their presence in sites like the Metropole. First, private life is mediated and outwardly broadcast through social media and encouraged by the spatial environments like the gallery in the Metropole space, ultimately shaping cultures and identities. Second, platforming occurs through the proliferation of spatial and financial data that ultimately shapes how the city is owned and for what purposes. While this network is diffuse and less immediately visible at the local scale, it reinforces existing power structures and consolidates ownership. Taken together, such processes reconfigure the domestic subject as a user, offering few options to increase agency or to reclaim a notion of the right to the city. Organizing within such frameworks requires a kinship with local populations and causes, to not only render visible the processes of platforming but also advocate for alternative forms of the domestic.

References

Accor Hotels. (2015). *Accor Hotels Feel Welcome: Graphic Guidelines*. [Online] Available at: http://travelofferz.com/EMAILS/accor/download%20040416/AH_graphicguidelines_GB_HD.pdf [Accessed 29 November 2021].

AirDNA. (2021). *Airdna Marketminder.* [Online] Available at: www.airdna.co/vacation-rental-data/app/us/ohio/cincinnati/overview [Accessed 13 September 2021].

Benjamin, W. (1999). *The Arcades Project*. (H. Eiland & K. McLaughlin, Eds.). The Belknap Press of Harvard Univ. Pr.

Bratton, B. (2014). *E-Flux Journal*. [Online] Available at: www.e-flux.com/journal/53/59883/the-black-stack/ [Accessed 23 September 2021].

Cincinnati Business Courier. (2009). *Cincinnati Business Courier*, 10 November.

de Cauter, L. (2005). *The Capsular Civilization: On the City in the Age of Fear*. Rotterdam: NAI Uitgevers Publishers.

Fox, J. T. (2018). Accor Hotels Grows US Footprint with 21C Museum Hotels Deal. *Hotel Management*, 31 July.

Foucault, M. (1984). Of Other Spaces: Utopias and Heterotopias. *Architecture Mouvement Continuité,* pp. 1–9.

Fraser, N. (1990). Rethinking the public sphere: A contribution to the critique of actually existing democracy. In *Public Space Reader* (pp. 34–41). Routledge.

Knight, C. (2017). Here's What a Cincinnati Mayor Yvette Simpson Would Do. *Cincinnati Enquirer*, 23 October.

Lefebvre, H. (1991). *The Production of Space*. Oxford: Blackwell, p. 368.

Oppenheim, L. (2016). Home is Where the Parking Lot is. *The New York Times*, 6.

Paulson, P. (2019). Making Kin: An Interview with Donna Haraway. Los Angeles Review of Books. Available at: https://lareviewofbooks.org/article/making-kin-an-interview-with-donna-haraway/

Schell, T. (2007). *Police-Community Relations in Cincinnati: Year Three Evaluation Report,* s.l.: RAND Corporation.

Sheridan, M. (2011). *The Urban Land Institute*. [Online] Available at: https://urbanland.uli.org/capital-markets/cincinnati-s-3cdc-a-model-for-urban-transformation/ [Accessed 29 November 2021].

The Metropole is Our Home. (2009). [Film] Produced by Rob Goeller, Josh Spring, and Barbara Wolf. Available at: http://vimeo.com/8127941. USA: s.n.

Wetterich, C. (2021). *Cincinnati Business Courier.* [Online] Available at: www.bizjournals.com/cincinnati/news/2021/08/13/2020-census-takeaways.html?utm_source=st&fbclid=IwAR1wp--CIJtjHALZGx3kzUUm9XCFUDXLgPcI2hK3wRpnL21EEkABEJfxToQ. [Accessed 13 August 2021].

Wilson, M. (2017). *Changing the Subject: Race and Public Space* [Interview] (June 2017).

Zhao, C., 2020. *USA: Cor Cordium Productions.* Available at: www.hulu.com/nomadland-movie [Accessed September 23, 2021].

3 Political Narratives of Shrinking Domesticities in Helsinki and Vienna

Johanna Lilius, Michael Friesenecker & Maximilian Krankl

Introduction

Cramped domesticities were problematized and put on the political agenda more than a century ago, when the majority of the working classes in many cities lived in extremely crowded conditions under late-19th-century industrial urbanization. This raised concerns: doctors and philanthropists worried about germs spreading when people lived so close to one another, and about what would happen to the physical and moral development of working-class children living together with an extended family or sharing a home with subtenants (Juntto 1990). In order to provide better living conditions, many cities including Vienna and Helsinki began to develop policies to provide adequate housing for their residents. Families became the target of housing policy.

Helsinki and Vienna, our two case studies, represent contexts where the cities carry historically rooted high levels of power over land use, planning decisions and housing production, yet we observe trends of shrinking domesticities in both cases. In this chapter, we explore narratives related to new trends of shrinking domesticities vis-à-vis changing social, demographic and economic contexts and housing policies in the two cities.

Helsinki and Vienna are particularly interesting to compare since both cities are substantial owners and producers of social housing and recently experienced a new wave of urbanization and immigration. While the remarkable population growth and share of single households is similar, the composition of apartment types and sizes tends to differ. Against this background, we ask: has there been a shift in housing production towards smaller dwellings? What debates have occurred around the production of new small apartments? And what are the policy responses and narratives to growing housing need? In answering these questions, we build on the assumption that housing and housing policy are socially constructed. Thus, how we discuss shrinking dwelling sizes and the production of dwellings influences our notion of them (Clapham 2012). Our exploration of recent developments in Vienna and Helsinki is empirically based on analysis of statistics on housing

DOI: 10.4324/9781003173052-5

conditions, housing and planning policy documents and current newspaper articles that focus on narratives about shrinking dwelling sizes.

We begin by reviewing literature on dwelling size. We then present our case studies sequentially starting with Helsinki, then Vienna. Last, we discuss similarities and differences in both cities and end with conclusions.

Narratives of Dwelling Size and Space

According to Ekstam (2013), the ways in which the state has been concerned about the size of dwellings in Europe has varied during the previous century. Her studies in Sweden show that, in a rather paternalistic way, the first standard of crowding from 1946 was defined to increase the size and quality of housing for the Swedish population. In 1965, when the population was defined as consumers, standards were again changed to meet the demands of larger sized homes. The final standard, which is still in use, claimed that having large enough homes is a social right. The norms reflect ideological assumptions regarding the individual in society and how this has changed over time. Since the 1980s, the question has more or less been if any norms are needed, as individuals should be allowed themselves to choose how they live.

Nevertheless, overcrowding is still perceived as an indicator of poor housing quality associated with health risks and poor living conditions. A well-designed home with a certain number of rooms and a certain amount of floor space offers dwellers possibilities for both a private and social life. When this is provided, there is an evidence of health and well-being benefits for residents (Carmona et al. 2010). Particularly in psychology, geography, sociology and anthropology, conclusions have been made about what people need in their homes. This includes enough space for "normal functions of living together: eating, sleeping, resting and maybe working" (Williams 2009, 90). In the midst of the COVID crises, it seems inevitable that the need to have space for working from home is an all the more important feature of homes for many households.

This narrative of adequate housing quality typically conceptualizes spatial needs per person measured as dwelling size by floor space or number of bedrooms. This easy measure of how much private indoor space a household consumes is widely used, and Madeddu et al. (2015, 75) refer to the Royal Institution of British Architects (2011) when they claim that the qualitative aspects of a home relate to floor space and dimension of rooms. The European Union, for instance, uses the so called "bedroom standard" that defines a household as overcrowded if it "does not have at its disposal a minimum number of rooms" for different household compositions (Eurostat Glossary 2014).

While it is statistically easy to follow up on the "bedroom standard" of all European countries, the need for floor space is also connected to cultural sensibilities and geographical considerations (Cohen, 2021). For example, families in cities may trade dwelling space in order to live in the more expensive inner city where the residential environment offers compensation for the smaller indoor living space (Lilius 2019). Yet Willliams (2009) argues that studies in the United Kingdom show most people feel that they don't have enough space in new housing. For example, people lack storage space, but also open plan layouts without separate rooms are considered to have implications for privacy.

A globally emerging "affordability crisis" driven by urban population growth, increasing fixes of capital in (urban) housing, cheap credit and social inequalities is strongly influencing the way in which housing is produced (Wetzstein 2017). Within this context, many cities emphasize the need to produce affordable housing, and one way to cut costs is to decrease dwelling sizes (Infranca 2014). Alongside these perspectives, housing policies have established the availability of housing as an issue for the private sector to solve (Ruonavaara 2017). Therefore, some argue that the production of smaller apartments is a developer-driven shift that aims to increase profit (Williams 2009, 90). Yet the majority of countries, and particularly most European Union countries, still have their own space standards and regulations for housing construction (Madeddu 2015; Tervo & Hirvonen 2020).Williams (2009, 90) claims it is a necessity, as developers will otherwise "try to reduce the size of the dwelling without reducing their value".

At the same time, housing needs have been diversified. Demographic shifts have increased discussion about the necessity to prioritize multiple needs in the function of dwellings, not only those of the nuclear family. A substantial number of households in cities consist of only one person, and a common claim by both policymakers and developers is that there aren't enough small apartments to meet the demand (Infranaca 2014). Yet Williams (2009, 86) and Tervo & Hirvonen (2020), for example, have claimed that the assumption that smaller households would prefer smaller homes is not always correct.

Nevertheless, the environmental narrative has also questioned how much dwelling space people in cities need, when many spaces can be shared. Shrinking floor space is a key measure for a sustainable consumption transition as decreasing dwelling sizes reduces the environmental impact of housing (Sandberg 2018; Cohen 2021). Lettenmeier et al. (2014, 497) emphasize that a reduction of 50 percent living space per person would be needed in Finland for more sustainable housing consumption. The Tiny Homes movement, on the other hand, which emphasizes downsized dwellings, could be understood – when ignoring the infrastructural expenditure – as a counterculture or alternative to the mainstream ideal of large homes and homeownership, a notion that other chapters in this collection explore (Colombini 2019, 449).

In the next sections, we analyse Helsinki and Vienna sequentially. We focus on (a) the historically rooted values of the city's housing policies,

(b) how available floor space and overcrowding along different tenures and social groups has developed in both cities and (c) which policies and narratives led to trends of shrinking domesticities.

Helsinki: Chicken Cages for Landlords or Homes for City Residents?

Helsinki began developing social rental housing in the 1920s, but an active national housing policy was developed only after World War II, when the housing need was vast. The so-called ARAVA system consisting of state-subsidized loans was introduced for the construction of both rental and owner-occupied apartments. It was based on particular housing norms and had a huge impact on the design of new apartments. The ARAVA system understood the ideal household as nuclear families consisting of a mother, father and children regardless of social class. The aim was that all family apartments should include a kitchen, one or two bedrooms (children were to sleep separately from their parents), a living room and a bathroom (Juntto 1990; Saarikangas 2002). In practice, however, almost 70 percent of all flats in Helsinki were 1–2 rooms (kitchen included) until the 1950s (Vihavainen & Kuparinen 2004, 11). The housing produced within the ARAVA system was typically of higher quality than private housing (Juntto 1990, 210), and the buildings included laundries, common saunas and high-quality outdoor spaces for recreation and play. Still today, residents in social rental housing always have access to laundries, common rooms and saunas.

Finland was urbanized in the 1960s, and Helsinki also grew substantially through suburbanization. The new suburban flats were more spacious, including even four bedroom flats. By the 2000s, the number of larger flats had increased and studios and one-bedroom flats accounted for only 41 percent of housing stock compared to 70 percent 30 years earlier (Vihavainen & Kuparinen 2004, 11).

Housing policies retrenched in the 1990s, and rent regulation was abolished other than for social rental housing. Since then, rents and the number of private landlords have grown substantially. The number of private rental flats grew by 17 percent in Helsinki between 2000 and 2017 (ARA 2020, 7), and housing prices more than doubled in the last 20 years (Marttinen 2020, 5). These developments have shifted housing production towards smaller units. Nevertheless, an important aim of current housing policy in Helsinki is to provide enough family apartments as well as meet the housing needs of different households (Asumisen 2020, 62). According to the city, zoning regulations are crucial to ensure development of new family apartments (defined as two bedroom apartments), as it is considered that the market does not produce enough otherwise. According to research conducted by the city of Helsinki, the most pressing housing issue among residents in the city is lack of space. Families in particular face affordability issues to purchase or rent one more needed room. Many respondents also described room cramming as a problem: rooms are simply too small to facilitate needs (Keskinen et al. 2019).

Contemporary Trends in Dwelling Size and Overcrowding

Today, the average size flat in Helsinki is 62.8 m^2 (in the rest of Finland it is 82.3 m^2). Yet tenure matters. Owner-occupied apartments are substantially (on average 20 m^2) larger than rental apartments (both private and social rented). The number of small flats has increased again, and studios and one bedrooms account for 58 percent of all flats (compared to 41 percent in 2000). More than 80 percent of private rental flats are studios or one-bedroom (Asumisen 2020, 22; 24). New housing also prioritizes smaller dwelling sizes. The majority have been studios or one-bedroom apartments. The level is higher in social rental housing production than in the private sector (which includes both owner-occupation and private rental flats) (see Table 3.1).

The number of new family units with at least two bedrooms has decreased from 60 percent to 40 percent between 2014 and 2018. The average apartment size has also decreased and is currently 54.6 m^2 (from 70 m^2 in 2010). It is particularly the size of family apartments that has decreased. The decline in apartment sizes has happened across all tenures, but is much higher in rental housing (Asuminen Helsingissä 2020a).The shares of household dwelling population, however, have remained fairly stable throughout the 2000s, and consist of 26 percent single households, 33 percent two-person households, and 41 percent of households living with three or more persons (Aluesarjat 2021; Asuntokuntien määrä 2020).

The amount of floor space per person grew in the Helsinki metropolitan area until 2010, when it began to decline. At the same time, overcrowding increased. In Helsinki, every tenth resident lives in overcrowded conditions. Households who rent typically live in smaller apartments than those who own their dwellings. More than 12 percent of those who live in social rental housing live in cramped conditions (Suomen virallinen tilasto 2019; Asumisen 2020, 20). It is particularly people with immigrant backgrounds and families with children that live in cramped conditions (Suomen virallinen

Table 3.1 Percentage of studios and one-bedroom flats of all the new production since 2010 in Helsinki (Aluesarjat.fi 2021)

	2010	*2011*	*2012*	*2013*	*2014*	*2015*	*2016*	*2017*	*2018*	*2019*
TOTAL	56	57	58	53	47	56	55	61	57	57
Social	67	64	67	61	60	56	59	69	64	62
Private	42	55	53	49	39	56	54	57	52	55

tilasto 2019). The dwelling space of singles has slightly grown (Asumisen 2020, 20).

Contested Narratives between the Growing Number of Small Households and Social Sustainability

One common narrative to explain the emphasis on smaller units is the growing number of single households in Helsinki (Karikallio et al. 2019, 12), and consequently their high demand for studio flats. According to the Landlord Association, the remarkably higher rents for studio apartments (average m^2 rent €26.20 compared to €19.90 for a one-bedroom flat) is a sign of the high demand (Rokkanen 2020, 13). To increase supply, and to tackle affordability issues, private developers have introduced new housing concepts that emphasize shrinking domesticities. The developer YIT brought "Mini Apartments", directed towards single and two-person households, to the market in 2014. "Mini" studio flats are 26 m^2 and "Mini" single-bedroom flats 35.5 m^2 (YIT homepage 2021). According to the major newspaper in Finland, Helsingin Sanomat, the apartments were immediately sold despite skyrocketing prices (between 6,200 and 6,980 Euros in 2014; Ala-Risku 2014). Smartti-homes by the same developer are micro-apartments where a good design makes it possible to place all functions of a home into 10 m^2 less space (YIT homepage 2021). Both concepts are owner-occupation which make them very suitable to be sold as buy-to-lets, in other words, investment products. Currently, it is estimated that 79–90 percent of all new small flats are sold to investors (Paananen 2021).

Institutional investors have also developed new concepts for the private rental market. "Studio Homes" consists of micro-apartments of 15.5 m^2, but with high ceilings allowing for an alcove for sleeping, and a common room for all residents to supplement the apartment space. Studio Homes was developed with an exemption from regulations. According to Decree 1008/2017 of the Ministry of Environment (2017), a residential apartment area must be at least 20 m^2. Studio Homes have been highly contested in the media. Researchers and social housing providers employ the narrative of adequate housing, addressing people's rights to proper homes, and naming the flats "chicken cages" and "conches" (Bäckgren 2018a; Linden 2018). The young, middle-class single-household residents of Studio Homes, however, claim high satisfaction with the homes in their current life situations (Bäckgren 2018b).

A quality dimension to new housing in Helsinki is the development of apartments with windowless bedrooms. This is connected to the aim of maximizing profit by building smaller units. Buildings that can be developed on small plots would often be better suited for larger apartments in which a room without a window could be replaced, for example, with an alcove. Yet the square meter price of an apartment with a windowless room is higher than that of a larger apartment (Taipale 2020).

Although the size of new flats has decreased in Helsinki, it has so even more in neighbouring municipalities. This is related to the stricter regulations in Helsinki (Asumisen 2020, 62). Between 2004 and 2012, an average area requirement of 75 m² of floor space was implemented in all new Helsinki apartment blocks. This limited possibilities for developers to build many small flats, but was highly contested and later abolished. Today the city uses a "flexible apartment type distribution control model". The city wants in particular to avoid concentrations of small flats, which is considered socially unsustainable for a neighbourhood: residents cannot stay put, if there are not apartments of different sizes for different life situations, and resident turnover is high in the private rental sector. In both cases attachment to the neighbourhood is reduced (Asumisen 2020, 63). Other municipalities have eased requirements on how many parking spaces are needed related to the number and size of apartments. It has been claimed that this has also encouraged the development of smaller flat sizes, as developers have been able to build more units (Suojanen 2019).

In Helsinki, we see a clear trend towards shrinking domesticities especially among families, an increase in the development of smaller units and a decrease in apartment sizes. The latter has to some extent been discouraged by current policies that seek to regulate apartment sizes through land transfer agreements. The city mentions the production of enough family housing as an important housing policy goal, yet family housing is defined as minimum two-bedroom flats, which would only suit small families.

Vienna: Shrinking Domesticities between Profit Interests and Affordable Housing

Countering the extremely poor housing conditions characterized by overcrowding and subletting of single beds in the private rental market after World War I, an ambitious housing programme by the social-democratic city government enabled the construction of 60,000 municipal flats between 1922 and 1934 (Blau 2014, 22). Although Vienna's municipal housing programme was extensive, economic hardship of the interwar period resulted in scarce standard apartment types that were used in different variations in countless buildings. One measured 38 m² and consisted of a kitchen-living room and an individual room; the larger one was 48 m² with an additional chamber (Ibid, 211). In contrast to other modernist examples of this era, which mostly focused on the promotion of individual living comfort, the confinement of flat layouts was compensated by the provision of generous communal spaces and functions (laundries, kindergartens, swimming and shower baths and libraries within these so-called superblocks). However, the gesture remains – despite some more radical and feminist undercurrents – essentially petit bourgeois and was meant to educate the residents in an almost paternalistic manner to live well together as a community.

After World War II, Vienna focused on the urgent restoration of its destroyed housing stock through mass production of small units and from the 1950s onwards on improving the quality of municipal housing, introducing a minimum dwelling size of 55 m^2 (Pirhofer & Stimmer 2007, p. 40). The mass production of social housing peaked in the 1970s (see Matznetter 2002 for details), and due to the focus on families and increased quality demands, the average flat size rose continuously during these years – for municipal buildings to 80 m^2 in the 1980s (Pramhas 1987, 77).

Population growth – driven partly by the fall of the Iron Curtain – from the 1990s onwards marks a key turning point fuelling shifting narratives in Vienna's housing policies. The city's housing policy discourses increasingly focused not only on meeting the rising demand for housing but also on managing the demographic and immigration-related diversification of housing needs. Phasing out construction of new municipal housing during the 1990s, which completely ceased in 2004, was another key moment of policy change. While still maintaining around 220,000 municipal housing units, subsidized social housing, usually built by limited-profit housing associations, became the main model in constructing new social housing (Kadi 2015). In doing so, the city still heavily controls its social housing production through housing subsidies, land banking policies and developer competitions. Within this setting, developer competition increasingly demanded a variety of floor plans beyond the nuclear family and the development of communal spaces (Reven-Holzmann 2019).

Recently, narratives regarding the affordability of Vienna's contemporary social housing approach emerged as land prices and quality requirements are rising, while at the same time commodification of the city's private housing landscape has increased (Kadi 2015, Aigner 2020). Both are important trends that affect dwelling sizes in the city's housing production.

Contemporary Trends in Dwelling Size and Overcrowding

The average flat size in Vienna (72.3 m^2) is almost 10 m^2 larger than the average apartment size in Helsinki, with the smallest apartments in municipal housing (60.2 m^2) and private rental (69 m^2), most of which date back to the pre-war period. Recently, the construction of smaller housing units increased, especially by commercial developers (Table 3.2). In social housing, the trend towards smaller apartments is moderate and production in this sector remains dominated by three- to five-room apartments (including kitchens larger than 4 m^2). This highlights that whilst housing construction in this tenure remains mostly orientated towards the nuclear family, smaller apartments have also become more important in this tenure.

Until 2001, average available floor space per person slightly increased to 38 m^2 (from 31 m^2 in 1981) and remained relatively stable (36 m^2 in 2020; Stadt Wien 2020, Statistik Austria 2020). While production of small

Table 3.2 Buildings permits for apartments per size and housing developer 2010, 2015 and 2020

		1–2 rooms	*3–5 rooms*	*6 and more rooms*
Private developers	2010	12 percent	45 percent	43 percent
	2015	23 percent	52 percent	38 percent
	2020	35 percent	44 percent	32 percent
Social housing (mainly LPHA)	2010	19 percent	67 percent	14 percent
	2015	27 percent	64 percent	10 percent
	2020	28 percent	61 percent	8 percent

Source: StatCube – StatistischeDatenbank der Statistik Austria; 2020 estimated, own calculations.

apartments is on the rise, the relatively stable household composition does not translate into substantially less space per person. The share of one-person households (44 percent), couples with and without children (each 21 percent) and single-family households (8 percent) remained persistent, although the number of households in general grew by around 15 percent from 2004 to 2020.[1] The number of single households is expected to grow, but the share will remain stable (Lebhart 2016). This development resembles the general narrative of Vienna's housing policy to meet a diverse set of demographic needs.

Nevertheless, like in Helsinki, around every tenth household lives in overcrowded housing. And it is the larger households, in particular multifamily households and couples with children, that have less available space per person: 23 m² for four and 17 m² for five and more person households (Statistik Austria 2016, 2020). Furthermore, families with a lower level of education and migration background are more at risk of living in overcrowded conditions (Verwiebe et al. 2020, p. 55). This trend tends to be related to a general growth of larger households. Although only accounting for 5 percent of all households, the share of two- or more family and multi-person households nearly doubled between 2004 and 2020, very likely contributing to higher rates of overcrowding. Given the socio-demographic profile of this group, the decreasing production of big apartments (> 6 rooms) in the social housing sector displayed in Table 3.2 very likely poses further affordability issues for very large households.

Available space for single households is stratified by age. Single households aged under 30 have on average 50 m², whereas 60+ households have nearly 70 m². Furthermore, young single households pay on average the highest rents of all household types: €10.7/m² including utility costs (Statistik Austria 2020, 48) suggesting that the situation for young newcomers is more compromised in terms of affordability and space availability.

Contested Narratives between Profit, Housing Quality, and Affordability

The trend towards expanding production of smaller housing units in Vienna largely relates to two dominant narratives: profit gains in the private real estate sector and affordable housing in the subsidized social housing sector. After the financial and economic crisis of 2007/08, an increasing trend towards buy-to-let apartments is observable in Vienna. According to Aigner (2020), almost a quarter of all advertisements on one of Vienna's largest real estate portals were buy-to-let apartments in 2019. At the same time, one of the biggest Viennese real estate developers announced that the 'perfect size' of buy-to-let apartments dropped from 55 m^2 to a range of 36–40 m^2 (Der Standard 2018a). These developers claimed that smaller units are preferred because tenants are not able to pay higher rents and therefore apartment size is adapted according to their 'needs'. Furthermore, due to increasing property prices, the construction of buy-to-let apartments spread from central neighbourhoods to all over the City and contributed to shrinking apartment sizes (EHL 2019). This trend very much resembles Williams' (2009) claim that shrinking apartments are a developer-driven phenomenon aiming at profit maximization and that space standard regulations are a necessity.

According to media reports, real estate unions argued for the abolishment of space standard regulations due to increasing alternative housing forms such as serviced apartments and temporary dwellings. The city government, nevertheless, maintained the standard, but debated its reduction from 30 to 25 m^2 during the building code reform of 2018. The Chamber of Labour, traditionally dedicated to tenants' rights, argued that 25 m^2 was too small for couples and especially for starting a family, and this would lead to an unnecessary residential relocation, which led to the City keeping the 30 m^2 rule (Der Standard 2018b). However, trends towards smaller residential units was strongly enabled when the obligation to construct parking spaces was reformed in 2014 (Wiener Garagengesetz, Novelle 2014). In practice, this meant a reduction of almost two thirds of parking spaces in residential buildings with many small flats and significantly contributed to reduction of building costs.

The rather moderate increase in the construction of smaller subsidized social housing units in recent years was discursively accompanied by a trade-off of affordability and quality. Experts and housing providers reported that property price increases led to higher one-time down payments that need to be made by tenants upon signing a contract, which include construction costs (up to 12.5 percent) and up to 100 percent of property costs capped at €300/m^2 (Marquardt & Glaser 2020; Gutmann & Huber 2014). Tenant contributions, therefore, became an increasing access barrier to subsidized social housing as construction costs and property prices increased during the 2000s. In 2012, Vienna started to experiment with caps on eligible construction costs, down payments and rent levels by limiting floor sizes.

Mainstreamed into the *SMART Housing Programme*, regulations demand that one third, and since 2019 one half, of all new units in big subsidized social housing developments are built as *SMART* units (Wohnfonds Wien 2019).

The programme specifically targets young people at the beginning of their housing career, senior citizens including accompanying services, young families and single parents and foresees a mix of five apartment types including studios with a maximum of 40 m^2, single bedrooms with a maximum of 55 m^2, up to five-room apartments with a maximum of 100 m^2 (Wohnfonds Wien 2019; Reven-Holzmann 2019, 26). At the same time, by drawing on its historical legacy in municipal housing, the city demands from project developers the provision of communal spaces (e.g. community kitchens, playrooms) and (semi-)public green space to compensate for smaller apartments.

In sum, contrary to profit-driven developments in buy-to-let apartments, discussion regarding compensating areas while reducing apartment sizes in subsidized social housing clearly leads to higher qualitative standards over the two-bedroom flats of the typical investor projects.

Discussion and Conclusions

In this chapter, we set out to understand shrinking domesticities in two growing European cities with strong housing policies. Helsinki and Vienna have been active housing providers for a century, aiming to improve the dwelling conditions of their residents.

Still today, city-led planning and housing regulation strongly influences housing production in both cities. Yet we find in both a growth in the number of small units, intended for the private rental market. Our results echo those of Williams (2009), emphasizing that without regulation, developers will aim to maximize profit, often at the cost of dwelling space. Private developers in both cities build on narratives around affordability and demographic changes to justify the trend. However, the flats are in the first place sold as investment products to landlords. This points to exacerbating affordability and quality issues in both cities. Yet we can see the effects of regulation in both. In Vienna, space minimum regulation (30 m^2 compared to 20 m^2 in Helsinki) has prevented the development of micro-apartments apart from houses for special groups of residents. In Helsinki, on the other hand, zoning regulations have been a key measure to prevent concentrations of small units.

Nevertheless, in both cities local social housing programmes are affected by trends towards smaller apartments. In Helsinki, the demographic narrative has emphasized the development of more small units. In Vienna, where the affordability narrative is dominant, SMART apartments have been justified by functionality, quality of living and compensating spaces. The provision of small SMART apartments are diversified according to the housing needs of various households. Overall, however, Vienna has maintained policies to also develop larger social rental apartments.

We also demonstrated that Viennese people on average have more dwelling space than those in Helsinki. This may relate not only to higher standards in minimum dwelling sizes, but also to the production of bigger dwellings before and after World War II. This suggests that regulation has had long-term importance for social sustainability in housing. The current trend of shrinking domesticities is a challenge also for future housing. The availability of new larger flats is also better in Vienna, while families in Helsinki are concerned with the quality of their housing, and this is particularly related to the lack of (affordable) space. It is particularly (bigger) families and multi-person households and those with immigrant backgrounds that have less space per person. Hence, these households are also more vulnerable to overcrowding, and not having enough private and social space has been shown to have negative health effects (Carmona et al. 2010). On the other hand, while single households may have more space, this may vary across different age groups. In Vienna, young single households pay on average higher rents than older single households, suggesting that newcomers live in lower quality housing

Exploring city-led housing and planning policies is important in order to highlight alternative narratives on shrinking dwelling sizes that prioritize residents' quality of life over economic rationales. Our cases, Helsinki and Vienna, show the importance of regulatory frameworks in maintaining accurate housing standards. Although the financialization of housing decreases dwelling sizes even in these context of relatively strong regulation, our analysis has shown that while not entirely preventing developers from trying to increase their profits by building smaller units, regulations do mitigate them.

Note

1 Own calculations, based on STATcube – Statistische Datenbank von STATISTIK AUSTRIA

References

Aigner, A. (2020). What's wrong with investment apartments? On the construction of a 'financialized' rental investment product in Vienna. *Housing Studies,* 37(3), 355–375. https://doi.org/10.1080/02673037.2020.1806992

Ala-Risku, P. (2014). Miniasunnot menevät kuin kuumille kiville –pikkukodissa sänky nousee seinälle. *Helsingin Sanomat* 17.9.2014.

Aluesarjat.fi. (2021). www.aluesarjat.fi/

ARA. (2020). Asuntomarkkinakatsaus 1/2020: vuokra-asunnot. Asuntomark kinakatsaus_1_2020_vuokra-asunnot.pdf

Asuminen Helsingissä. (2020a). Asuntojen koko. https://asuminenhelsingissa.fi/fi/content/asuntojen-koko

Asuminen Helsingissä. (2020b). Talotyyppi. https://asuminenhelsingissa.fi/fi/content/talotyyppi

Asumisen ja siihen liittyvän maankäytön toteutusohjelma. (2020). City of Helsinki. https://dev.hel.fi/paatokset/media/att/57/575b338de14f698c1228a244265057ed428f7ed4.pdf

Asuntokuntien määrä. (2020). Asuminen Helsingissä. https://asuminenhelsingissa.fi/fi/content/asuntokuntien-määrä-ja-tyyppi

Bäckgren, N. (2018a). Asuntomarkkinoilla on yksiökuplan riski- "Kanankoppeja" rakennetaan liika, turhan kauas keskustasta ja väärillle ihmisille. *Helsingin Sanomat* 5.10. 2018.

Bäckgren, N. (2018b). Voiko tätä edes kutsua kodiksi? Nuoret pitävät 15 neliön miniasuntoja ekologisia, vanhojen mielestä "kanakopit" eivät sovi ihmisasumukseksi. *Helsingin Sanomat* 29.3.2018.

Blau, Eve. (2014). *Rotes Wien Architektur* 1919–1934. Vienna: Ambra.

Carmona, M., Tiesdell, S., Heath, T., & Oc., T. (2010). *Public Places Urban Spaces, The Dimensions of Urban Design*., 2nd edn. London: Routledge.

Clapham, D. F. 2012. 'Social Constructionism and Beyond in Housing Research', in D. F. Clapham, W. Clark, & K. Gibb (eds.), *The SAGE Handbook of Housing Studies*. New Delhi: Sage, pp. 174–187.

Cohen, M. J. (2021). New Conceptions of Sufficient Home Size in High-Income Countries: Are We Approaching a Sustainable Consumption Transition? *Housing, Theory and Society*, 38(2), 173–203, doi:10.1080/14036096.2020.1722218

Colombini, C. (2019). The Rhetorical Resistance of Tiny Homes: Downsizing Neoliberal Capitalism. *Rhetoric Society Quarterly*, 49(5), 447–469, doi:10.1080/02773945.2019.1658213

Decree 1008/2017 of the Ministry of Environment. (2017). www.finlex.fi/fi/laki/alkup/2017/20171008

Der Standard. (2018a). Tausend Wiener Wohnungen gehen an Anleger. www.derstandard.at/story/2000074255943/vorsorgewohnungen-tausend-wiener-wohnungen-gehen-an-anleger

Der Standard. (2018b). Größerer Disput um kleinere Wiener Wohnungen. www.derstandard.at/story/2000087522579/groesserer-disput-um-kleinere-wiener-wohnungen

EHL. (2019). Vorsorgewohnungen in Wien – Marktbericht 2019. www.ehl.at/fileadmin/user_upload/EHL_Vorsorgewohnungsmarktbericht_2019.pdf

Ekstam, H. (2013). Om trångboddhet. Hur storlekenpåvårabostäderblevettvälfärdsroblem. *SociologiskForskning*, 50(3–4), 199–222.

Eurostat Glossary. (2014). Overcrowding Rate. https://ec.europa.eu/eurostat/statistics-explained/index.php?title=Glossary:Overcrowding_rate

Gutmann, R. & Huber, M. (2014). Die Sicherung der „Sozialen Nachhaltigkeit" im zweistufigen Bauträgerwettbewerb – am Beispiel der dialogorientierten Verfahren „Wohnen am Marchfeldkanal" und „In der Wiesen" sowie des zweistufigen Wettbewerbs „Preyersche Höfe" Eine Evaluierung der soziologischen Aspekte. Eine Zwischenbilanz.

Infranca, J. (2014). Housing Changing Households: Regulatory Challenges for Micro-Units and Accessory Dwelling Units. *Stanford Law & Policy Review*, 25(1), 53–91. Available at www-cdn.law.stanford.edu/wp-content/uploads/2018/03/infranca_25_stan._l._poly_rev_53.pdf

Juntto, A. (1990). *Asuntokysymys Suomessa: Topeliuksesta tulopolitiikkaan.* Helsinki: Valtionpainatuskeskus.

Kadi, J. (2015). Recommodifying housing in formerly "Red" Vienna? *Housing, Theory and Society*, 32(3), 247–265.

Karikallio, H., Keskinen, P., Kiviholma, S., Reijonen, J., Ruuskanen, O.-P., Vuori, L., Härmälä, V., & ja Lamminkoski, H. (2019). *PTT raportteja 262: Pienten asuntojen osuus asuntotuotannossa ja vaikutukset asuinalueiden eriytymiseen.*

Keskinen, V., Väliniemi-Laurson, J., & Hirvonen, J. (2019). *Helsinki-barometri 2019: kaupunkilaisten kokemuksia Helsingistä.* www.hel.fi/hel2/tietokeskus/julkaisut/pdf/20_04_01_Tyopapereita_01_Keskinen_Valiniemi_Laurson_Hirvonen.pdf

Lebhart, G. (2016). *Entwicklung der Privathaushalte in Wien und in den 23 Wiener Gemeindebezirken.* www.wien.gv.at/statistik/pdf/statistik-journal-1-2016.pdf

Lettenmeier, M., Liedtke, C., & Rohn, H. (2014). Eight Tons of Material Footprint: Suggestion for a Resource Cap for Household Consumption in Finland. *Resources*, 3: 488–515. DOI: 10.3390/resources3030488

Lilius, J. (2019). *Reclaiming Cities as Spaces of Middle Class Parenthood.* Singapore: PalgraveMacmillan.

Linden, J. (2018). Kodista kotiloon? Blogpost 23.02.2018. www.a-kruunu.fi/blogi/kodista-kotiloon

Madeddu, M., Gallent, N., & Mace, A. (2015). Space in New Homes: Delivering Functionality and Liveability Through Regulation or Design Innovation? *Town Planning Review*, 86(1), 73–96.

Marquardt, S., & Glaser, D. (2020). How Much State and How Much Market? Comparing Social Housing in Berlin and Vienna. *German Politics*, 1–20.

Marttinen, R. (2020). Asuntojen hintojen ja vuokrien vuosijulkaisu 2019. Tilastoja 2020:9. www.hel.fi/hel2/tietokeskus/julkaisut/pdf/20_08_25_Tilastoja_9_Marttinen.pdf

Matznetter, W. (2002). Social housing policy in a conservative welfare state: Austria as an example. *Urban Studies*, *39*(2), 265–282.

Paananen, V. (2021). Tässä ovat Helsingin kallein ja halvin uusi yksiö – Sijoittajat hamuavat nyt jopa 90 prosenttia kaupungin pienistä uudisasunnoista. *Helsingin Sanomat* 15.2.2021.

Pirhofer, G., & Stimmer, K. (2007). Pläne für Wien: Theorie und Praxis der Wiener Stadtplanung von 1945 bis 2005. Stadtentwicklung Wien, MA 18.

Pramhas, E. (1987). Der Wiener Gemeindebau. Birkhäuser: Basel.

Reven-Holzmann, A. (2019). 10 Jahre Soziale Nachhaltigkeit. Bestandsaufnahme und Ausblick.

Rokkanen, S. (2020). Suomen Vuokranantajien kesän 2020 vuokramarkkinakatsaus. Suomen vuokranantajat.

Royal Institution of British Architects (2011). *The Case for Space: The Size of England's New Homes.* London: Royal Institution of British Architects.

Ruonavaara, H. (2017). Retrenchment and Social Housing: The Case of Finland. *Critical Housing Analysis*, 4(2), 8–18. DOI: 10.13060/23362839.2017.4.2.382

Saarikangas, K. (2002). *Asunnon muodonmuutoksia: Puhtauden estetiikka ja sukupuoli modernissa arkkitehtuurissa.* Helsinki: Suomalaisen kirjallisuuden seura.

Sandberg, M. (2018). Downsizing of Housing: Negotiating Sufficiency and Spatial Norms. *Journal of Macromarketing*, 38(2), 154–167.

Stadt Wien. (2020). Statistisches Jahrbuch 2020. www.digital.wienbibliothek.at/wbrup/download/pdf/3128807?originalFilename=true

Statistik Austria. (2016). Wohnen 2016 – Zahlen, Daten und Indikatoren. www.statistik.at/wcm/idc/idcplg?IdcService=GET_NATIVE_FILE&RevisionSelectionMethod=LatestReleased&dDocName=112751

Statistik Austria. (2020). Wohnen 2019. http://statistik.at/wcm/idc/idcplg?IdcService=GET_PDF_FILE&RevisionSelectionMethod=LatestReleased&dDocName=123361

Suojanen, A. (2019). Vantaan parkkipaikkamitoituksen höllennus johti kaaokseen uusilla asuinalueilla – Pienten asuntojen määrä yllätti. Vantaan Sanomat 20.3.2019.

Suomen virallinen tilasto. (2019). Asunnot ja asuinolot [verkkojulkaisu].ISSN=1798–6745. 2019, Liitetaulukko 3. Asuntokunnat asumisväljyyden mukaan 31.12.2019, maakunnittain. Helsinki: Tilastokeskus [viitattu: 19.2.2021].

Taipale, T. (2020). Nyt rakennetaan ikkunattomia huoneita – "Onko valosta tulossa luksusta?" *Helsingin Sanomat* 24.3.2020.

Tervo, A. & Hirvonen, J. (2020). Solo dwellers and domestic spatial needs in the Helsinki Metropolitan Area, Finland. Housing Studies, 35(7), 1194–1213, DOI: 10.1080/02673037.2019.1652251

Verwiebe, R., Haindorfer, R., Dorner, J., Liedl, B., & Riederer, B. (2020). Lebensqualität in einer wachsenden Stadt: Endbericht an die Stadt Wien [Quality of life in a growing city: Final report to the City of Vienna]. Vienna: Department of Sociology, University of Vienna.

Vihavainen, M., & Kuparinen, V. (2004). ASUNTOJEN VUOKRAT HELSINGISSÄ TAMMI–MAALISKUUSSA 2004. Available online: https://www.hel.fi/hel2/tietokeskus/julkaisut/pdf/04_07_12_vihavainen_vj18.pdf

Wetzstein, S. (2017). The global urban housing affordability crisis. Urban Studies, 54(14), 3159–3177.

Wiener Garagengesetz, Novelle. 2014 (2021). www.wien.gv.at/wohnen/baupolizei/pdf/stellplatznovelle-2014.pdf

Williams, K. (2009). Space per person in the UK: A review of densities, trends, experiences and optimum level. review. Land Use Policy, 26S, S83–S92. DOI: 10.1016/j.landusepol.2009.08.024

Wohnfonds Wien. (2019). "SMART-wohnen". www.wohnfonds.wien.at/media/Websitepercent20PDF-INFOpercent20Downloads/Publikationen/Neubau/2019_SMART-wohnen_Folder_web.pdf

YIT homepage. (2021). www.yit.fi/asunnot/uuteen-kotiin/kotimuotoilu.

Part II

Narrativising Shrinking Domesticities

4 Shrinking Aspirations

The Potential Impact of Build to Rent Models on Housing Transitions

Daniel Durrant & Frances Brill

Introduction

There has been growing interest amongst both policy makers and investors in different models of rental housing as an alternative to increasingly unaffordable homeownership. This issue is acute in cities like London where demand is high and capital from around the world flows into housing, further driving up prices. The development industry has put forward a number of new products, or forms of housing, that are promoted as solutions to the problems faced by people seeking to secure appropriate housing. In this chapter, we examine one of these products, Build to Rent (BTR), and the form of domesticity it offers. We use the term domesticity to describe the capacity for housing not only to be affordable, well located and of an acceptable standard but also to meet the aspirations of the people who make it their home. BTR takes inspiration from the US multi-family model, and is often driven by the same actors (Brill & Durrant, 2021). As a result of lobbying by the sector, it has been defined in policy terms as both a new form of tenure and an asset class that is exclusively for the rental market and under a single management regime (Brill & Durrant, 2021). In material terms, particularly so in London, developments are relatively large, up to 6,000 units, and are often located in more peripheral locations (where land prices are lower) which are still well connected to the urban core.

We argue that BTR as a form of housing shrinks the domestic realm in three interconnected ways. First at the level of individual households, the buildings contain a specific configuration of domestic, shared and public space. Private space is reduced, and activities from leisure to relaxing and entertaining are increasingly shifted to the shared areas. Second, at the level of the development, the active management of activities and amenities creates a unique form of *curated domesticity.* This is integral to the model and its marketing as it is aimed at attracting and retaining tenants and their rents as a steady source of revenue. Finally, the model seeks to embed itself in a certain form of domesticity which for many may be specific to one stage in their 'housing career' (Clark & Huang, 2003). But due to the high

DOI: 10.4324/9781003173052-7

costs and limits imposed by the material form of developments, this risks shrinking the domestic aspirations of tenants.

Theoretically, this chapter develops the idea of domesticity based on the notion of housing as a home. Housing, when bought and sold, has been described as a 'composite good' (Andrew, 2012) in that it serves a number of functions above the basic one of shelter. For example, it can at the same time be an investment, a home, place of work and status symbol. Its composite nature, therefore, affords multiple ways of seeing it. One useful distinction is between housing as a noun (a material object) or as a verb (a social process), used recently in analysing other new and alternative housing models (Turner, 1972, cited in Thompson 2020). Our analysis of domesticity cuts across this distinction. There are the material features, the quantum of domestic space, the configuration of urban space and the various amenities with which different forms of housing and locations are endowed. There is however also the lived experience of the individual people who make up households and their changing aspirations, at some points in the course of a life for flexibility, and at others for security. It is at this domestic level we suggest that individuals and the housing they inhabit are firmly embedded in a crucial social process: the transformation of housing into homes.

Much of the appeal of BTR to policy makers is the way it offers (as we discuss below) a relatively rapid supply of new high-quality housing in areas where there is high demand. Yet as Rachel Weber (2016) has shown, urban property markets are never simply the interaction of supply and demand. At one level, there is the mix of quantitative and qualitative calculations of investors that constitute the market (Raco, Livingstone & Durrant, 2019). Yet we would argue this sits atop a domestic level. Here the composite nature of housing and the different practices involved also constitute the market from the quantitative and qualitative calculations of individuals, their different relationships, the agency this affords them (Callon, 1998) and the households they form.

Empirically, we focus on the social processes of production and promotion of this particular form of housing. We draw upon research conducted since 2016 as part of the WHIG project (2021). This has included over 50 interviews with developers, investors, brokers, private sector researchers (for large real estate firms), public and private sector planners and representatives of civil society and tenant organisations. We have also undertaken an analysis of the discourses through which London has been promoted as a destination for international capital (Raco, Livingstone & Durrant, 2019) and policy discourse around BTR (Brill & Durrant, 2021). Through this research, we have sought to analyse the multiple social processes through which housing systems are co-created. At one level, there are the practices of the development industry, its regulators and the aspirations of investors which frame housing in abstract, quantitative and ultimately financial terms. At the more domestic level, we draw upon our own experiences visiting BTR developments and the way this furthered our understanding of the interview data, especially around the configuration of space and the curation of amenities. These visits also left us with questions about the model and the extent to which it would or would not meet our own, different, domestic needs now and in the future.

In the following sections, we set out the concept of a housing career in relation to the ability of housing systems to meet the domestic aspirations at different life stages within it. We then discuss London as an example of a city where this has become increasingly difficult. The section on the 'Making and Marketing of BTR' describes the way this model has evolved, been promoted as a solution to the problems of housing in London whilst being marketed to a mix of transitional and key workers with an additional generational element in the way developments target 'millennial minded' tenants. We then describe the way both the internal and communal space within developments is managed, before concluding with a discussion of the extent to which a form of housing that is predominantly shaped by the interests of investors may ultimately shrink the domestic aspirations of tenants.

Housing Careers

In order to understand the way in which domestic aspirations are influenced by the material form housing takes, it is important to appreciate how domestic needs and housing interact over the course of a lifetime. Most of us will begin life in some form of household, and between leaving that household and forming another it is common to have a period in which some form of 'transitional housing' (Clark & Huang, 2003) will meet our needs, either during higher education or in the early stages of a career. As we begin to establish our own households through more permanent relationships, employment and particularly if bringing up children is part of the process, the need for domestic space changes. Other life changes such as the breakdown of relationships, shrinking households and particularly deteriorating health change the demands placed on domestic space again. There are two ways a housing system can accommodate these changing needs. Either individual housing units can be sufficiently adaptable, or households can move between them. Thus, an important measure of an effective system is its ability to marry domestic space with domestic need for people with different incomes and at different stages in their lives.

In countries like the United Kingdom, household mobility is the most common solution, although real-world 'housing careers' (Clark & Huang, 2003; Lennartz & Ronald, 2019) may well contain a mix of strategies. Certainly, some properties can be expanded or subdivided. Whilst initiatives and concepts such as 'Lifetime Homes' (Rooney, Hadjri & Craig, 2013) are an acknowledgement that a degree of adaptability within individual units is desirable, there are limits to this, particularly as households grow. In theory, there is no reason why the lifetime needs of an individual cannot be met by social housing. However, in the United Kingdom, in practice, the options, and crucially the ability to benefit from the investment component of housing, is greatest for those whose housing careers see them become at some point owner occupiers. Indeed, wealth is a key determinant of the ability of households to move within the UK's housing system, with those at one end of a very broad spectrum able to access housing with luxury amenities, domestic space and good location. At the other, a combination of high price and deregulation sees households increasingly pushed into housing that lacks any of these (Clifford et al., 2018)

Housing in London

In a city such as London, the vast inequalities in wealth result in considerable disparities in housing accessibility. As a hub in the global economy, the employment it offers draws in workers at all levels and from around the world, all of whom require housing. This inward flow of workers includes young people at the start of professional careers for whom rental accommodation may have traditionally been seen as an interim stage before homeownership. Yet for potential owner occupiers, the flow of wealth into the city's property market (Gallent, Durrant & May, 2017) has pushed the price of housing beyond the reach of many. Consequently, there is a large group who lack the wealth or income necessary to amass the large deposits required to become owner occupiers whilst still earning too much to qualify for social housing. The latter provides only a partial safety net due to a limited supply, as decades of privatisation (see Boughton, 2019) and underproduction have limited social housing provision in the city. Consequently, eligibility is restricted to those with the very greatest housing need and on the lowest incomes. This leaves a large group which includes relatively high earners for whom London's housing system offers limited options. As one developer put it, London's future resilience depends on it providing

> a place for the rich, a place for the poor but there has to be a place for the middle and I don't think, at the moment, London provides for its middle very well at all.
>
> (Landowner and Developer)

In response to this situation, the landowner, involved in a high-profile BTR development, estimated that around thirty percent of the estate they manage is now targeted towards catering for this 'squeezed middle'. This concept acknowledges that rising costs of 'core goods and services' such as housing is a global phenomenon making the maintenance of 'middle-class lifestyles' increasingly precarious (OECD, 2019). One particularly salient feature of this squeeze in the United Kingdom has been declining rates of homeownership. This grew to a peak of seventy percent in 2001, but has since slipped to just under sixty-five percent in a country where it is still the preferred model and one that is prized politically and socially (Jackson, 2005).

In this way, the middle class are enrolled into the wider housing crisis as they are pushed out of traditional owner occupation. A long-standing phenomena in London is that the to-buy (for owner occupiers) and to-let (in which often quite small private landlords, in contrast to the institutional landlords driving BTR, make up a significant proportion of the private rented sector) markets suffer from crises of both affordability and quality. Attempts to stimulate the to-buy market through supply-side policies such as credit guarantees and direct subsidies have been orientated towards the bottom end of the market. These are intended to help people (implicitly younger buyers) get on the housing ladder. As a result, these subsidies have maintained high prices creating a *de facto* minimum sale price for houses. At the same time, in contrast to pre-2008, stagnant wages and rapidly increasing prices across the rest of the London market have meant that the average house price to wages ratio is 12.5, nearly double the rest of the United Kingdom as a whole (MCHLG/ONS, 2021). Unable to buy a home, many people have turned to the private rental sector (PRS), which has become the default tenure for 'Generation Rent' (McKee et al., 2017). Despite this, the PRS remains a tenure of last resort, characterised by insecurity and instability, poor quality, rogue landlords and a lack of affordability. There is a growing consensus, across national government, tenant activist and city-level politicians, that the rental market needs reforming.

Making and Marketing of BTR

For both national and city-level governments, BTR has emerged and been promoted as a solution to this housing crisis across the United Kingdom, particularly in London. With over 82,700 BTR homes in the capital, proponents of the model orientate its attributes around the well-identified failings of the PRS (British Property Federation, 2021). They argue that the institutionally owned and professionally managed quality of the property ensures tenants are happy and looked after. In our interviews, developers and investors alike made the point that BTR units offered the stability that alternative renting from small landlords did not: "almost everyone has a [negative] story of a landlord" (Investor). In light of this, local authorities and the Greater London Authority have sought to develop supportive policy frameworks, backed up by national government recognition in the National Planning Policy Framework. This growth in the acknowledgement within the 'corridors of power' of BTR's role in the housing system is one of many features that makes the London market increasingly attractive for institutional investors and BTR specific developers. Continuing their efforts to develop political support, a number of the features of London's housing market have in recent years converged to the point that BTR professionals have been able to promote the model as offering one solution to the crisis (Nethercote, 2019).

At the local level, two other features of the BTR model make it attractive to policy makers: the speed of delivery and management regimes. Economies of scale for developers and investors drive larger developments. Whilst this limits BTR's suitability for the most central London Boroughs, the model allows for large numbers of homes to enter local housing markets effectively as a block. This is something that is impossible with the conventional house building model which is dependent on income from sales and thus manages the supply for fear of depressing local house prices. Even on the largest developments, supply is dribbled out for this reason. This enhances the attractiveness of BTR to local authorities facing high levels of demand, mandatory housing targets and pressure from central government to meet them.

From the perspective of those responsible for managing housing at the local level, there is a further feature of the model that increases its attractiveness. BTR is defined by (and indeed this is mandated in policy) the way it is managed by a single organisation. In practice, this means at the very least a concierge service and maintenance regime. This stands in strong contrast to the challenges of developing communities and a sense of place more generally in urban development where the management of the (broadly understood) public realm is something that local authorities struggle with after a decade at the sharp end of a fiscal austerity programme. As such, the management of the housing stock itself casts the model in a favourable light in comparison to the existing private rented sector which is often seen as fragmented and, due to poor management and maintenance, often detrimental to the public realm.

The marketing of BTR has targeted three main groups or categories. First are transitional workers. In early interviews with financial advisors to BTR firms, interviewees reflected that the key demographic are those who do not want to stay in a place for a long time, but expect and demand high-quality urban realm and the professionalised services BTR sites deliver. One interviewee, who had recently advised local authorities on how to facilitate BTR developments, explained that he saw high-income jobs in urban centres and the internationally mobile workers they attract as a key market:

> It is really suited to high-end jobs, like research jobs where people move in for two, three years and they just want to start their job and life when they get here.
>
> (Economic Advisor)

Another interviewee repeatedly returned to the value of BTR in creating labour market flexibility and the importance of appealing to mobile, transitional populations to ensure good returns for investors. Indeed, this practice of attracting relatively short-term lets based on the offer of amenities in order to maintain the levels of occupancy such returns require was likened by a number of interviewees to the business model of hotels. There was even evidence of a transfer of staff and knowledge from this sector into BTR where one developer noted that their senior management was "straight out of the hotel industry" (Developer).

A second category identified, into which both of the other two groups could easily fall, refers less to occupational status than to a particular stage in life and the aspirations that come with it. This is what interviewees referred to as the 'millennial-minded' occupant. Whilst this generally referred to the attractiveness of the bundle of amenities on offer in a particular development, it reflects an acknowledgment that the offer of BTR is targeted towards a particular age group, that is, those who reached adulthood in the first two decades of the twenty-first century.

The final group targeted by BTR developers, evident in the shift in narrative particularly post-COVID-19, is key workers. As has been argued elsewhere (see Brill et al., 2022), workers with state-backed incomes were seen as increasingly attractive in the face of uncertainty posed by changing market trends – particularly the apparent decline in the appeal of high-rise buildings typical of BTR. This was not totally new. In interviews in 2019, developers remarked that key workers such as nurses were the ideal occupants because they had guaranteed stable jobs that tracked inflation and therefore investors' liabilities to pension funds. When pushed about the ability of such workers to afford the homes, interviewees reflected that these groups still remained key to delivering the site in its entirety because they created stability and prevented excessive 'churn' (tenants moving out being replaced by those moving in). The provision for this section of the market was also about meeting planning requirements to provide affordable housing, with marketing often making explicit the targeting of this group, for example, Grainger's tag line is "Providing homes to key workers and those with the greatest housing need" (Grainger Trust, 2021).

Shrinking Private Space

There are a number of material features of the BTR model that appear to reconfigure the relationship between private (potentially) domestic space and communal or what may or may not be public space. In some cases, this takes the form of on-site amenities such as spaces for working, socialising and exercising – access to which is included in the rental price. Our research also showed a number of additional management practices and design elements. In isolation, these could be seen as little more than the extension of efficient management practices, albeit ones designed from the perspective of asset owners and managers. However, these measures appear slightly different if they are seen as placing BTR tenants within a spectrum of housing options. At one end, individuals and households with high levels of housing wealth have considerable private space in which they are free to determine their own form of domesticity. Those with sufficient wealth may even be able to extend their existing accommodation or move to a larger home in the same area thus retaining the amenities that attracted them in the first place. At the other end of the spectrum, this flexibility is reduced. In the case of BTR, tenants may be much more dependent on the amenities provided by the developer. Private space may be relatively constrained with limited freedom to manage it independently. And at the far end of the spectrum, related rental models such as dormitory style co-living sees private space reduced to a single room.

The first of these features is known as the *dumbbell model*. This is a direct import from the United States and refers to the way individual flats are designed with two identically sized bedrooms. This is so the flats can be marketed to professionals sharing, with each having the same amount of space and thus splitting the rent equally. This is a principle that can be seen extended to the way space within flats is configured, with the doubling up of appliances such as fridges and washing machines so again each individual has their own appliance with only some domestic activities such as cooking shared between them.

The second feature is the emphasis on high-quality fittings. All fittings we have seen on our visits to multiple sites have been marketed as and are genuinely high-quality. Brands are specifically chosen that are identifiably higher end than traditional 'high street' ones, and on our tours of sites, managers and developers pointed to brands such as Bo Concept. This is part of the developers' demonstration of a commitment to providing a quality product and evidences' attempts to appeal to a particular target audience: young, relatively high-income, professionals. Additionally, flats are generally rented fully furnished, and here the principles of well-managed, high-quality environments extend into the private realm. As a number of developers pointed out, this level of management, one not normally seen in private landlords, is seen to be as much about ease of maintenance as the needs of the tenants.

An ongoing emphasis on maintenance and management, either via technology or through on-site staff, is a third feature. In interviews and during site visits, developers and operational managers stressed their continual involvement in the project. For example, they reflected on the valuable role of 'smart' technologies that enable easy maintenance of products and communication with tenants. Such technologies also shape the relationship between the landlord and the tenant whereby the professionalisation leads to a de-personified interaction across a digital interface which is justified as more efficient. On a more mundane level, in other developments, practices such as a site-wide programme for refilling the salt in every dishwasher is conceived of as a long-term cost saving measure that is mutually beneficial. Maintenance shapes the physical form of the development in other ways. For example, corridors wrap around the buildings allowing cleaners to clean in one direction and return to the lift. Planners traditionally try to avoid these in blocks of flats due to security concerns associated with long empty spaces. However, one interviewee described how local authorities have been won over by the developers' claims that the combination of regular cleaning and the concierge service creates a presence and oversight of these areas that addresses concerns with security.

Curated Domesticity

Particularly in the larger developments, organisations with names such as Get Living, Fizzy Living and Tipi see themselves very much in the business of 'curating' an experience or what one developer termed "experiential living". This active curation is most evident in the offering of amenities such as a high-quality public realm, and a mix of retail and leisure opportunities often supplemented with a programme of activities. This includes everything from yoga and meditation classes through to summer events such as outdoor cinemas and community barbeques. As such, BTR promoters emphasise these dimensions in their marketing, highlighting the potential 'buzz' of the development and the facilities offered, rather than the wider amenities of a local area. Indeed, the relatively peripheral locations of BTR developments means the wider area often lacks many of the features, restaurants, bars and cafes that typically attract young professionals. In one walking tour, the operational manager repeatedly pointed to the way they, as a developer, were providing and actively managing these types of facilities within the site, rather than relying on existing urban spaces. For example, the conversion of the former Olympic Village in Stratford, East London, into BTR includes emphasising the novelty of the experience and the place:

> It's a new way to rent and to live in London's newest neighbourhood: East Village. ... We understand the importance of making a place your own.
>
> (Get Living, 2021)

What is created are quasi-public spaces which if not specifically closed are targeted at those living in the developments rather than functioning as part of a broader public offering made by the scheme. These are not exclusively for residents, but rather their physical layout and range of amenities on offer are designed to prioritise the BTR occupants over the wider area. What is noticeably lacking from such environments is the retail and social facilities catering for different age, ethnic and, crucially, income groups.

Discussion: Shrinking Aspirations?

So far, we have focused on the way London's housing system caters for the needs and domestic aspirations of young professionals who in other circumstances might find it relatively easy to meet those needs through renting or buying. Initially, at least, it is a group that is more flexible, less bound by long-term commitments and thus more able to move to find a location that has the combination of amenities they are looking for. However, as people amass commitments, the question of the extent to which the material elements of housing are able to adapt or facilitate transition to a more suitable form re-emerge. Therefore, in this discussion section, we argue that it is important to consider whether or not BTR can adequately accommodate changing domestic aspirations.

On the one hand, the investment-driven model of BTR is, in part, a response to a range of failures in London's housing system to meet the needs of Londoners. On the other, there are risks in the way its promotion has been accepted, uncritically, as a solution to them. Within the wide range of needs London's housing has to cater for, we focus now on the question of transition. The managed, curated domesticity offered by BTR in its current form may well meet the needs of young professionals at the early stages in their housing careers. Yet it appears to be targeted and configured around domestic aspirations that are likely to change.

The increased post-COVID attractiveness of key workers as a reliable source of revenue for investors suggests again that for some this model is increasingly seen as something other than a transitional one. BTR is also evolving, with proponents keen to develop more suburban family housing (see Brill et al., 2022). This is partly a reflection of what, in response to COVID-19 and in the short term at least, has been a shift in the relative attractiveness of a central location that is often traded off against the benefits of increased domestic space. It may also reflect the possibility that as the BTR sector develops it will be feasible for people to transition to housing that meets their domestic needs at different stages in their life *within* the BTR universe. The Greystar model in the United States provides a precedent here as it is specifically designed to facilitate geographical mobility, with tenants able to easily move their Greystar accounts between schemes in different cities.

Where this is problematic is that traditionally the offer of rental accommodation is either the convenience of transitional housing or the lower cost. This is because renters are automatically excluded from any benefit from the investment component of housing. But BTR is relatively expensive, with a premium paid over rental accommodation in similar areas – these are on average fifteen percent above comparable rents (Da Silva, 2019) and in some areas in London as much as forty-four percent higher (Cottrell, 2019). Such costs must therefore be justified in terms of the amenities, or the form of domesticity, that is offered.

For the model's advocates, it is these amenities that are central to its attractiveness. The often voiced assumption is that, in individuals' calculations of their domestic needs, the premium for BTR compared to other rental housing is considered worth paying. Furthermore, it was often assumed that quality would be maintained through a form of market discipline with developments that failed either to deliver or to keep up with the competition punished by tenants willing to switch in order to take up a better offer. Yet from the developers' and investors' perspective, this requires balancing the cost of amenities that attract occupants in the first instance, and ensuring costs do not escalate beyond investors' margins. The strategies around the quality and quantity of additional features provided as part of a standard BTR site was continually addressed at industry events attended, with professionals often questioning how and why some of the more comprehensive packages initially offered are able to sustain themselves financially. The immediate impact of COVID has, in some instances, been that the full range of amenities are relatively difficult to provide. This sort of calculation is by no means unique to BTR.

Whether the calculation made by tenants to trade limited, highly managed, domestic space for all the benefits of a well-connected urban location reflects a permanent shift in values for the millennial generation is unclear. Certainly, what is acknowledged in the concept of a housing career is that these calculations are likely to change. It is here that we believe the model fails to stand up to scrutiny. First, there is little scope for adaption given the limited quantum of private space, although this is something the increasing choice of suburban locations may begin to address. Second is the higher rental costs which will, for some, inhibit the ability to save the amounts required for the high deposits necessary for homeownership and thus inhibit transition.

Conclusion

It could be argued that the concerns of those able to access BTR are relatively narrow, certainly compared to those whose most basic housing needs are unmet. We acknowledge this, although the inclusion of key workers as one of the groups targeted suggests the model is not restricted to those higher-than-average earners able to pay the BTR premium. In response, we would make two points. First, as it is common for a wide range of people to require transitional housing at some stage in their housing careers, and cities such as London often attract people at that point in their life, it is hard to disagree with the general principle that such housing should be of good quality, well managed and enable transition as it is required. The second is that such groups are indicators of how widespread the problem of constrained housing aspiration has become. They reveal the extent to which the material elements of housing in London appear unable to accommodate the social processes of creating a home.

What becomes the critical question is whether the amenities on offer are really an adequate compensation for key workers and professionals for whom salary increases or access to family wealth are insufficient to allow them to access other forms of housing. This is a calculation which may well change if individuals find themselves trapped between the high rents of BTR, the high costs of owner occupation and the limited offer of the rest of the PRS. Individuals and even households may end up unable to move on from the curated form of domesticity offered by BTR – something based on a set of domestic calculations which may have been appropriate at a particular stage in a career and/or lifetime but no longer remain so. The targeting of 'generation rent' in particular becomes a little more insidious given the existing intergenerational transfer of housing wealth from the young to the old associated with the rising costs of owning a home. Likewise, if limited housing options and the domestic space required for everything from bringing up children or owning pets through to simply adequate private space actually inhibit the movement through different phases of life, the form of domesticity offered by BTR appears superficial. What is instead revealed is a shift in power with the users of housing asked to limit their domestic aspirations. These may well be complex, and differ between individuals and over time. Nevertheless, implicit in the notion of housing as a home are domestic calculations and aspirations that are undoubtedly greater than simply the provision of a revenue stream for investors.

References

Andrew, M. (2012). 'Neoclassical models of the housing market', in Smith, S. J. (2012). *International Encyclopedia of Housing and Home*. Elsevier Ltd. doi:10.1016/B978-0-08-047163-1.00649-4

Boughton, J. (2019). *Municipal Dreams: The Rise and Fall of Council Housing*. Verso.

Brill, F. & Durrant, D. (2021). The emergence of a Build to Rent model: The role of narratives and discourses. *Environment and Planning A: Economy and Space*, 53(5), 1140–1157.

Brill, F., Raco, M., & Ward, C. (2022). Anticipating demand shocks: Patient capital and the supply of housing. *European Urban and Regional Studies, 0(0)*. https://doi.org/10.1177/09697764211069837

Callon, M. (1998). Introduction: The embeddedness of economic markets in economics. *The Sociological Review*, 46(1_suppl), pp. 1–57. doi: 10.1111/j.1467-954x.1998.tb03468.x

Clark, W. A. V. & Huang, Y. (2003). The life course and residential mobility in British housing markets. *Environment and Planning A*, 35(2), pp. 323–339. doi:10.1068/a3542

Clifford, B. P., Ferm, J., Livingstone, N., & Canelas, P. (2018). Assessing the impacts of extending permitted development rights to office-to-residential change of use in England. Available at: www.rics.org (Accessed: 24 March 2021).

Cottrell, A. (2019). Build to rent market is better value for money for renters. *Real Homes*. Available at: www.realhomes.com/news/build-to-rent-market-is-better-value-for-money-to-renters (Accessed: 31 August 2021).

Da Silva, M. (2019). Build to rent homes cost 15% more than other private .... *Landlord Today*. Available at: www.landlordtoday.co.uk/breaking-news/2019/6/build-to-rent-homes-cost-15-more-than-other-private-rentals?source=newsticker (Accessed: 31 August 2021).

Federation, B. P. (2021). Green light for record-breaking number of new build-to-rent homes. *Press Release*. Available at: https://bpf.org.uk/media/press-releases/green-light-for-record-breaking-number-of-new-build-to-rent-homes/ (Accessed: 30 August 2021).

Gallent, N., Durrant, D. & May, N. (2017). Housing supply, investment demand and money creation: A comment on the drivers of London's housing crisis. *Urban Studies*, 54(10), pp. 2204–2216. doi:10.1177/0042098017705828

Get Living. (2021). Available at: www.getliving.com/ (Accessed: 31 August 2021).

Grainger Trust. (2021). Contact US. Available at: https://corporate.graingerplc.co.uk/properties/grainger-trust/grainger-trust-team

Jackson, B. (2005). Revisionism reconsidered: "Property-owning Democracy" and egalitarian strategy in post-war Britain. *Twentieth Century British History*, 16(4), pp. 416–440. doi:10.1093/tcbh/hwi053

Lennartz, C. & Ronald, R. (2019). 'Chapter 1', in Ronald, R., & Lennartz, C. *Housing Careers, Intergenerational Support and Family Relations*. Routledge, pp. 1–13.

MCHLG/ONS. (2021). Ratio of house prices to residence-based earnings. Available at: www.ons.gov.uk/peoplepopulationandcommunity/housing/datasets/ratioofhousepricetoresidencebasedearningslowerquartileandmedian%0A.

McKee, K., Moore, T., Soaita, A., & Crawford, J. (2017). 'Generation rent' and the fallacy of choice. *International Journal of Urban and Regional Research*, 41(2), pp. 318–333.

Nethercote, M. (2019). Build-to-Rent and the financialization of rental housing: Future research directions. *Housing Studies*, 35(2), pp. 1–36. doi:10.1080/02673037.2019.1636938

OECD. (2019). *Under Pressure: The Squeezed Middle Class*. OECD. doi:10.1787/689afed1-en

Raco, M., Livingstone, N. & Durrant, D. (2019). Seeing like an investor: Urban development planning, financialisation, and investors' perceptions of London as an investment space. *European Planning Studies*, 27(6). doi:10.1080/09654313.2019.1598019

Rooney, C., Hadjri, K. & Craig, C. (2013). Assessing lifetime homes standards and Part M building regulations for housing design in the UK. *The Design Journal*, 16(1), pp. 29–50. doi:10.2752/175630613X13512595146871

Thompson, M. (2020). *Reconstructing Public Housing: Liverpool's Hidden History of Collective Alternatives*. Liverpool, UK: Liverpool University Press.

Weber, R. (2016). Performing property cycles. *Journal of Cultural Economy*, 9(6), pp. 587–603. doi:10.1080/17530350.2016.1212085

5 Glamorising the Materiality of Living Small

De-stuffocation, Storage, and Tiny Living Aesthetics

Jennifer Owen

Introduction

It is estimated by geographer Danny Dorling that the amount of 'stuff' in the average home is six times that of the previous generation (BBC 2014). This reflects both changes in consumption practices and wider social changes, such as less stable partnerships and precarious living arrangements. These shifts in consumption practices have not gone unnoticed, and several movements and forms of value-driven living[1] have developed over the decades in response to apparent overaccumulation, of which tiny living could arguably be the most recent popular incarnation. Living in a small home means choosing what you can live with or without and, intentionally or not, subscribing to a certain way of 'living with things' (Gregson 2007). More often than not, shrunken domestic spaces require a difficult balance between comfortable, functional living and the 'comfort of things' (Miller 2010). This chapter will examine the material movements, services, and aesthetics which have been employed to portray and manage 'living small' as a lifestyle choice rather than a limitation of choice.

Books, blogs, and articles about living small are intertwined with a particular culture of consumption. Whilst there are enthusiasts, many people living in small homes are not fortunate enough to have the resources or autonomy to live in the highly glamourised forms by choice. This chapter will focus on those who buy – in to branded small homes and alter their materiality to reflect a chosen lifestyle, deliberately deviating from the norm, rather than those who are forced by circumstance into smaller, arguably inadequately sized, dwellings. However, the three areas discussed – minimising possessions, storage solutions, and pared-back aesthetics – are often common between those who live in small dwellings by choice or necessity. Choice, of course, is relative; labour and housing markets still dictate what is available and attainable, and living in a smaller dwelling, even if glamorised, may be the best of a set of bad options.

DOI: 10.4324/9781003173052-8

Understanding Materiality and Small Homes

The tiny house movement shares similar ideals with two other movements: the voluntary simplicity movement and minimalism (Mangold & Zschau 2019). Voluntary simplicity, historically influenced by the Puritans, Quakers, and transcendentalism,[2] is a lifestyle that is described as "outwardly more simple and inwardly more rich" (Elgin & Mitchell 1977: 2). It provides a blueprint to a more fulfilling life through the reduction of clutter and minimisation of activities that one does not find meaningful (Grigsby 2004: 2). In comparison, minimalism is a philosophy of intentionally eliminating excess things in order to live a simple life, which places focus on items of importance and value, again in the pursuit of a more meaningful life. In recent years, there has been a popular reinvigoration of minimalism by Marie Kondo (2014) who, through her best-selling book and subsequent Netflix series 'Tidying Up with Marie Kondo', extols the benefits of only having items at home which 'spark joy', and therefore fit within value-driven ideals.

Scholarship on the importance of material possessions to our ideas of identity, family, and home is well developed. The home is commonly understood as comprising a great array of material objects which collectively create "a dwelling experience that is greater than the sum of its parts" (Hecht 2001: 123). Hence the home contains a person's most special objects, where they can be close at hand and a permanent feature in identity production, or be freely discarded if they produce too much conflict with the self (Csikszentmihalyi & Rochberg-Halton 1981). This work suggests that materiality is a central component to making the home a secure base around which our identities are constructed, tried on, and remembered, and we gain a sense of ontological security from this when external forces are threatening or uncontrollable (Dupuis & Thorns 1998). These conceptualisations are true of all dwellings, but constraints such as space put a limit on the number of possessions which can be kept in the home, and as such can heighten or disrupt how meaning is attributed to things and the home itself.

Home-making, as an ongoing project of the self, is a way for people to actively engage with creating and recreating the meaning of their homes, and a means to narrate identity through home consumption (Miller 1998). Hollows (2008: 76) states that it is how we relate to our possessions and chose to arrange them that creates the foundations for our everyday practices and ways of relating to the home. So the home is materially created through the use and placement of objects – 'living with things' (Gregson 2007), and therefore the 'comfort of things' is a fundamental part of the creation of home (Miller 2010). For those who subscribe to the tiny living lifestyle, meaning-making around the home occurs less from appropriating mass-produced objects (see Miller 1998), but intentionally choosing to have fewer things and actively not owning what is thought to be 'wasteful' or 'thoughtless' (Summers 2021: 8). As Summers describes, tiny home enthusiasts therefore symbolically construct an alternative narrative of what home is and should be. Co-living, in comparison, sits within a broader field of 'compensatory' homemaking that attempts to rebrand inadequate housing opportunities as aspirational, thereby reworking what is understood as an adequate home (Harris 2019; Harris & Nowicki 2020).

Moving into a tiny home is an intentional choice to slim-down possessions, un-making the traditional idea of the home in favour of re-making the ideal *small* home. Tiny living enthusiasts see their alternative way of living with things as a "practical roadmap to the Good Life: a simpler life characterized by more security, autonomy, relationships, and meaningful experiences" (Mangold & Zschau 2019: 1). However, far from un-making or abandoning the idea of home, these individuals subscribe, legitimise, and manage their mode of living as a (sometimes temporary) lifestyle choice through different movements, services, and aesthetics away from the mainstream. These are discussed in turn in the following three sections with reference to the website and social media presence of The Collective and Apt Living, co-living schemes located in London, and the bestselling book 'Tiny House Living – Ideas for Building and Living Well in Less than 400 Square Feet' by Ryan Mitchell. Many tiny living books follow the same themes, and Mitchell provides commentary and inspiration based on interviews with tiny home dwellers across the United States, as well as his own experiences of living in a tiny home of only 150 square feet that he built in 2012.

Prioritising Experiences over Possessions

Living small is linked with particular values around possessions, influenced by popular representations, and born out of necessity. Any living arrangement with limited space often requires the dweller(s) to minimise the things in their home so that it is liveable and comfortable – a cluttered tiny home might feel claustrophobic for even the more tolerant person. Therefore, unsurprisingly, the pursuit of small living often goes hand-in-hand with the principles of minimalism. One co-living scheme in London, Apt Living, makes strong connections with minimalism through its tagline: "Maximising space by minimising the things we don't need". This mantra extends beyond its website branding to social media, where on Instagram Apt Living regularly posts inspirational quotes from well-known historical and contemporary figures relating to minimalism and that praise simpler, more fulfilling ways of living:

> The greatest wealth is to live content with little.
>
> (Plato)

> Simple can be harder than complex: You have to work hard to get your thinking clean to make it simple. But it's worth it in the end because once you get there, you can move mountains.
>
> (Steve Jobs)

Simple pleasures are the last healthy refuge in a complex world.
(Oscar Wilde)

However, framing intentional and well-curated ways of owning stuff in small dwellings as aspirational is somewhat at odds with the field of 'compensatory' homemaking as a whole, because often reductions in standards – such as size – come from a lack of choice within a limited housing pool rather than a lifestyle choice (Harris 2019; Harris & Nowicki 2020). The practices of managing possessions 'out of place' in small homes are discussed later in this chapter but rely on a discourse which reinforces this categorisation.

Deliberate 'simplification' of home, materially, has been found to be one of five significant motivators to live in a tiny home (Mangold & Zschau 2019), but, in his book, Mitchell (2014: 75) warns that this requires "more than simply selling all your belongings and moving into your house" but a process of soul-searching and realignment of values. Tiny living enthusiasts desire a version of simple living, similar to voluntary simplicity and minimalism in its aversion to a consumerist lifestyle, that is an alternative to the conspicuous consumption they are accustomed to (Cherrier & Murray 2002; Grigsby 2004). Therefore, they embrace practices of downsizing and decluttering as a way of achieving "functionally adequate and experientially liberating" small spaces (Mangold & Zschau 2019: 15). Unlike minimalists, who view downsizing as an ongoing process (Millburn & Nicodemus 2015), tiny home dwellers may buy new items if they will enhance their experiences of small living, and this pragmatism and experiential focus overrides the essentialism of minimalism or adherence to certain values as proposed by voluntary simplicity.

Unlike other movements, however, tiny living often puts a physical limit on the number of things in the home, as there is simply not enough room for a typical household's worth of stuff whilst maintaining the usability of the space. Mitchell (2014: 176) describes the reduction of possessions to fit within limited space "a welcome task" in response to the negative impact of clutter and the associated stressors of buying, caring, organising, and storing stuff. Mangold and Zschau (2019: 7) also noted this with their participant, Andrea, who felt her abundance of items was weighing her down, and this realisation led to a process of introspection: that more stuff does not equal happiness. Indeed, there is growing evidence that clutter negatively impacts upon mental well-being and can increase levels of the stress hormone cortisol (Ferrari & Roster 2018). In fact, more than half of Mangold and Zschau's participants expressed that they wished to get rid of stuff they never used or needed, in order to have less stressful, less complicated, and more efficient lives. The prioritisation of simplicity, intentionality, and essentialism over consumption is central to the approaches of voluntary simplifiers, minimalists, and tiny home dwellers, albeit to differing degrees and resulting in different practices of living with things.

In practice, as Mitchell (2014) points out, even with a strong motivation to reduce the number of possessions for a tiny home, ridding is a difficult task for many because it is counter to "our culture [which] has instilled a perceived need for more and more stuff" (176). Therefore, to be able to live a simpler lifestyle in a small space means "finding ways to reduce their belongings to the most essential, letting go of knick-knacks, and/or reconsidering the stuff they bought or were bringing home" (Mangold & Zschau 2019: 12). By implementing decluttering strategies set out in his book, Mitchell (2014) suggests that over time:

> you will end up with a collection of items that you value more and more, because you are constantly refining and re-evaluating each thing. [And] the result [...] is hopefully a set of things that you find very useful, very valuable, very beautiful, and highly sentimental.
>
> (153)

Importantly though, he stresses that ownership of items must be intentional, using things not just storing them, to fit within the lifestyle chosen by the tiny home dweller, whether for hobbies, work, or family life.

In the neoliberal capitalist context, any principles – including those followed by tiny home enthusiasts – which advocate detachment from material possessions and the prioritisation of experiences have taken on new meaning. All the participants in Mangold and Zschau's (2019) study "expressed a passionate desire to have more experiences within the simplicity of their newly found lifestyles" (13). With the time and resources made available by having less, and less to manage and worry about, tiny home dwellers, according to Mitchell, are able to pursue hobbies and passions, travel and see the world, and take enjoyment from other things in life, which reflect the principles of essentialism. However, no matter how 'ideal' this focus on experiences over possessions, for tiny home dwellers the prioritisation can also be a necessity, making up for what is not possible in their small quarters. As there is limited space at home, some traditionally domestic activities must take place outside the home. Mitchell, of course, puts this in a positive light, describing how socialising with large groups at a nearby bar, instead of having them over to a tiny home, allows for opportunities to engage with the local community. This is a similar framing and lifestyle choice for those in co-living schemes who trade-off domestic space for the ability to be "adaptable, flexible urban citizens" close to the action in city centre locations (Harris & Nowicki 2020: 595–6). Everyday life in a small home is therefore "characterised by a series of particular spatial and relational negotiations", whereby leaving the home is both a way of engaging with the eventfulness of city-living and a crucial coping mechanism (Preece et al. 2021: 3). Co-living schemes offer a site of community within shared spaces, both for co-working and through planned social activities. These experientially-focused spaces are promoted as both satisfying a desire for alternative living situations and addressing circumstances of precarious housing or unaffordable housing stock, despite often being positioned and experienced as a short-term solution.

As I discuss later in this chapter, focus on the practical and functional is central to the appeal of tiny home living. However, as we've seen here, 'living simply' also resonates with individuals because it frees up time and resources that can be directed towards having more experiences and nurturing better relationships. Though before we see small homes through only rose-tinted glasses, it is important to remember that whilst "simple living may eventually become the existential modus operandi, for many enthusiasts, the decision to go tiny is often much less voluntary" (Mangold & Zschau 2019: 15). Proponents of voluntary simplicity and minimalism often begin their journeys with a conscious act of rebellion against perceived shallow consumerism, yet many come from more privileged backgrounds; so unlike the majority of small home dwellers, they simplify and minimise not because they have to, but because they can (Fagan 2017).

Managing Materiality in a Small Home

When discussing how to reduce possessions to fit into a tiny house, Mitchell (2014) is clear that people should be wary of falling for the trappings of storage solutions seen on television, the Internet, and in stores. He warns that "to think that you can fix your problem by just organising better will get you nowhere", and that whilst space-saving solutions should be executed in tiny homes, they should not be used to hide possessions (145). There are several examples in Mitchell's book of families and individuals finding ways of maintaining order within their home, through carefully designed and allotted space for certain items or to each person. This echoes research on everyday life in small homes, in which participants describe being unable to leave items out (of place), meaning there is a constant "sense of movement as objects [are] shifted to make way for other functions" (Preece et al. 2021: 9). The Odom family, featured in Mitchell's book, share a closet which measures 4″ × 4″ and holds the current season's clothes, which are swapped over seasonally with those stored in a small shed. Having storage space for items that are not in use all the time, bulky things like bikes or tools, and seasonal clothes, in peripheral spaces, such as lofts, cellars, and garages, is not unusual in traditional homes (Hirschman et al. 2012), but in a tiny home, where all available space is required for living, storage becomes either integral to the design of the space or even more peripheral, requiring people to go outside to access their things. Indeed, Mitchell (2014: 117–18) argues that "outdoor spaces are key to tiny homes [because] they can increase your usable space". Reimagining the storage of things as part of innovative home design, or not part of domestic space at all, allows tiny home dwellers to maintain their ideal vision of living minimally.

Mitchell, on the one hand, argues against the utilisation of additional storage space, as it can produce feelings of stress and goes against the principle of finding happiness away from material things. Yet on the other, he includes several examples of tiny living dwellers utilising external storage spaces. In another form of micro-living, co-living schemes like Apt Living attempt to reassure prospective residents that they have adequate storage space, carefully highlighting 'clever', 'integrated' storage in plans of apartments and providing optional bike storage at an extra charge, but really to maintain the clean, pared-back design of the apartments, one would need to subscribe to living with less. The Collective, one of the most well-known co-living schemes, also based in London (and New York), openly acknowledges the disconnect between the living and storage space in its apartments by advertising a deal it has with Spaceways, which provides subsidised rates of storage for its residents. Spaceways is an alternative form of self-storage which provides durable plastic storage boxes for free, delivers and then collects these to/from the customer for free, charges a rate for storage per 67 litre box (£4.41 per month) or larger item (£9 per month), and then charges a fee for redelivery (£49 if stored under three months and £19 thereafter). This type of self-storage fits in with the subscription-style all-inclusive co-living lifestyle, which is central to its appeal, but also shows that space is lacking for tenants as they need to find it elsewhere outside of the home.

Except for the most disciplined, adhering to the keeping of only minimal things is perhaps an unrealistic expectation. By distancing itself from external storage space, it could be argued that small living attempts to uphold a falsity around having the bare minimum, when in actuality domestic needs ebb and flow and require the corresponding space to allow for this (see Owen 2019). Self-storage, as an industry, has grown exponentially over the last 15 years and even surpassed expectations though the recession and COVID-19 pandemic where other businesses failed. Its popularity could arguably result from a societal trend toward precarity, and is not only an expression of storage space deficiencies in small homes but also housing stock as a whole (see RIBA 2011). Small homes are disproportionately inhabited by younger households (Mckee et al. 2017), but the material hangover of this is felt across generations, as parents store the things their children cannot yet accommodate in their homes (Owen & Boyer 2019).

Function over Form?

The fringe counterculture of micro-living has been brought to mainstream attention through coverage by publications like *National Geographic* and *The New Yorker*, as well as reality shows and documentaries, and furnished displays in shops like Ikea; and as Colombini (2019: 449) states "[t]o no small degree, the popular appeal of tiny homes is constituted by a unique aesthetics". These media representations "invite appreciation for endearing aesthetics and clever economies of scale" (Colombini 2019: 462).

By virtue of its scale, the tiny home occupies a child-like place in people's imaginations, often being described as 'adorable' or 'whimsical' (Colombini 2019: 461), since as Chollet (2015) puts it "[t]here is a playful, adventurous aspect to the small house, like being suddenly inserted into a dolls house". Other popular imaginings of tiny homes describe a certain mix of materials and proportions, which mark them out from traditional homes. Mitchell (2014: 261) describes that "when people think of tiny houses, they often think of the iconic small house built on a trailer, wider cedar siding, and a red metal roof". These elements – the sloping roof, as well as well-placed windows, and correct proportions – are employed intentionally to provide visual cues that it is in fact a home, and not something less permanent like a shed, recreational vehicle, or trailer. Communicating that the structure is indeed a home is important not only for inhabitants' sense of home, but also central to a symbolic battle attempting to distance tiny homes from low-status and stigmatised forms of living (Summers 2021: 13). The participants in Summers' study (2021: 14) emphasised the importance of respectable aesthetics in marking out their tiny homes as 'real' and socially accepted. High-quality materials, in particular, made the permanence of the dwelling very clear compared to 'ugly, aluminium can' mobile homes. Also, having the capacity for choice, customisation, and self-expression in both the look and function of their tiny homes – qualities associated with the middle class – also distinguished them from lower status forms of housing.

The intentional use of materials, along with light and furnishing, is a central component of the Hygge movement, which has strong links with small spaces and therefore the tiny living aesthetic. Linnet (2011: 34, 27) describes Hygge as always "connected with the smallness of scale" and "antithetical to excess". Looking through the images of tiny homes included in Mitchell's book, the majority fit with the Hygge aesthetic – clad inside and out with bare wood, clever use of natural light, and pared-back, well thought out furnishings. Producing hominess is what McCracken (1989: 172) calls 'the embracing property' whereby "the surfaces of the homey environment exhibit a pattern of descending enclosure". This is not confined to tiny homes but their small scale lends itself easily to this and both the Hygge-style aesthetics and principles. Following this approach justifies a sense of homeliness which is comfortable with very little, but different from the somewhat coldness of stripped-back minimalism (both of which are forms of consumption in their own right). In comparison, the design of co-living apartments is much more similar to boutique hotels, combining muted walls with in-vogue jewel-toned tiling, carefully chosen furniture and artwork, and indoor plants. The importance of interior décor is apparent as 'Interior and Furniture Design' is included as one of eleven categories in the annual Coliving Awards, which received over 100 applications in its first edition of the awards. Whilst fashionable, and presumably meeting the aspirational tastes of many tenants, these apartments lack the opportunities for meaningful personalisation, also missing from much of the private rental sector (see Soaita & McKee 2019), which has consequences for tenants' ability to produce and convey meaning and relationships (see Miller 1998).

Self-building is common in the tiny living movement, with 84% of respondents in Summers' study (2021) having either built their home themselves or been heavily involved in the design process. Born of individual stylistic choices and practical necessities, the counterculture of tiny homes "promotes artful innovation with functional space" (Colombini 2019: 229). Mitchell (2014: 69) proudly describes how the tiny living movement has prompted common citizens to pick up hammers to build a better future for themselves. Research on the home has largely been concerned with interior design and furnishings, but the choice and use of building materials by the homeowner are also relevant to homemaking, bound up in specific cultural and historical contexts (see Cox 2016). The use of certain materials for tiny homes reflects not only their availability and cost but also their 'fit' with idealised imaginary of what a (tiny) home should look like. Building a home then is an iterative process whereby self and desired home are made together, and in this act producing and confirming valued identities and relationships (Cox 2016: 70). However, the confirmation of the identity of tiny home builder/dweller through the rejection of consumerism and undertaking of DIY is difficult to reconcile in the context of globalised media and industry influences (Leonard et al. 2004). The DIY market in particular has, over recent decades, become "utterly co-opted by commercial culture" through a proliferation of YouTube tutorials, reality shows, and websites like Pinterest (Farmer 2013: 47). Several works on symbolic consumption show that the value of homemade products lie in their opposition to commercially produced counterparts (see Curasi et al. 2004), yet tiny home dwellers make intentional choices in the design of their homes which allow them to adhere to their principles, as far as possible, whilst also making a homey place to live. An antipathy for the mass market can only go so far when the biography of production supports identities which go beyond 'correct consumption'.

Conclusion

This chapter has briefly examined how the origins and popular imaginaries of tiny homes and co-living apartments shape the justification of material practices and strategies by enthusiasts and dwellers in reality. Mitchell (2014) defines a tiny house as meeting the following three principles: (1) focusing on effective use of space, (2) relying on good design to meet the needs of residents, and (3) serving as a vehicle to a lifestyle that a resident wants to pursue. Whilst chosen to define the uniqueness of tiny homes, these principles are also applicable to other glamorised types of small homes, and notably lacking in the normal, substandard, and unromanticised. Each of the sections in this chapter has covered these three principles from the perspective of domestic materiality, in the form of possessions, storage, and design, respectively.

First off, we have seen how tiny living principles differ from voluntary simplicity and minimalism yet, at their heart, share a rejection of conspicuous consumption and the pursuit for a more meaningful life. An overall utilitarian angle on consumption is central to tiny living principles, but unlike other movements, having a small domestic space imposes reflection born out of necessity over everything else. Like any other home, practices of decluttering and slimming down occur, but to a more drastic degree so that the tiny home is made and maintained as a comfortable place to reside. The orientation away from possessions towards experiences also is central to the tiny living way of life but, as Mangold and Zschau (2019: 17) point out, this has a risk of becoming commodified as blogs, TV shows, and products increase in number. It would be somewhat ironic for the most anti-consumerist tiny living enthusiasts to inadvertently become users – and proponents – of new forms of consumption through the experience industry. Co-living schemes, however, do just this and occupy a contradictory space between experientially focused accommodation and reinforcement of minimalist ideals – which are achievable only through short-term material and relational negotiations.

In the second section, I discussed the contradictory advice on, and positioning of, storage. On the whole, minimising and disposing of possessions is the preferred option, but concessions are made for particularly significant items, bulky seasonal things, and anything which enhances the possibility for meaningful experiences or hobbies. The line between domestic and non-domestic space is drawn differently for tiny homes, where traditional storage spaces such as lofts, cellars, and garages are not included, or repurposed to make the most of limited square footage. As a result, dwellers have to make use of external storage, such as outbuildings, and therefore perceive it as outside of the domestic space. This way of viewing storage space maintains the sanctity of the tiny home and keeps ideas of the 'correct' number of things in line with the principles of the movement. Similarly, co-living schemes link-up with providers of self-storage to maintain the pared-back, fuss-free image of the youthful, urban citizen.

Finally, this chapter examined how following a certain aesthetic plays out in differentiating and justifying the existence of tiny homes in relation to traditional and lower income forms of housing, as well as the ideals the lifestyle is aligned with and against. Tiny homes, through their scale, are seen as not only endearing and picturesque but also 'not real homes', so attempts are made to include traditional elements in their construction, so they appear more like traditional homes than caravans or trailers, with which they actually share many elements. The use of materials and light inside a tiny home is also intentional and fits with the look and basis of the Hygge movement, in its simplicity, essentialism, and focus on the experiential. The design of co-living apartments is also central to their appeal but follows a different set of trends more akin to boutique hotels, fitting given the potential brevity of rental periods.

Whilst this chapter has painted a generally positive impression of tiny living, since accounts of prolonged difficulties and challenges are largely missing from Mitchell's book and representations of co-living found on websites and social media, it is important to end on a warning about glamorising the materiality of 'living small' that differentiates between aspirational small homes and insufficient space. As one critic puts it, we should avoid applauding people – and particularly Millennials – for 'living in boxes' (Harris 2015), and the sacrifices that are necessary to do so, since it maintains the illusion that precarity and instability are equal to opportunity and innovation, thereby glossing over the lack of choice and opportunity in a harsh housing market (Colombini 2019: 465). In a culture that, on the one hand, "stresses success, hard work and material comfort" and, on the other, "encourage[es] individuals to strive for happiness and fulfilment", adopting the tiny home lifestyle or occupying a plush co-living apartment offers a way to navigate the world orientated by a new moral compass (Mangold & Zschau 2019: 4). Yet the material realities that attract small home dwellers are a glossy representation that fails to acknowledge race, class, and other deeply entrenched issues with the housing economy. So we must provide accounts which are more than a fascination with living small, but highlight the discomforting capacity of the tiny- and co-living - movements and voice our collective 'claustrophobic horror' of the wider issues it represents (Colombini 2019: 465).

Notes

1 Value-driven living here is understood as making decisions on what to consume (products, experiences, accommodation etc.) in line with one's personal values, in order to move towards, or maintain, a more fulfilling life which is unique to the individual. Certain movements or lifestyles, such as minimalism, have shared values at their core.

2 Puritans and Quakers were denominations/reform movements of English Protestant Christianity which emerged in the 16th and 17th centuries. Transcendentalism is the name given to a loose philosophical movement of writers and philosophers which developed in the United States in the 19th century. Adherents of these three religious and philosophical movements placed particular value on living simply as means to being closer to God or nature.

Bibliography

BBC Two. 2014. Real Storage Wars. Business Boomers. Series 1, Episode 1, 14th April.

Cherrier, H. and Murray, J. 2002. Drifting away from excessive consumption: A new social movement based on identity construction. In Susan M. Broniarczyk and Kent Nakamoto (eds.), *Advances in consumer research*. Volume 29. Valdosta, GA: Association for Consumer Research, pp. 245–47.

Chollet, M. 2015. Whatever happened to the Tiny House Movement? *Counterpunch*. 29th May. Available online: www.counterpunch.org/2015/05/29/whatever-happened-to-the-tiny-house-movement/. Accessed 19/04/2021.

Colombini, C. 2019. The rhetorical resistance of tiny homes: Downsizing neoliberal capitalism. *Rhetoric Society Quarterly, 49*(5), pp. 447–469, doi:10.1080/02773945.2019.1658213

Cox, R. 2016. What are homes made of? Building materials, DIY and the homeyness of homes. *Home Cultures, 13*(1), pp. 63–82.

Csikszentmihalyi, M. and Rochberg-Halton, E. 1981. *The meaning of things: Domestic symbols and the self*. Cambridge: Cambridge University Press.

Curasi, C., Price, L., and Arnould, E. 2004. How individuals' cherished possessions become families' inalienable wealth. *Journal of Consumer Research, 31*(3), pp. 609–622.

Dupuis, A. and Thorns, D. C. 1998. Home, home ownership and the search for ontological security. *The Sociological Review, 46*(1), pp. 24–47.

Elgin, D. and Mitchell, A. 1977. Voluntary simplicity. *Co-Evolution Quarterly* (Summer), 5–18.

Fagan, C. 2017. Minimalism: Another boring product wealthy people can buy. *The Guardian*, 24th March. Available online: www.theguardian.com/lifeandstyle/2017/mar/04/minimalism-conspicuous-consumption-class. Accessed 19/04/2021.

Farmer, F. 2013. *After the public turn: Composition, counterpublics, and the citizen bricoleur*. Logan: Utah State UP.

Ferrari, J. and Roster, C. 2018. Delaying disposing: Examining the relationship between procrastination and clutter across generations. *Current Psychology, 37*, pp. 426–431.

Gregson, N. 2007. *Living with things: Ridding, accommodation, dwelling*. Oxford: Sean Kingston.

Grigsby, M. 2004. *Buying time and getting by: The Voluntary Simplicity Movement*. Albany, NY: SUNY Press.

Harris, E. 2019. Compensatory cultures: Post-2008 climate mechanisms for crisis times. *New Formations*, 99, pp. 66–87.

Harris, E. and Nowicki, M. 2020. "GET SMALLER"? Emerging geographies of micro-living. *Area, 52*, pp. 591–599.

Harris, M. 2015. Where should a good millennial live? *Splinter*, 23rd November. Available online: https://splinternews.com/where-should-a-good-millennial-live-1793853071. Accessed 19/04/2021.

Hecht, A. 2001. Home sweet home: Tangible memories of an uprooted childhood. In: Miller, D. ed. *Home possessions: Material culture behind closed doors*. Oxford: Berg, pp. 123–145.

Hirschman, E., Ruvio, A., and Belk, R. 2012. Exploring space and place in marketing research: Excavating the garage. *Marketing Theory, 12*(4), pp. 369–389.

Hollows, J. 2008. *Domestic cultures*. Maidenhead: Open University Press.

Kondo, M. 2014. *The life changing magic of tidying up: The Japanese art of decluttering and organising*. Berkeley, CA: Ten Speed Press.

Leonard, L., Perkins, H., and Thorns, D. 2004. Presenting and creating home: The influence of popular and building trade print media in the construction of home. *Housing Theory and Society, 21*(3), pp. 97–110.

Linnet, J. T. 2011. Money can't buy me hygge: Danish middle-class consumption, egalitarianism, and the sanctity of inner space. *Social Analysis, 55*(2), pp. 21–44.

Mangold, S. and Zschau, T. 2019 In search of the "good life": The appeal of the tiny house lifestyle in the USA. *Social Sciences, 8*(1), pp. 1–21, doi:10.3390/socsci8010026

McCracken, G. 1989. Homeyness: A cultural account of one constellation of consumer goods and meanings. In: Hirschman, E. ed. *Interpretive consumer research*. Provo, UT: Association for Consumer Research, pp. 168–183.

McKee, K., Moore, T., Soaita, A., and Crawford, J. 2017. 'Generation rent' and the fallacy of choice. *International Journal of Urban and Regional Research, 41*(2), pp. 318–333.

Millburn, J. and Nicodemus, R. 2015. *Minimalism: Live a meaningful life*. Montana: Asymmetrical Press.

Miller, D. 1998. *A theory of shopping*. Cambridge: Polity.

Miller, D. 2010. *The comfort of things*. Cambridge: Polity.

Mitchell, R. 2014. *Tiny House Living: Ideas for building & living well in less than 400 square feet*. Ohio, CT: Betterway Home Books.

Owen, J. 2019. 'Out of sight, out of mind' – The place of self-storage in securing pasts, ordering the present, and enabling futures. PhD Thesis, Cardiff University.

Owen, J. & Boyer, K. 2019. Holding on to childhood things: Storage, emotion, and curation of children's material biographies. *Social & Cultural Geography*, online, pp. 1–18, doi:10.1080/14649365.2019.1705992

Preece, J., McKee, K., Robinson, D., and Flint, J. 2021. Urban rhythms in a small home: COVID-19 as a mechanism of exception. *Urban Studies*, online, pp. 1–18.

Reimer, S. and Leslie, D. 2004. Identity, consumption, and the home. *Home Cultures, 1*(2), pp. 187–208.

RIBA. (2011). The Case for Space: The Size of England's New Homes. Available online: www.architecture.com/-/media/gathercontent/space-standards-for-homes/additional-documents/ribacaseforspace2011pdf.pdf Accessed 31/8/2021.

Seeley, J., Sim, A., and Loosely, E. W. 1956. *Crestwood heights: A study of the culture of suburban life*. Toronto: University of Toronto Press.

Soaita, A. and McKee, K. 2019. Assembling a 'kind of' home in the UK private renting sector. *Geoforum, 103*, pp. 148–157.

Summers, N. 2021. The socioeconomic concentration of intensive production interest: Lessons from the tiny home community. *Journal of Consumer Culture, 22*(2), 476–494, doi:10.1177/1469540520982360

6 Freedom or Dispossession?

Imaginaries of Small, Mobile Living in the Film *Nomadland*

Ella Harris, Mel Nowicki & Tim White

Introduction

Nomadland (Nomadland, 2020) was released in 2020 and met with high acclaim, winning best drama and best director at the Golden Globes, and arguably Hollywood's most prestigious prize, the 2021 Best Picture Oscar. The film is based on the 2017 book of the same name about people living nomadically in contemporary America. It follows characters who have opted out of conventional housing and made homes in vans, moving from place to place. That this film had such resonance with audiences and critics is perhaps not surprising at a time when opting out of conventional housing models became increasingly common, and increasingly present in collective imaginaries of the good life. In America, the Tiny Housing phenomenon continues to accelerate, promoted as a desirable alternative to the traditional American dream of suburban home ownership.

Like Tiny Housing, van living in *Nomadland* is discursively constructed as enabling freedom – freedom to move when and where you please, freedom to be closer to nature, freedom to work flexibly and freedom from the confines of conventional domestic life. In this chapter, we explore notions of freedom in *Nomadland*, in particular considering how this style of living both enhances and prohibits freedom. We do this with a view to better understanding the contemporary imaginaries of freedom circulating around small and mobile housing in America and beyond. We argue that, although tiny living is narrativised as enabling increased freedom, it often reflects a diminishment of choice. As such, it perpetuates a tradition of mobile homes as caught between being 'on the one hand a symbol of untethered freedom' and on the other 'a small, cheap, confined way of life' (Isenberg, 2017, p. 241).

Freedom and Housing Systems

In academic explorations of home and housing, notions of freedom remain underexplored, with some disjointed exceptions (Makhulu, 2015; King, 2003). This is strange considering how closely tied housing has been,

DOI: 10.4324/9781003173052-9

historically, to personal and political freedom. Until the early 1800s, property ownership was a requirement to vote in most American states, a prerequisite for the freedom to partake in political decision making. Going back further, the system of serfdom in medieval Europe also tied freedom to housing, as tenant farmers were enslaved to the landlords of the plots of land they worked on.

Although direct links between land ownership and political participation aren't operative in contemporary society, homeownership is still seen as a pathway to freedom. As well as having more autonomy over home design, homeownership relieves people of subservience to the timescales and decisions of landlords. However, imaginaries of freedom linked to homeownership are tied to the idea of paying off a mortgage, an ambition which can now take a lifetime or more. The strain of this was famously depicted in Arthur Miller's play *Death of a Salesman* (Miller, 1949) in which the main character Willy is so broken down by his perceived failure to achieve the American dream of homeownership and success in business that he has already resolved to end his life by the time of the last payment on his 25 year mortgage. This was the case already in 1949, and the unaffordability of housing has worsened significantly in the decades since.

Indeed, many have found that pursuing homeownership makes them feel considerably less free. High costs of housing mean that saving enough to put down a deposit and secure a mortgage requires curtailing other freedoms. For example, it requires you to limit choices of work to jobs that provide enough money and contractual security to obtain a mortgage. It also entails limiting choices of where to live, according to where housing is affordable, and forgoing leisure and consumption to save enough money for deposits. Finally, once a deposit has been saved and a mortgage obtained, homeowners are ultimately left tied into long-term indebtedness to a bank.

House prices have risen exponentially over recent decades as housing has become primarily viewed as an asset to invest in. This has made homeownership less accessible for even the relatively well off, and less desirable for those who can just about manage it. In this context, (ostensibly) more affordable, alternative forms of housing have entered the picture. Alongside Tiny Housing, micro living and co-living similarly purport to maximise freedom by lowering overhead costs of homeownership and enabling looser ties to place. These are all growing industries. Mobile homes represent 66% of new affordable housing produced in the United States and make the greatest share of unsubsidised low-income housing in the country (Sullivan, 2018). According to a 2019 real estate industry report, global funding in the co-living sector had increased by more than 210 percent annually since 2015, totalling over US$3.2 billion. Recent data suggest that between 2011 and 2021 as many as one in 15 new build flats in London fell below the national minimum standard of 37 m^2. Media representation and promotion of tiny living is also increasing. Popular series like Tiny House Nation make living in small, mobile properties seem aspirational, aligned with enhanced creativity and better relationships. In the 'Tiny House' extension pack for the video game The Sims, characters rack up points for creativity, well-being and relationships faster if they live in a Tiny Home. This kind of depiction positions Tiny Housing as enriching, not just different but better than traditional housing options.

Yet the rise of tiny living is arguably just part of an expansion of recreational vehicle (RV) and trailer park housing that has been around for decades and undergone several rebrandings. In the late 20th century, trailer manufacturers tried to reimagine trailer 'parks' as 'well-manicured, family-friendly garden sites' to 'cast off the temporary-sounding, refugee-bearing trailer "camps" of World War II"' (Isenberg, 2017, p. 243) and then as a kind of 'private club' (245). However, whereas this previous rebranding sought to 'domesticate' trailers and make them seem more like conventional housing, contemporary rebrandings focus on alterity.

Freedom as Alterity

Freedom has long been aligned with the ability to problematise and consciously opt into or out of convention. This was at the core of how the Cynics, a school of ancient Greek philosophers, defined freedom and runs through the conceptions of freedom informing philosophies and movements such as existentialism, situationism and hippie culture. Tiny Housing and van life are positioned as free in this sense of being alternative, outside the box ways of living, appropriate for freethinkers with the courage to subvert societal norms and expectations. Yet the extent of this freedom is questionable given that many of those opting to live in these ways have, like the characters in *Nomadland*, done so largely because financial, vocational and familial situations have made more conventional housing choices untenable.

Freedom is also commonly associated with mobility, which is key to the narratives of freedom in *Nomadland*. While some mobility is obviously forced or coerced (Sheller, 2008), an imaginary pervades of movement as equitable with freedom. In relation to housing, mobility has been framed as a resistance to the claustrophobia of domestic life and the heteronormativity and mononormativity tied to ideals of homeownership and nuclear family. As Cresswell (1993) explores, Jack Kerouac's novel *On the Road* depicts mobility as a form of resistance to these expectations. Physical mobility is aligned with the mental autonomy that alternative housing types connote, the ability to think for oneself and contest societal norms.

Homeownership and the American Dream

Mobility as freedom is also a crucial part of the nebulous aspirational imaginary of the American Dream. The movement of Europeans to America, en-masse, between roughly 1500 and 1800, was driven by hopes of a better life. These migrants mostly arrived on the East coast of America, leading to large, industrialised cities like New York and Washington, DC, where poverty and unemployment became rife. Idealised mobility then became a movement *within* America, an imperative to 'go west!' in search of greener, fertile lands and a better quality of life. Here, mobility is linked to agency, to having the opportunity to seek out the good life and shape one's own future.

Yet home ownership is also a key part of the American dream (Cullen, 2004). In an apparent contradiction, the American Dream not only encourages movement and growth but also presents predictable, suburban domesticity as the ultimate aspiration. Small, mobile housing marries together these two elements of the American dream, promising not only a sense of home and belonging but also mobility and adventure.

However, as Cullen has argued, the American Dream in all its iterations is arguably a construct that 'lulls people into ignoring the structural barriers that prevent collective as well as personal advancement' (Cullen, 2004, p. 6). Small, mobile housing can be read as a reproduction of this false promise of the American Dream and as a 'compensatory culture' (Harris, 2020). People are encouraged to think they can attain happiness through small and mobile housing, distracting them from structural issues that have shut them out of traditional housing models.

The notion of freedom attached to small and mobile living is focused on freedom *from* the prescriptions of authorities (although clearly these cultures have their own figures of authority and structures of power). But freedom, as Isaiah Berlin notably defined it, is also about freedom *to*. Whereas negative freedom is about what you're not subjected to or constrained by, positive freedom is about what you have the ability to do; and much of this requires infrastructures that give us shelter, stability and support. It's therefore important to think about what freedoms small and mobile housing enable both in relation to negative and positive freedom.

Nomadland

In exploring imaginaries of small, mobile living in *Nomadland*, we work within a tradition of cinematic geographies and geographies of film. Within this subfield, scholars have explored geographies of cinematic production and consumption as well as undertaken textual analysis of films and their construction of geographical meanings (Lukinbeal & Zimmermann, 2008; Sharp & Lukinbeal, 2015; Cresswell & Dixon, 2002). There have been longstanding calls to read film texts *through* the geographies of their production and exhibition (Zonn, 2007; Roberts, 2012; Aitken & Dixon, 2006) considering how meanings are generated through the interactions between the 'reel' and the 'real.'

In our analysis of *Nomadland*, the production of the film is especially important in understanding the meanings it attaches to small and mobile living. In particular, it's crucial to note that the film, while not a documentary, is based on a nonfiction book, features real nomads alongside actors and includes non-staged scenes. A decision was also made to film inside the small vans, rather than recreating them on a film set, despite the practical challenges.

However, alongside these 'real' elements, the 'reel' – the drama, technology and aesthetics of cinema – is also, according to the production team, key to its representation of small, mobile living. In a documentary about the making of *Nomadland*, it's argued that "the magic of the film is that you should have no idea what's staged and what is reality" and that the film would not have worked as a straight documentary, because a cinematic lens was needed to show the appeal of nomad life. The team suggests that a straight documentary would have made RV dwellers look like strange, societal outsiders whereas a cinematic approach captures the beauty in their emotional attunement to place and mobility.

Anti-essentialist approaches to film emphasise that films don't capture a pre-existing meaning of the world – there is no such meaning out there. Rather, they are part of the process through which collective meanings are constructed (Aitken & Dixon, 2006). We approach *Nomadland* in this way, as a cultural artefact that constructs meanings attached to small, mobile living. Interestingly, the film purposefully didn't include depictions of younger people living in vans, the kind of millennials who hashtag #vanlife in Instagram posts. Presumably, the makers saw this group as distinct from the outsider nomads it focuses on. Nevertheless, we argue that the meanings attached to small, mobile living through *Nomadland* relate to a broader discursive field that includes this more glamorised version. In the sections that follow, we explore tensions between freedom and constraint in *Nomadland* in three key areas: labour, mobility and materiality. We show how the elements of small mobile living imagined as freeing also represent precarity and constriction.

Labour

Nomadland is set in the early 2010s, in the aftermath of the 2008 global financial crash and its devastating impacts on industry-centred housing and communities. The protagonist, Fern, initially makes the decision to take up van living when she loses her job at the US Gypsum (a manufacturer of construction sheetrock) plant in Empire, Nevada. Fern worked in the plant's human resources department for many years and later held posts as a teacher and cashier in the town, while her husband worked at the mine. Empire is a real former company town that housed approximately 750 US Gypsum workers and their families from 1948 to 2011. "We had an airport, public pool, a golf course" Fern recalls during the film, reminiscing about the family's home there – "nothing special ... just a company tract house", she remembers, before correcting herself – "actually it was special, we were right on the edge of town and our backyard looks at this big open space ... it was just desert, desert, desert, all the way to the mountains, there

Figure 6.1 At the end of the film Fern visits the (now largely abandoned) former company town Empire where she used to live.

was nothing in our way…". In 2011, the mine and plant were closed, and Empire's population as of 2021 is estimated to be 65.

Fern's relationship with freedom is inextricably linked to her position within a changing labour market. After decades tied to a fixed location defined by a singular industry, the dissolution of Empire suddenly enables Fern total freedom to live wherever she wants. In this sense, her employment no longer dictates her home. Making the switch to tiny, mobile living establishes a sense of freedom in not being defined, personally or geographically, by her work. Instead, Fern takes on a range of temporary, zero-hour jobs, starting with seasonal work at an Amazon fulfilment centre, and eventually including camp leader, tour guide and restaurant worker. Her shifting engagement with the labour market is reflective of the rise to prominence of flexibility in contemporary labour markets. In the postindustrial, post-crash era, flexibility has come to define employment practices. As 'job for life' approaches to working-class livelihoods have become defunct, insecurity and temporariness have become the norm in the globalised capitalist system, yet this insecurity has been glamorised and reconstituted as flexibility – a labour pattern to be celebrated not just tolerated.

Flexibility – to work whenever and wherever – has become a key cultural logic in recent decades, especially within labour economies in the post-Fordist landscape. What the imaginary of flexibility overlooks, however, is that the malleability of work schedules and locations for workers goes hand in hand with the ability of bosses to also change schedules and locations of labour for employers, often without much notice or alternative. Flexibility imaginaries include an expectation that people should be willing to take work as and when, and where, it is on offer, retraining and/or relocating if necessary. This is the kind of flexibility that the British politician Norman Tebbit gestured to in his now much quoted speech, in which he described how

Figure 6.2 Fern approaching an Amazon warehouse, an employer she relies upon several times for temporary work in the film.

his unemployed father did not riot during the depressed interwar period of the 1930s but instead 'got on his bike and looked for work'. The statement captures a sentiment very much alive in contemporary work cultures – one which suggests that rather than responding to hard times with depression or anger, workers should be infinitely flexible and optimistic, willing to proactively make their own opportunities. One example of this kind of worker is the 'digital nomad' – denoting a person who (enabled by technology) can work from anywhere. The digital nomad is particularly prevalent in popular culture and marketing for new service-oriented real estate products like co-working and co-living. This term celebrates the agency of workers (particularly those in the cultural and creative sectors) in an individualised culture of merit-based competition – mythologising the autonomous worker and glorifying 'passionate work' (McRobbie, 2015). Home and work as fixed in time and space is framed as burdensome and outdated, while housing uncertainty and flexibility is adventurous and innovative.

Yet, clearly, Fern is not the glamorous digital nomad. The work she undertakes in the film is mostly manual labour in warehouses, not part of the glamorised imaginary of flexible jobs. Equally, she is at a different stage in her life. She should be retiring but needs the money, requiring her to keep moving around following low-paid work. Fern's story is an important insight into how small and mobile living is linked to more obviously precarious kinds of flexible labour as well as to glamorised ones.

That's not to say Fern doesn't experience flexibility positively. She has the freedom to detach herself from Empire and live life on the open road, immersed in epic natural landscapes. However, Fern's experience can also be read as emblematic of the highly restrictive shift in working-class livelihoods, from secure, well-paid, unionised work, to that which is highly insecure and unprotected. She represents a growing body of 'informal' workers, afflicted by cuts in welfare provisions and the escalating casualisation of labour – outside of established welfare regulations, unable to join healthcare and pension schemes, and lacking in collective representation. Whilst Fern's varied temporary jobs, on the one hand, indicate freedom from stationary and limited work in a particular industry, on the other, they denote her submersion into insecure labour markets. Guy Standing (2011) has termed this new category of working class labourers as "the precariat": people whose long-term work patterns consist of insecure jobs interspersed with regular unemployment. Such instability has subsequently impacted other aspects of everyday life, reducing access to and the maintenance of housing, and the erosion of paid leave and other work-based social welfare such as pensions. The normalisation of precarity within the labour market has also led to the dismemberment and fragmentation of people's sense of work-based identity. Standing argues that this in turn begins to impact on wider aspects of social identity, inciting alienation not only towards employers and the labour market but also with people's relationship with the state itself and their own sense of citizenry. He concludes that as more and more people see their rights associated with citizenship dismantled, precarity becomes an entrenched condition that produces socially and politically disenfranchised subjects. Fern's shifting experience of labour as she moves from company town to nomadic lifestyle is emblematic of both the reconstitution of working-class employment as inherently precarious and of the complex dynamics between freedom and work.

Mobility

Nomadland is structured around a journey. Fern is constantly 'on the road' – entering new landscapes, communities, etc. – sometimes simply passing through, sometimes stopping off for a night, sometimes staying for a week or two. Freedom to move one's body from one place to another at will is perhaps the purest form of freedom. And Fern's life is, in many ways, one of constant discovery and exploration. The conversations she has with people on the road centre around the places they've serendipitously roamed to, witnessing a new natural event or landscape. At times she departs abruptly and unexpectedly. Towards the end of the film, for example, we watch her sitting uneasily in her friend's huge quiet, sterile house. Suddenly, in a flash – and without so much as a goodbye – she has left for the coast, finding freedom and solace in the aggressive waves and wind – an environment contrasting acutely with the silent, immaculate domestic interiors of the previous scene. Clearly there is a sense in which she is empowered by this untethered existence, which stands in stark opposition to her previous life at Empire – work, home, community, social infrastructure strictly contained and geographically constrained. This freedom is romanticised by her sister later on in the film, who comments "I think that what the nomads are doing is not that different to what the pioneers did. I think

Figure 6.3 Fern's life is one of constant movement – shifting through different landscapes and communities.

Fern's part of an American tradition. I think it's great". But to what extent does this mobility – also a central way of framing freedom in the tiny house movement – truly represent freedom? Choice and agency must be closely considered.

Mobility is constrained – or imposed – to a large extent by the fact that those in mobile and tiny homes do not own the land beneath their unit, and are subject to the whims of those who do. For starters, they can only settle within strict legal and geographical parameters. Exclusionary zoning has long relegated mobile home parks to peripheral areas – particularly commercial and industrial districts lacking in adequate social infrastructure – and they are also subject to strict visual screening/containment rules (Sullivan, 2018). It is this peripheralisation that makes them so vulnerable to displacement via urban growth pressures – a phenomenon documented in depth by Sullivan (2018). Crucially, in what she identifies as the "central tension between mobility and rootedness", she explains how physical mobility is far from the norm for Americans living in mobile homes. The vast majority aren't in fact mobile at all – once set in place, they are difficult, costly, or impossible to move, hence why they are often forced to leave their homes behind when parks close. Indeed, the (im)mobile structures themselves are discovered as an opportunity to make profit from their poor residents: homes that can't be moved are often resold by park owners – profiting massively off their losses. Those assessing, moving, repairing and/or scrapping them have created a sub-industry from these evictions – which Sullivan refers to as the "mobility marketplace" – including park owners renting out abandoned (im)mobile homes to displaced renters waiting for their mobile home to be reinstalled elsewhere, forcing this captive market to pay a higher rent on homes that their former owners were forced to leave behind. Sullivan explains how the mobile home park industry thrives "precisely because it capitalises on a captive and needy population". While tiny homes are painted in a very different light (aspirational and empowering), and their occupants often have greater financial freedom – they do not solve the central constraints of land and law.

We see in Nomadland how staying outside the confines of designated parks is unpredictable, insecure and harsh – with Fern's life on the road marked by a constant struggle to find safe places to park. For example, in one scene following a shift picking beetroots in Nebraska, Fern is settling in for the evening when she receives a sharp tap on the window and a man wearing a hi-vis shouts "No overnight parking, you can't sleep here". She and the nomads she meets along the way rely heavily on lenient, kind or nonexistent gatekeepers in Walmart car parks etc. – and the sharing of information on safe places via social media. One scene features a lecture from a van dweller on the "10 commandments of stealth parking", which includes a demonstration of how to pretend you have a flat tyre when the authorities ask why you've stopped. The fine line between mobility and immobility in this form of dwelling is illustrated by the scenes when Fern has problems with her van – including when she gets a flat tyre and is forced to knock on a fellow nomad's door asking for a drive to a garage, who warns "you can die out here, you need a way of finding help". Later on, her van breaks down entirely. The garage she takes it to says it'll cost several thousand dollars to repair and recommends getting a new vehicle – 'it's my home', she eventually admits. All of a sudden, she's forced to leave her van and everything at the shop as she can't afford the repair.

Nomadland encourages us to ask the question: is mobility really freeing if forced? We see this tension playing out particularly in the relationship between mobility, labour and home in the film. Fern travels from place to place not in search of leisure activities but (temporary, often seasonal) work, first at an Amazon fulfilment centre, then at a camp, then at a restaurant, before taking up another post at the Amazon warehouse towards the end. In opposition to Empire, where there was a forced immobility linked to her employment, now her work is characterised by a forced mobility. While the former is not without its flaws, the latter is insecure, unstable, unpredictable – and it's clear that the mobility facilitated by these workers' homes allows them to better service the globalised corporations of late capitalism. Fern's access to a safe parking space with amenities – that is, her home – is also still intimately tied into her employment. This is made particularly apparent in a tense scene early on in the film where Fern is forced to leave a parking space provided by Amazon when her temporary contract comes to an end. When she asks if she can stay, the receptionist tells her there's no other jobs going, offering as consolation "Since you're in a van it's easy for you to move and to go south to a warmer place". Similarly, later in the film a friend encourages her to take a job at Wall Drug, a key selling point being the "great space to park". Fern is not 'off-grid' as in romantic imaginaries of nomadism – she's reliant on the wages, land and amenities provided by companies that offer her little in the way of security.

The freedom of mobility that life on the road is often aligned with "is usually connected with masculinity while place and home are femine" (Cresswell, 1993, p. 258). In classic depictions of nomadic life like Jack Kerouac's *On the Road*, men are often escaping the constrictions of domesticity. Films like *Thelma and Louise* counter this with a feminist mobility, showing women undertaking their own journeys on the road, escaping abusive men and other oppressive elements of domesticity. Yet *Nomadland* shows a different kind of mobility in which the alignment with freedom is less clear. Fern is not escaping domesticity; her domestic lifestyle has evaporated with the death of her husband and demise of her town. She has been forced into nomadic single life. Equally, she is older than most cinematic nomads, and the physical discomforts of living in a van and doing manual labour are subtly presented as taking their toll in the film. While she celebrates her freedom to roam around the American landscape, the films' close-ups of her sleeping on a thin mattress amidst her pots and pans, or diligently shifting heavy materials, her face pale from the cold, seem to point as much towards a domestic comfort that is lacking in her life.

Stuff

For Fern, as with the majority of people who make the shift to tiny living, freedom from the material, from 'stuff', is an important part of her journey into nomadism. At the beginning of the film, she sells the majority of her belongings in order to buy her van. There are continual shots throughout of her small home and limited belongings, set against the backdrop of the vast, spacious landscapes of US national parks and open highways. One scene, for example, shows her defecating in a bucket right by her kitchen – pan hanging inches to her left, bed inches behind her – shortly followed by scenes of her wild swimming and standing looking out across a vast expanse of trees and mountains. As a number of the contributions in this collection have discussed (Meissner, Owen, Lutke & Elbract), the shedding of material objects and adherence to minimalism have become an increasingly popular lifestyle choice for many in the West in recent years – much of it appropriated from East Asian traditions of reuse and de-centring the material from happiness and success. The growing popularity of de-stuffification and minimalism has gone hand-in-hand with the rise in tiny living. Both centre on the idea that stuff doesn't make you happy and that the shedding of unnecessary belongings can free you from the trappings of capitalist measures of success.

This is emphasised particularly at the end of *Nomadland* when Fern returns to Empire to dispose of the remaining belongings she has been keeping in a storage unit. "You sure you don't need any of this stuff?", the storage guy asks. "No, don't need any of it, I'm good. Not gonna miss one thing", she responds. Elsewhere in the film, she suggests that retaining stuff made her spend 'too much of my life just remembering, I couldn't pack up

Figure 6.4 and 6.5 Vast, stunning landscapes are juxtaposed with the interior of Fern's small, cramped van throughout the film.

and move on', implying that being free from physical things is a way to free herself from being stuck, emotionally, in a past life, and to move forward after her husband's death. Fern's disregard of material possessions is framed as what enables her to remember her past but also look to her future on her own terms. She is not bound by the values the objects of her past life connote, including domesticity and the association of status with material possessions.

This sentiment is shared in other recent works on tiny living, such as Catrina Davies' 2019 memoir *Homesick*. Davies recounts her decision to leave an overpriced shared room in Bristol (a mid-sized city in the UK) and move into a remote shed owned by her father on the Cornish coast. Much of the memoir speaks to the freedom gained from shedding stuff and living with only the material possessions that matter: a small bag of clothes, a treasured guitar. Davies spends much of the early chapters of the book recounting the unnecessary junk she disposes of as she prepares for tiny living, referring to unworn clothes as 'languishing', an array of unused objects stuck to her 'like burrs' (p. 44). Her depiction of these objects connotes drudgery and constraint, particularly when juxtaposed with her decision to embark on her Thoreaudian adventure of off-grid tiny living.

However, as Meissner has argued (Meissner, 2019, 2021), de-stuffification and minimalism, while modelled on the rejection of capitalism and the promotion of degrowth, have themselves become a lucrative market in and of themselves. Joshua Fields Millburn and Ryan Nicodemus, otherwise known as the minimalists, have built something of a popular culture empire through their website, podcast, book deals and two Netflix films. A brief browse on online marketplaces such as Etsy reveals a myriad of tiny living merchandise, including T-shirts celebrating freedom from materialism with slogans like "You don't need more space, you need less stuff" and "keeping it simple". This somewhat paradoxical commodification of de-commodifying one's life draws us back to the complexities of searching for freedom from dominant economic systems. Similarly to the previous discussion on labour, freedom from one system can ultimately lead to being subsumed into a parallel version of what was being escaped in the first place.

Despite the constant avowals of being free from material possessions, the importance of stuff is also a recurring theme in Nomadland. For example, Fern cherishes a set of plates given to her by her father and is furious when her admirer Dave accidentally smashes them. In another scene, she gives away a pile of her stuff, instructing someone who takes an item "my grandmother gave that to me, so take care of it", and there are numerous scenes of her looking through old photos. These scenes show the emotional importance of stuff as a way of holding onto the past/memories – and reflect the contradictory nature of de-stuffification, which can represent a traumatic loss just as equally as an empowering 'moving on'. Again, we see a tension between the freedom that renouncing stuff enables and the downplayed persistence of desire for comfort in things that small, mobile living doesn't really allow for.

Conclusion

Across key themes in the film, we see a persistent tension between freedom and constraint within small, mobile living. Fern lives a life unrestricted by ties to one place for work, where she can move through countless places having manifold fresh experiences, and where she is unburned by the traditional prescriptions of domestic life – its upkeep, its gendered duties. Yet she also lives a life of insecurity, where work is always being chased and never promised, where friends come and go, where her movements are often dictated by work and finances and where the very vehicle that enables her mobility can also leave her stranded when it falters or breaks. These inadequacies and constraints call into question the recent glamorisation of tiny living, particularly within the Tiny House Movement. While these supposedly new ways of living are promoted as offering escape from unjust housing systems, we argue that they disguise, entrench and expand forms of precarity and insecurity that mobile home communities have long suffered.

Equally, on a structural level, the freedom that small and mobile living offers is shown to play into dominant economic and social logics that actually reinforce constraints. As Cresswell (1993) has argued, 'forms of resistance are themselves subverted and redirected by flexible and adaptive forms of power' (p. 252). Resistance can be part of, rather than a threat to, the neoliberal agenda. We see this distinctly in *Nomadland*, where opting out of traditional neoliberal lifestyles to live in small, mobile housing actually provides precarious neoliberal labour with the mobile, eager work force that it needs and props up a failing housing economy that cannot provide affordable homes for a significant number of people. For small mobile living to be truly emancipatory, it therefore needs to actively confront – rather than support and entrench – unjust political economic structures.

References

Aitken, S. C. & Dixon, D. P., 2006. Imagining Geographies of Film. *Erdkunde,* 60, pp. 326–336.

Cresswell, T., 1993. Mobility as Resistance: A Geographical Reading of Kerouac's 'On the Road'. *Transactions of the Institute of British Geographers,* 18(2), pp. 249–262.

Cresswell, T. & Dixon, D., 2002. *Engaging Film: Geographies of Mobility and Identity.* Lanham: Rowan & Littlefield.

Cullen, J., 2004. *The American Dream: A Short History of an Idea that Shaped a Nation.* Oxford: Oxford University Press.

Davies, C., 2019. *Homesick: Why I Live in a Shed.* London: Riverrun.

Harris, E., 2020. Compensatory Cultures: Post-2008 Climate Mechanisms for Crisis Times. *New Formations,* 2020(99), pp. 66–87.

Isenberg, N., 2017. *White Trash: The 400 Year Untold History of Class in America.* London: Penguin.

King, P., 2003. Housing as a Freedom Right. *Housing Studies,* 18(5), pp. 661–672.

Lukinbeal, C. & Zimmermann, S., 2008. *The Geography of Cinema – A Cinematic World.* Stuttgart: Franz Steiner Verlag.

Makhulu, A.-M., 2015. *Making Freedom: Apartheid, Squatter Politics and the Struggle for Home.* Durham: Duke University Press.

McRobbie, A., 2015. *OpenDemocracy.* [Online] Available at: www.opendemocracy.net/en/transformation/is-passionate-work-neoliberal-delusion/ [Accessed 24/11/2021].

Meissner, M., 2019. Against Accumulation: Lifestyle Minimalism, De-growth and the Present Post-Ecological Condition. *Journal of Cultural Economy,* 12(3), pp. 185–200.

Meissner, M., 2021. Towards a Cultural Politics of Degrowth: Prefiguration, Popularization, Pressure. *Journal of Political Ecology,* 28(1), pp. 511–532.

Miller, A., 1949. *Death of a Salesman.* s.l.:s.n. London, UK: Penguin Plays.

Nomadland. 2020. [Film] Directed by Chloe Zhao. USA: s.n. Los Angeles: Searchlight Pictures.
Roberts, L., 2012. *Film, Mobility and Urban Space, A Cinematic Geography of Liverpool*. Liverpool: Liverpool University Press.
Sharp, L. & Lukinbeal, C., 2015. Film Geography: A Review and Prospectus. In: S. Mains, J. Cuppers & C. Lukinbeal, eds. *Mediated Geographies and Geographies of Media*. Dordecht: Springer, pp. 21–35.
Sheller, M., 2008. Mobility, Freedom and Public Space. In: T. Sager and S. Bergmann (Eds.), *The Ethics of Mobilities*. London and New York: Routledge, pp. 25–39.
Standing, G., 2011. *The Precariat: The New Dangerous Class*. London: Bloomsbury.
Sullivan, E., 2018. *Manufactured Insecurity: Mobile Home Parks and Americans' Tenuous Right to Place*. Berkeley, California: University of California Press.
Zonn, L., 2007. Going to the Movies: The Filmic Site as Geographic Endeavor. *Aether: The Journal of Media Geography*, 1, pp. 63–67.

Part III

Experiencing Shrinking Domesticities

7 Decent Homes in Compact Living?

Conventional Ideals in Unconventional Contexts

Anne Hedegaard Winther

Compact living is currently receiving increasing attention in housing and urban planning, and this novelty often ignites an assumption that dwellings targeted at compact living should revolutionise the idea of home. However, the present study shows that the making of unconventional housing choices does not automatically entail unconventional ways of making home.

This chapter is based on a case study of six examples of compact living in a Danish context. By prioritising living in the city higher than domestic spaciousness, these households deviate from conventional norms of the home; yet the chapter concludes that despite making unconventional housing choices, the households under study are highly aware of conventional social ideals of domestic spaciousness, and being spatially restricted, they apply other elements of conventional ideals of the home, namely, comfort, functionality and aesthetics.

Introduction

Average Danish households spend nearly 38% of their income on housing related expenses[1] (Statistics Denmark 2019). In combination, a voluminous home decor market and a substantial popularity of home decor television, magazines, social media communication, etc., provide very strong indications of the immense importance of our homes and the clear presence of ideals about what a proper and a decent home is. A key element in such ideals of the home is spaciousness. Throughout the evolution of the Danish welfare society, expansion of domestic living space has been a key element in the enhancement of general housing standards (Bech-Danielsen & Stender 2015; Lind & Møller 1996). Even today, the City of Copenhagen has a minimum size requirement for new housing units (City of Copenhagen 2019). Standing as the ideal type of spacious dwelling is the detached single-family house – residents of detached houses have a 32% larger living space than residents of flats (Statistics Denmark 2021), and nearly 80% of the population rates this housing type as their favourite (Kristensen & Andersen 2009). Since the 1960s, detached houses in the form of standard houses have been a core element of the welfare state (Bech-Danielsen & Gram-Hanssen 2004),

DOI: 10.4324/9781003173052-11

steadily increasing in size to reach an average of 205 m^2 today (Statistics Denmark 2020). This strongly suggests a preference for large dwellings amongst those who have the choice, and settlement patterns support this by revealing that middle-income and high-income households live in detached houses to a substantially larger extent than low-income households (Møller 2001). Small dwellings are often associated with low social status (apart from student housing).

Despite conventional ideals about domestic spaciousness, however, some households choose to go in a different direction: Danish cities (and cities in other countries) have recently witnessed middle-class households living in much less space than the majority of this population group. In the present context, this is termed 'compact living'. The domestic lives of these households are spatially condensed or compressed compared with those of other households in the surrounding society. This chapter is part of a research project doing a case study on such households (A. H. Winther 2021b). They have much less available living space than the 40 or 46 m^2 per person making up the averages of Denmark's two largest cities (Dansk Byggeri 2020). The study has shown how living in the city is of such high priority to these households that this drives their housing choice (A. H. Winther 2021a). Housing prices in urban areas have recently risen to unprecedented levels, making it difficult for middle-class households like those of the case study to afford large dwellings in central urban neighbourhoods (City of Copenhagen 2018). Thus, by choosing to live in unconventionally little space in the city instead of relocating out to where they could afford much larger dwellings, these households deviate from general macro trends and social ideals of the home that prioritise space very highly in housing choice.

Such findings give rise to considerations of whether conventional ideals of the home are in fact unimportant to these households, yet the study indicates that matters may not be that simple. Consequently, this chapter sets out to explore this by answering the following question: *Do conventional ideals of the home play a role for the case study households?* Secondly, given the general preference for spacious dwellings in conventional ideals of the home, there is an immediate misfit between these and compact living. The chapter thus further asks: *How does compact living affect the realisation of conventional ideals in the homes under study?*

Practicing Homes: Establishing the Theoretical Framework

Making Home

The above 200 m^2 average size of newly built houses in Denmark strongly indicates that the meaning of our dwellings reaches far beyond basic functions like offering a roof over our heads and a place to sleep, cook or store possessions. A broad body of literature has stressed this by analysing and investigating the concept of 'home'. As put clearly by Després (1991) 30 years ago and continuously underlined by proceeding scholars (see Boccagni & Kusenbach (2020) for overview), the layers of home reach beyond the material and include the social, the affective, the sensorial, etc. (Blunt & Dowling 2006). As pinpointed by anthropologist Gullestad (1989), our dwellings are simultaneously a symbol of our lives and the place of their continuous formation and consolidation. Thus, through our choice of dwelling and location, and through our way of using our dwellings, our homes become a way of both showing and consolidating ourselves and our lives in relation to our surroundings. 'Home' is relational; it is embedded in a specific socio-structural and cultural context (Boccagni & Kusenbach 2020). The choice of housing type and neighbourhood type, the decoration style and the organisation and usage of our dwellings are far from meaningless; they contain expressions of our lifestyle and tastes, and they position us in relation to our surroundings (Sparke 2010; Karsten 2010; Bech-Danielsen & Gram-Hanssen 2004; Reimer & Leslie 2004). Along these lines, Douglas (1991) terms home as "space under control" (289), yet this control, she holds, is contested. Humans are not fully in control over their homes. Firstly, for most people, economy puts up limitations to our freedom of choice in terms of acquisition, renovation and decoration of dwellings. Additionally, other factors can set up obstacles too, e.g. structural, societal or physical conditions of the home (Özüekren & van Kempen 2002). Consequently, a mismatch between dwellings and occupants is the rule more than an exception, though to highly varying extents (see, for instance, Lancione (2019) or Højring and Bech-Danielsen (2021) on public space home-making of the homeless).

Though home is often perceived as based in a dwelling, this does not always hold. In some cases, the feeling of home is strongly related to places outside the dwelling, for instance, a neighbourhood, a city or even a country. As shown in A. H. Winther (2021a), the neighbourhood and the city as a whole are core elements (alongside the dwelling) in the perception of home of the case study households. Home can also relate more to emotions or practices than to a geographical location as demonstrated by e.g. I. W. Winther (2013) pointing to the phrases 'feeling at home' or 'making oneself at home', which are not restricted to refer to an individual's dwelling. Thus, homes are not static material housing units. Homes are practiced and perceived: they are constantly in the making, continuously activating and connecting past, present and future (Pink et al. 2017) and renegotiating usage and perceptions of different spaces (Meagher 2017).

People, Practices and the Physical Environment

In this making of homes, people interact with the physical environment around them, yet the social sciences and humanities, i.e. the sciences working precisely with the social and the human, have traditionally perceived the physical world as merely a backdrop for human life (as described by Warf & Arias, 2009). However, within recent decades, scholars have increasingly begun dealing more thoroughly with the physical surroundings of people as opposed to the people only and as something which actively impacts human life[2] – a development often phrased as the spatial turn, e.g. by Warf and Arias (2009). Applying the idea of the non-human as acting, Norman (2013) has examined the design of everyday objects through their interaction with humans by reinstating and reformulating the concept of "*affordances*": Originally introduced in 1979 by Gibson (2015), affordances refer to the way in which physical elements prompt or invite certain actions from humans (Chong & Proctor 2020). For instance, solid ground prompts standing or walking; and when added an adjacent raised level, it prompts sitting. In other words, affordances are objective. However, proceeding scholars have criticised this objectivity, most notably Norman (2013) arguing that the way humans perceive and interact with the physical environment does not depend on the affordances of this alone; it also depends on human cognition and thus involves interpretation. Interaction with a given physical element, for instance, a dwelling, a room or a piece of furniture, will not be identical for all humans. According to Norman, "affordances provide strong clues to the operations of things" (Norman 2013, p. 9), but are not determinant of perception. Norman thus distinguishes Gibson's physical affordances from "perceived affordances" (Norman 2013).[3] Consequently, as Højring (2018, p. 65) puts it, studying affordances entails studying not only the physical elements which prompt or impede human action but also those who act and their actions.

Studying homes thus reaches far beyond studying material dwellings. As Pink (e.g. Pink et al. 2017 or Pink 2012) argues from a practice-theoretical approach, what we generally think of as a kitchen, i.e. an indoor room equipped with a fridge, a cooker, tableware, etc., would not be a kitchen without being practiced as such, i.e. being cooked in, being used to store food, etc. Yet practices in themselves do not determine whether they are performed in one way or another; this depends on their relation to the world in which they are performed and to the humans performing them. In other words, humans perform practices in multiple ways, depending on who they are, and how they relate to the world around them – including the physical environment. Places, on their part, situate practices and humans in the world (Pink 2012). Correspondingly, a dwelling without people or practices would not be a home, but simply be a volume filled with air and certain material elements (walls, furniture, etc.). The historical development in visual arts and architecture demonstrates clearly the way in which human understanding and perception of the spatial have become more refined over time: As stated by Bek (2010), it has elaborated from a simple and static understanding to an organic in-motion understanding tied to senses and experiences. The spatial is lived and experienced, not merely observed. This applies to the spaces in a dwelling too.

Altogether then, homes are practiced by people, meaning they are produced through our bodily, cognitive and social practices, all rooted within the given context. At the same time, homes actively practice back, so to speak, they are much more than passive, material backdrops of human life. Accordingly, the object of analysis of this study must be the interaction between people, practices and the non-human environment.

Methods and Cases

The paper is based on a qualitative ethnographic study methodologically designed to produce in-depth, detailed and situated knowledge rather than broad-spectrum knowledge. Consequently, it takes qualitative case study as its method, as the strength of this lies in the detail, the depth and the power of the good example (Flyvbjerg 2015; Thomas 2011). The approach is explorative in order to allow for situating and contextualising the collected data (Thomas 2010), and the purpose is to capture the concrete, the experienced, the reflected and the perceived set within space and time. Accordingly, the methodology lends from everyday life ethnographies on the home (like those collected by Pink et al. [2017] or the work of Madsen [2017]).

The dataset covers six carefully selected cases, each consisting of a dwelling, its occupants, its surroundings and the life led in and around the dwelling. They are presented in Figures 7.1–7.6 below.[4] In other countries, these dwellings might hardly be perceived as small, but the relation to

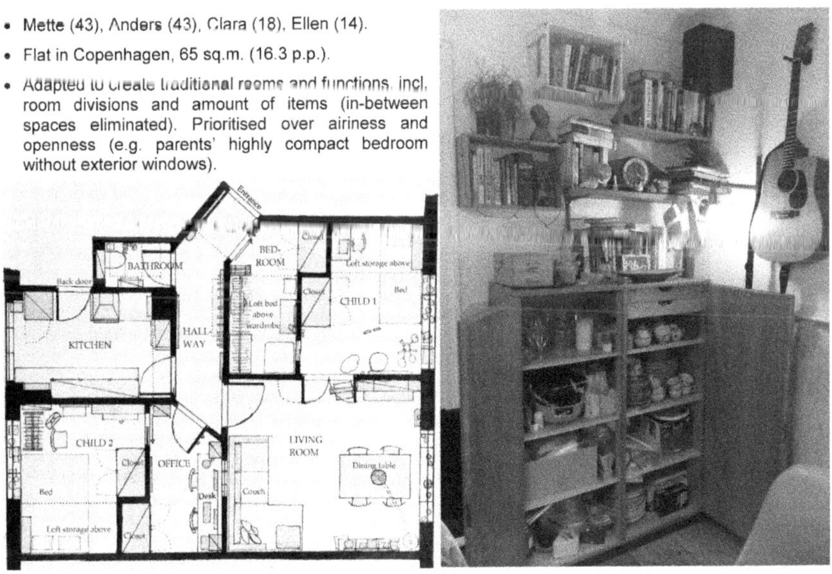

Figure 7.1 Presentation of cases 1–6.

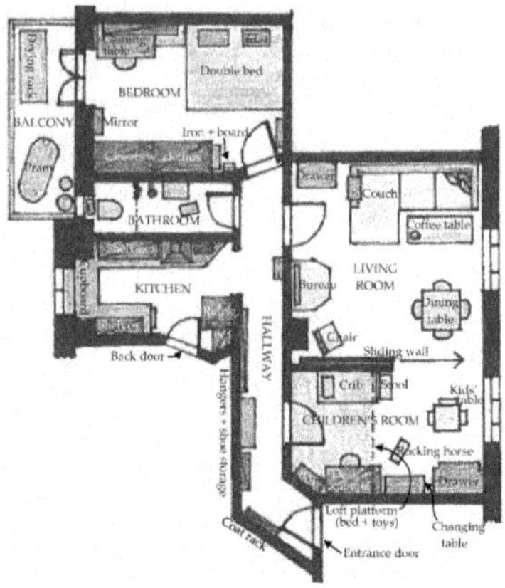

- Emil (32), Johanne (33), Karla (5), Lauge (1).
- Flat, Copenhagen, 56 sq.m. (14.0 p.p.)
- Different needs of four individuals + making room for sociability. Physical structures restrain reorganisation of the dwelling. Flexibility: A sliding wall btw. children's room and living room has preserved the social + granted temporal privacy for parents and children.

Figure 7.2

- Stine (42) + Barbara (14) and Ursula (12) who live there every second week.
- Flat in Copenhagen, 53 sq.m. (17.7 p.p.).
- High prioritisation of airiness, openness, light. Flat adapted to this by using an open plan divided into zones. Stine sleeps on sofa bed = temporal privacy (exists only every other week).

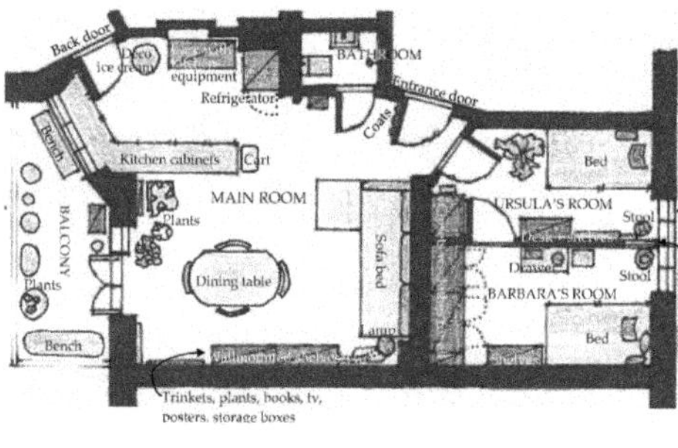

Figure 7.3

general housing patterns in the surrounding society is key, and Denmark has very high averages of available living space, also in urban areas (Eurostat, 2018). For instance, in Case #1, each family member disposes of 16.3 m², which is much lower than the Copenhagen average of 40 m² (Dansk Byggeri 2020). Each case is studied through a palette of methods, namely, qualitative,

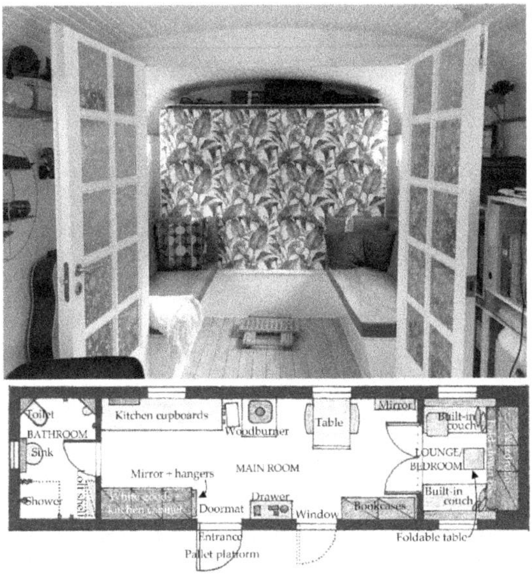

- Majbrit (44).
- 28 sq.m. tiny house on wheels, rural location.
- Included despite non-urban location, because it holds unique information about purpose-built compact living (difficult to find in Danish cities).
- Home to Majbrit = freedom (geographically, economically, materially) and self-determination and independence.Contains all traditional functions (sleeping, dining, kitchen, full bathroom), connected to water and electricity, isolated and heated.

Figure 7.4

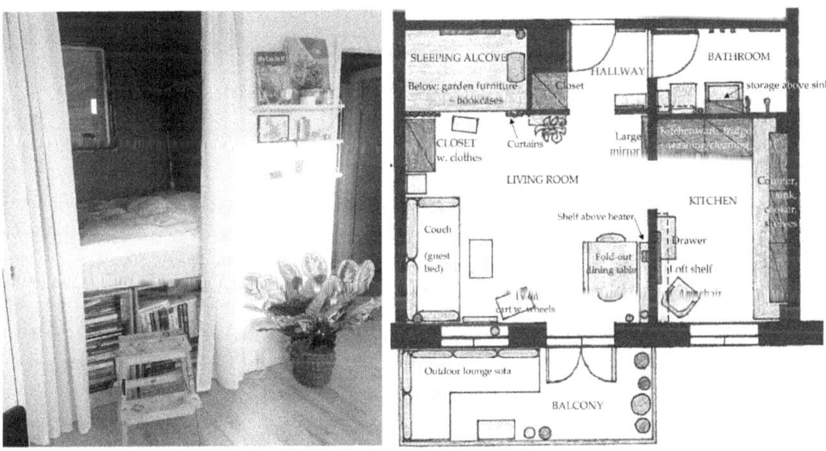

- Agnes (31).
- Studio in Copenhagen, 29 sq.m.
- Key feature: Abundance of light (large balcony, large glazed areas + unblocked view). Living alone makes fit btw. compact physical environment and Agnes' ideals of home easier; yet the open alcove makes sociability a challenge.

Figure 7.5

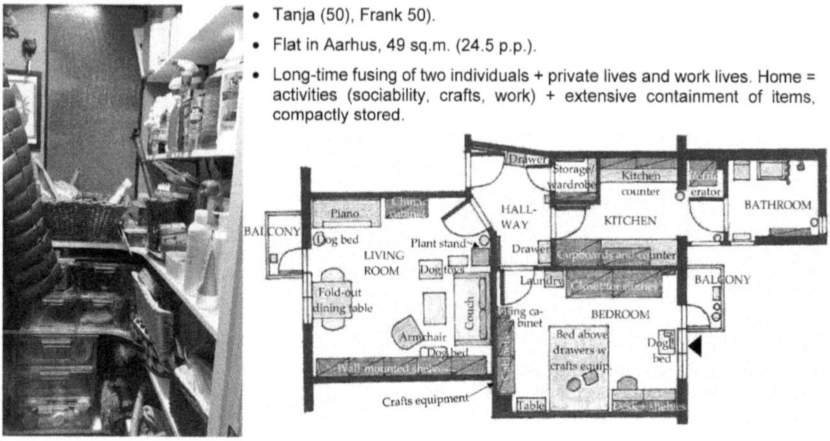

Figure 7.6

semi-structured, in-depth interviews taking place in the homes and including a tour of the home; registration of dwelling layouts and arrangement of dwellings (functions, furniture, etc.); households photographing least and most favourite parts of their home; and seven-day journal-keeping of all activities in the homes.[5] Data was collected between August 2018 and December 2019.

Findings from Life in Six Compact Homes: Making Decent Homes under Spatial Restrictions

The following section analyses the six cases of the study to examine, first, which role conventional ideals of the home play for the compact living households. Second, the section examines how the case study households set out to realise such conventional ideals of the home within the particular context of compact living. Such conventional ideals are to be understood as the generalised ideals prevailing in the surrounding society with regard to the home. This is not to say that such ideals are dictating of social acceptance, but that they are closely linked to social status and the assessment of ourselves in relation to others (Boccagni & Kusenbach 2020). Social ideals play key roles for the definition of socio-cultural contexts of normality, acceptability and status.

Do Conventional Ideals of 'A Decent Home' Matter at All?

Compared to conventional ideals of the home and prevailing residential settlement patterns of the surrounding society, the households under study have made very unconventional housing choices. Does it then follow that their ideals and perceptions of home are unconventional too?

Urban inhabitants generally live on less space than inhabitants of other types of environments. This applies to Danish cities too. This might cause ideals of domestic spaciousness to be moderated amongst urban inhabitants. Literature on home has clearly demonstrated how home is embedded in socio-structural and cultural contexts – this applies on multiple scales. One only needs to consider the vast differences between different parts of the world and different countries to grasp how ideals of home are context-dependent (see Meagher [2017] or Sobh & Belk [2011] for intercultural studies of home). Home is thus also about feelings of belonging and fitting in (Sobh & Belk 2011). The impact of such contextual conditions on local norms about the home is clearly noticeable to the case study households. For instance, the family of Case #1 states that:

METTE: Other families live relatively small too; it's not like if we lived in the middle of a detached-house neighbourhood

ANDERS: It's really not that unusual here; we've just taken things a little step further

Similar reflections are expressed by the study participants when accounting for their decisions to remain in a flat in the city instead of taking the conventional road and settling in a house in the suburbs: Being surrounded by other households that have made the same choice (living in the city) has made it feel less controversial (see A. H. Winther [2021a], which examines these processes). However, the study clearly shows that though local urban contexts may moderate macro-scale ideals of the home, they do not supersede them to the case study households. A finding that cuts across the cases are the aspirations of the households to create "*decent*" homes or "*proper*" homes (in their own words). Examining the meanings of such terms thoroughly reveals that these are highly social phenomena, closely linked to more common or conventional ideals of the home: This is evident, for instance, in Case #1, where the household has simply shrunken and condensed the topology of a conventional dwelling instead of seeking to recast and revolutionise it (see Figure 7.1). Another example is that of Majbrit's (Case #4) assessment of her caravan home. She bases this on distinguishing her dwelling from the trailers of alternative communities of squatters, marginalised groups, etc.:

> It feels like a home-home, like a home for real, you know. [...] My house doesn't look like an appalling trailer, which is all filthy and cold and clammy, I mean, it's bright and nice – it's an actual home.
>
> (Majbrit, Case #4)

The case study households show strong awareness of the generally lower social status of small dwellings. Homes play key parts in the self-perception and positioning of individuals in relation to others, and accordingly, Agnes (Case #5) sees an extended risk for small homes, compared with 'normal' homes, of becoming shabby and indicates that having a shabby home will translate into a feeling of being shabby yourself:

> Things are normally sized in my flat; it feels normal to be here ... You owe yourself, when you live in a small space, to avoid your home becoming shabby.
>
> (Agnes, Case #5)

Thus, space grants social status, and the study clearly demonstrates that these compact living households are highly aware of this. Conventional ideals about home and what constitutes a decent or a proper home are very evident and very important to the households.

But being short on square metres, the households are off to a poor start in producing what they perceive as 'decent' homes. The next section examines the strategies applied by them to take up this challenge, identifying how they turn to alternative means for meeting the ideals of a 'decent' home.

Practicing Decent Homes Without Spaciousness at Hand

The case study households are highly aware of being behind on points regarding ideals of spaciousness in the home. This section will examine how they instead turn to other ways of practicing what they perceive as a 'decent' home within the context of compact living. In particular, they look to comfort, to functionality and to aesthetics.

Understood as a domestic feature, comfort is considered to be a core element in contemporary standards of home and to have almost come to represent the basics of housing qualities in the Westernised world (see Madsen 2017 for a literature overview). Comfort being a key element in the case study households' perceptions of a decent home thus supports such arguments. In the home, comfort contains multiple layers like thermal comfort, sensory comfort, cosiness, physical convenience and ease (Madsen 2017). Similarly, comfort takes many shapes to the households under study. In Case #2, an insistence on making room for a voluminous sectional couch in the living room is a way of creating comfort in terms of relaxation (bodily and cognitively) and cosiness (see Figure 7.7). Such large couches have become common in Danish homes in recent years as opposed to smaller, more upright sofas in a mid-20th-century design. Accordingly, this choice of furniture is a way of keeping up with modern-day standards of domestic family life, despite living in a small dwelling that would seemingly *afford* opting for more compact furniture. Additionally, the household insists on making room for kitchen appliances that functionally speaking are dispensable, but that grant the family an added convenience in their kitchen practices:

Figure 7.7 The family of Case #2 has prioritised a large sectional couch even though their living room is relatively small.

> Let's just call it a luxury problem, I mean, we don't actually need a stand mixer or a milk steamer, and they take up a lot of counter space, but they are luxury elements that we enjoy, so I wouldn't trade them for anything. And a dishwasher – one could of course live without it, but I would just never give that up either.
>
> (Emil, Case #2)

At first hand, compact dwellings appear to be affording an elimination of inventory that is not utterly indispensable, and adding extra comfort to the home often takes up extra space. However, the households of the study interpret their dwellings differently and insist on prioritising comfort, on the face of it *in spite of* the restricted spatiality, but perhaps more precisely *because of* the restricted spatiality. The physical affordances of the homes thus differ from the perceived or interpreted affordances, in the terms of Gibson (2015) and Norman (2013). As Norman argues, affordances provide strong clues to the interaction between the physical environment and the people living in it, but they are not determinant of it. Here, prevailing social ideals of home act in as well, affecting the human interpretation of the compact dwellings. To the case study households, consciously prioritising an upholding of certain levels of comfort becomes a means for increasing the decency of the home.

Besides comfort, the households of the study look to functionality as a means for approaching the ideals of home. In fact, domestic functionality can be said in a way to be a form of comfort – relating to the layers of physical convenience and sensory or bodily comfort (Madsen 2017) and is likewise perceived by literature to be a central element in modern Westernised standards of housing qualities. A key source of the challenges to domestic functionality in the dwellings under study is what could be termed compact functionality, that is, the way multiple functions are physically compressed in the home. Especially, practical rooms like kitchens, bathrooms and hallways present compact functionality – for instance, the kitchens contain multiple items each affording different practices (washing up, preparing meals, filling and emptying the dishwasher, sometimes eating too), and given their small sizes, this compact functionality is intensified further. Moreover, in some of the cases, practices conventionally performed in other rooms are relocated to the kitchen, for instance, tooth brushing, which in Case #1 is relocated from the bathroom due to the similarly intense compact functionality of this (see Figure 7.8). As a consequence, the household has embodied adapted ways of conduct and regulations of behaviour in the kitchen and the bathroom – "like on a submarine", one of the residents say. A symbolic materialisation of such lack of domestic functionality is when the case study households experience physically bumping into things in their homes or physical items repeatedly bumping into each other, because of the restricted spatiality and compact functionality. Frank and Tanja (Case #6) have consciously prioritised making room for their abundance of physical possessions as opposed to sorting out and arranging their home more airily. Nevertheless, when they experience the lack of functionality through physical collisions like edging through the narrow space between the bed and the closet or

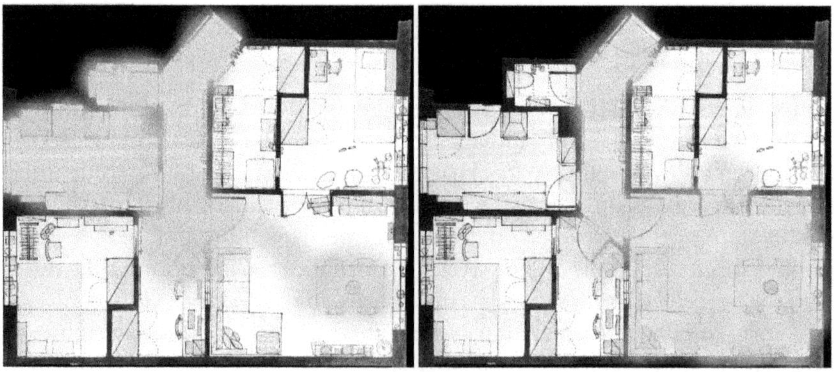

Figure 7.8 The pink clouds depict the busy areas of the flat on mornings and afternoons/evenings, respectively. Especially in the mornings, the family adapt their practices into what resembles a choreography. Illustrations by author.

Figure 7.9 Frank (Case #6) has photographed the collision between a drawer and a door as one of his least favourite features of the home: “Notice the wear marks!”, he writes. Photo by Frank.

repeatedly bumping the opening cabinet door into the drawer, leaving wear marks on both, it is a clear source of irritation and linked to perceptions about decency in the home. In fact, Frank identifies the physical traces on the drawer and the cabinet door as one of his least favourite things about his home(see Figure 7.9). Thus, Frank and Tanja’s ideals about the functionality of a decent home collides with a feeling of homeliness rooted in surrounding themselves with meaningful material objects. As a consequence, the compact physical environment of their dwelling puts up obstacles for their practicing of home – figuratively *and* literally. Altogether, the challenges to creating functionality in the compact dwellings under study demonstrate how the physical environment acts, affording changed practices and interpretations and challenging the realisation of human ideals of the home.

Finally, the households of the study look to aesthetics as a means for making decent homes. At first hand, this seems self-evident, as the beautiful home is the contrast of the ugly and unappealing home. However, aesthetics is largely a matter of taste, making the venture into creating domestic beauty a more uncertain one, at least on the face of it, because questions of taste or style have to do with socially relative questions of identity or lifestyle (Boccagni & Kusenbach 2020; Sparke 2010). In this perspective, homes can thus be perceived as displays of the identity, lifestyle and social positions of their occupants (Reimer & Leslie, 2004; Sparke, 2010). To Stine in Case #3, creating bright, airy and uncluttered environments is key to her aesthetics, and consequently, she has compromised on a key element of domestic space, according to, e.g., Lawson (2001), namely, privacy:[6] Instead of creating a separate bedroom for herself, she has combined all functions of her sleeping area, living room, dining room, kitchen and hallway in one main room, in which she sleeps on a sofa bed (see Figure 7.3). Her privacy is thus temporal – restricted to the weeks in which her daughters stay at their father's – rather than sensory or spatial (Pink 2012). In return, Stine has maximised the brightness and airiness in the main room of the flat. To other households conversely, like Case #1, creating small, dense nooks in the flat and filling it with trinkets and curiosities is key for their aesthetics and perceived as a means for creating cosiness and atmosphere (see Figure 7.1). Of course, prioritising individual privacy for the four household members is the firsthand purpose of subdividing their flat into small separate rooms instead of creating an open plan. However, their aesthetic preferences for physical condensity in the home make this topological solution appealing aesthetically too and are an important additional reason for organising their flat in this manner. To this family, Mette in particular, the aesthetic ideals are the eclectic, the bohemian, the patinated and the disorganised. To Stine (Case #3), on the other hand, the aesthetic ideals are the simplistic, the light, the Scandinavian and the designed. In both cases, these ideals are clearly expressed in the interior and organisation of their homes. Homes become materialised expressions of the personal in context, that is, of what a desirable and appropriate home *for someone like them* is (Boccagni & Kusenbach 2020). Accordingly, the household of Case #2 attribute nearly human characteristics to their home, making strong links between it and their own tastes, personality and lifestyle (see Winther, 2021 submitted, for elaboration):

> This flat has some charm; everything's a bit unorthodox. And we've done things like painting the floors green, putting up a 'bounty' beach wallpaper. Adding a bit of humour, the flat has a little craziness to it.
>
> (Emil, Case #2)

Altogether, the study demonstrates how the case study households consciously set out to realise widespread, conventional ideals of the home by different means than the domestic spaciousness, which they strongly lack in their compact living context. Furthermore, the study supports claims that comfort, functionality and aesthetics are core elements in prevailing ideals of the home.

Conclusion

The significance of home is immensely large. This is strongly identified by a broad body of literature. Home is an integral part of our self-perception, self-assessment and self-expression in relation to others. The home becomes a material translation of the identity of its occupants. In contemporary Denmark, overarching housing trends go clearly in the direction of expansion of dwelling sizes, and domestic spaciousness is a key element in conventional ideals of the home. Such ideals play key parts in defining socio-cultural contexts of normality, acceptability and status, and though domestic spaciousness is not dictating of social acceptance, it does function as a key driver of social status. This chapter is based on a case study of six examples of compact living in a Danish context. The households under study have prioritised living in the city highly enough to compromise substantially on the spaciousness of their homes. Hereby they deviate from conventional norms of the home, and this chapter consequently examined the role (if any) of such ideals for the home-making practices of the case study households. Furthermore, most of them live in highly urbanised areas where living space is generally more limited than in other parts of the country, suggesting that ideals of spaciousness may be moderated locally. Even though this assumption is confirmed by the study, the main finding is that conventional ideals of the home remain important to the households. Despite making unconventional housing choices, the households under study are highly aware of conventional social ideals of domestic spaciousness. Furthermore, they are highly aware of being behind on points, because they live compactly. Consequently, they look to other elements of conventional ideals and consciously apply these in order to create 'decent' homes, as they phrase it themselves, within the context of compact living. By prioritising comfort, functionality and aesthetics, the households integrate elements in their compact homes, which (as the chapter demonstrates) are key features of current ideals of the home.

Homes must be understood in the dynamic nexus of the human, the practiced and the physical environment. The key point of this chapter is to demonstrate both the importance and the relativity of social ideals of the home. Compact living is currently receiving increasing attention from developers, planners, architects, policy makers and the general public, particularly as a possible tool for meeting the challenges of boiling-point housing markets in urban areas across the world. This development can be identified in Denmark too, reflecting urban planning tendencies of densification applied to urban as well as suburban environments during the past decades. Densification as an approach thus spreads from urban planning to housing development in the current context of increasing urban housing shortage. Yet the novelty of compact living often ignites an assumption that dwellings targeted at this should revolutionise the idea of home. Numerous examples of radical and highly innovative design and architecture targeted at compact living demonstrate this. However, the present study shows that the making of unconventional housing choices does not *automatically* entail unconventional ways of making home. In the cases of this study, compact living becomes a means for living in the city, not an end in itself. This knowledge is of key importance for future approaches to compact living as a part of urban housing. Compact living holds valuable potential for innovation and creativity. The challenge lies in avoiding to compromise residential opportunities for *making home*.

Notes

1 Calculated as the share of variables housing use [boligbenyttelse] and furniture, household equipment and services [møbler, husholdningsudstyr og husholdningsservices] of total private consumption [forbrug i alt] at Statistics Denmark (2019).
2 One of the most radical and renowned approaches is that of actor-network-theory as instigated by Latour (e.g. 1988). ANT shares the idea of the non-human as acting with approaches such as Norman's.
3 Gibson did in fact touch upon this (Chong & Proctor 2020), but without specifying it or following the matter through: For instance, he described how children often interact differently with objects than adults due to children's smaller physical size (see Højring 2018). But then, one might ask, why not because of children's different way of perceiving the world? A chair may be interpreted not as something to sit on, but to climb on, by a child's playful mind.
4 See Winther (2021b) for an elaborative analysis of the spatiality, organisation and usage of the six case study dwellings.
5 Additionally, photographs, routes and activities of each household member in the surrounding neighbourhood were collected too. This data type is however less relevant for the current paper, as this focuses on the dwelling units and not their surroundings.
6 Creating privacy for the individual household members is a challenge identified across the cases – also those of single-person households, as this also concerns privacy towards visitors in the home. Dealing more thoroughly with the challenges of creating privacy falls beyond the scope of this chapter, however, but such analysis can be found in Winther (2021b).

References

Bech-Danielsen, Claus & Kirsten Gram-Hanssen, 2004. House, Home and Identity from a Consumption Perspective. *Housing, Theory and Society, 21:1*, 17–26.

Bech-Danielsen, Claus & Marie Stender, 2015. *Et lille hus i byen. Fortællinger om Arbejdernes Byggeforening – nostalgi eller fremtid? [A little house in the city. Stories of the Labourers' Building Society – nostalgia or future?]* Copenhagen, Denmark: Historika.

Bek, Lise, 2010. *Arkitektur som synlig tale [Architecture as visible speech]*. Aarhus, Denmark: IKAROS Press.

Blunt, Alison & Robyn Dowling, 2006. *Home*. Oxon and New York, NY: Routledge.

Boccagni, Paolo & Margarethe Kusenbach, 2020. For a Comparative Sociology of Home: Relationships, Cultures, Structures. *Current Sociology, 68:5*, 595–606.

Dansk Byggeri, 2020. Københavnerne bor dyrt og småt, jyderne bor stort og flot [Copenhageners live small and expensively, those from Jutland live large and fancily]. Available from: www.danskindustri.dk/ brancher/di-dansk-byggeri/nyheder/arkiv/pressemeddelelser/2020/1/kobenhavnerne-bor-dyrt-og-smat-jyderne-bor-stort-og-flot/ [Accessed 01 December 2020].

Chong, Isis & Robert W. Proctor, 2020. On the Evolution of a Radical Concept: Affordances According to Gibson and Their Subsequent Use and Development. *Perspectives on Psychological Science, 15:1*, 117–132.

City of Copenhagen, 2018. *Status på København 2018. Nøgletal for København [Status of Copenhagen 2018. Key figures on Copenhagen]*. City of Copenhagen, The Financial Administration, Velfærdsanalyseenheden. www.kk.dk/sites/default/files/status_paa_kbh_2018_aug.pdf

City of Copenhagen, 2019. *Retningslinjer for Boligstørrelser. Københavns Kommuneplan 2019 [Instructions on Dwelling Sizes. City Plan Copenhagen 2019]*. City of Copenhagen, The Finance Administration. https://kp19.kk.dk/sites/kp19.kk.dk/files/uploaded-files/retningslinjer_boligstoerrelser.pdf

Després, Carole, 1991. The Meaning of Home: Literature Review and Directions for Future Research and Theoretical Development. *Journal of Architectural and Planning Research, 8:2*, 96–115.

Douglas, Mary, 1991. The Idea of a Home: A Kind of Space. *Social Research, 58:1*, 287–307.

Eurostat, 2018. "EU Buildings Database" [Interactive statistics database]. Retrieved from: https://ec.europa.eu/energy/en/eu-buildings-database [Accessed 25 May 2020].

Flyvbjerg, Bent, 2015: Five Misunderstandings About Case-Study Research. *Qualitative Inquiry, 12:2*, 219–245.

Gibson, James J., 2015. *The Ecological Approach to Visual Perception. Classic Edition published 2015*. New York, NY and East Sussex: Psychology Press.

Gullestad, Marianne, 1989. *Kultur og hverdagsliv [Culture and everyday life]*. Oslo: Oslo University Press.

Højring, Laura H., 2018. *Hjemløse og hjemlighed [Homeless and homeyness]*. Thesis (PhD). Aalborg: Aalborg University Press.

Højring, Laura H. & Claus Bech-Danielsen, 2021. Homelessness and homeliness. Collage technique as a way of studying relations between homeless and the place they live. In Marie Stender, Claus Bech-Danielsen & Aina Landsverk Hagen (eds.), *Architectural Anthropology: Exploring Lived Space*. London: Routledge, 76–89.

Karsten, Lia (2010). Housing as a way of life. Towards an understanding of middle-class families' preferences for an urban residential location. In R. Paddison & W. Ostendorf (eds.), *Urban Studies. Society. – Vol. 1: Cities as social spaces*, pp. 357–372. Los Angeles, CA: Sage Publications.

Kristensen, Hans & Hans Skifter Andersen, 2009. *Befolkningens boligønsker [Housing Preferences of the Population]*. Copenhagen: Centre for Housing and Welfare – Realdania Research.

Lancione, Michele, 2019. Weird Exoskeletons: Propositional Politics and the Making of Home in Underground Bucharest. *International Journal of Urban and Regional Research, 43:3*, 535–550.

Latour, Bruno, 1988. Mixing Humans and Nonhumans Together: The Sociology of the Door-Closer [written under the pseudonym of Jim Johnson]. *Social Problems, 35:3*, 298–310.

Lawson, Bryan, 2001. *The Language of Space*. Oxford: Architectural Press.

Lind, Olaf & Jonas Møller (1996). *Bag hækken. Det danske parcelhus i lyst og nød [Behind the Hedge: The Danish Standard House for Better or Worse]*. Copenhagen: Arkitektens Forlag.

Madsen, Line Valdorff, 2017. *Energy consumption in the comfortable home: Practices, perceptions and conventions*. Thesis (PhD). Aalborg: Aalborg University Press.

Meagher, Caitlin, 2017. Constructing an Interior Public: *uchi* and *soto* in the Japanese Sharehouse. *Home Cultures, 14:2*, 113–136.

Møller, Bo (2001, August 9). *Indkomst, forbrug og priser [Income, consumption and prices]*. Statistics Denmark. www.dst.dk/ext/876103163/0/pris/1997-1999-Husstande-med-hoej-og-lav-indkomst--pdf

Norman, Donald A., 2013. *The Design of Everyday Things. Revised and expanded edition*. Cambridge, MA: MIT Press.

Özüekren, A.S. & R. van Kempen (2002). Housing Careers of Minority Ethnic Groups: Experiences, Explanations and Prospects. *Housing Studies, 17:3*, 365–379.

Pink, Sarah, 2012. *Situating Everyday Life. Practices and Places*. London: Sage Publications.

Pink, Sarah, Kerstin Leder Mackley, Roxana Morosanu, Val Mitchell, & Tracy Bhamra, 2017. *Making Homes: Ethnography and Design*. London: Bloomsbury Academic.

Reimer, Suzanne & Deborah Leslie (2004). Identity, Consumption, and the Home. *Home Cultures, 1:2*, 187–208.

Sobh, Rana & Russell W. Belk, 2011. Privacy and Gendered Spaces in Arab Gulf Homes. *Home Cultures, 8:3*, 317–340.

Sparke, Penny 2010. Modern Interior: A Space, a Place or a Matter of Taste? *Interiors, 1:1*, 7–17.

Statistics Denmark, 2019. *Statistikbanken. FU02 [The Statistics Bank. Table FU02] [online]*. Available from: www.statistikbanken.dk/fu02 [Accessed 25 November 2020].

Statistics Denmark, 2020. *Statistikbanken. BYGV06 [The Statistics Bank. Table BYGV06] [online]*. Available from: www.statistikbanken.dk/bygv06 [Accessed 25 May 2020].

Statistics Denmark, 2021. *Statistikbanken. BOL106 [The Statistics Bank. Table BOL106] [online]*. Available from: www.statistikbanken.dk/bol106 [Accessed 29 June 2021].

Thomas, Gary, 2010. Doing Case Study: Abduction Not Induction, Phronesis Not Theory. *Qualitative Inquiry, 16:7*, 575–582.

Thomas, Gary, 2011. A Typology of the Case Study in Social Science Following a Review of Definition, Discourse, and Structure. *Qualitative Inquiry, 17:6*, 511–521.

Warf, B. & Arias, S., 2009. *The Spatial Turn: Interdisciplinary Perspectives*. London and New York, NY: Routledge.

Winther, Anne Hedegaard, 2021a. Choosing Urban Compact Living. A Case Study of an Unconventional Housing Choice of Families in Contemporary Denmark. *Journal of Housing and the Built Environment, 36*, 925–941. https://doi.org/10.1007/s10901-021-09839-8.

Winther, Anne Hedegaard, 2021b. *Urban compact living: Making home in the city. An ethnographic case study of compact living in an urban Danish context.* Thesis (PhD). Aalborg: Aalborg University Press.

Winther, Ida Wentzel, 2013. *Hjemlighed: kulturfænomenologiske studier [Homeliness: Cultural Phenomenological Studies].* Aarhus: Aarhus University Press.

8 The Tiny Home Lifestyle (THL)

A Contemporary Response to the Neoliberalisation of Housing

Megan Carras

Introduction

The Tiny Home Lifestyle (THL) gained popularity in the United States amidst an affordable housing crisis, ignited by irresponsible housing practices and policy interventions rooted in the contemporary neoliberal mentality of rule. This chapter provides an investigation of the rise of this small-space, alternative housing option in this post-recession era. The 'contemporary neoliberal mentality of rule' refers to an infiltration of mentalities and rationalities by neoliberal discourse and governing practices to steer how individuals come to understand themselves as free and autonomous (Foucault,1988; Rose, 1999a, 1999b; Lemke, 2001). The THL arose amidst this mentality, whereby individuals are 'called' to take responsibility over their livelihoods to reduce reliance on the state. In contrast to mobile homes and trailers, tiny houses are often aesthetically appealing, miniature versions of traditional American homes. Tiny house builders are reporting prolific growth and substantial expected increase in sales; an onset of markets in Canada (Belmonte, 2020), Australia (Zhuang, 2020), and the United Kingdom (Wilson, 2020); and an increase in popularity amidst COVID-19 (Chang, 2020). Houses typically range in size from 10 m^2 (~ 100 ft^2) to 37 m^2 (~ 400 ft^2), as opposed to the average 2019 newbuilt American single-family house size of 214 m^2 (2,301 ft^2) (United States Census Bureau, 2019).

This lifestyle is marketed as providing a cost-effective, less regulated, and more mobile housing and lifestyle option that challenges traditional housing and debt models (Shafer, 2010; Anson, 2014; Mitchell, 2014, 2018). However, the actualities of these provisions and outcomes are uncertain, as empirical investigation is lacking. The lack of systematic academic scholarship on the THL is perhaps unsurprising given the newness of the phenomenon and its rate of growth. There is thus a significant, and pressing, opportunity to engage with and understand it. Yet it is of vital importance to dig beyond relatively superficial benefits to question where the desire for homeownership comes from, and the way in which this shapes the THL. Taking this step to delve deeper into such debates has the potential to contribute to the following gaps identified: actualities of financial ease and

DOI: 10.4324/9781003173052-12

legalities; reasons for increased popularity amidst an economic crisis; and the potential for long-term impact on housing trends. This was achieved by exposing the nuanced happenings at play around this lifestyle and giving credence to the voice of the THL dweller.

The chapter is structured as follows: firstly, I review the THL, including its suggested benefits. I then provide details of the theoretical understanding which lends to the development of the research approach. In the Results section, empirical findings on motivations and experience of the THL amidst the contemporary neoliberal mentality of rule are presented. The penultimate section provides a discussion of findings, placing them amidst the theoretical understanding of this research. Finally, concluding remarks are provided to position the THL within a wider contemporary housing context.

An Affordable, Simple, and Fulfilling Choice?

The THL is often framed as offering affordable housing outside the financial burden of traditional housing (Shafer, 2010; Mitchell, 2014, 2018), while at the same time, it is promoted as providing freedom, resilience, self-reliance, happiness, and fulfilment. This is exemplified in media attention such as *The Washington Post*'s article entitled 'Tiny house, big benefits: Freedom from mortgage and worries – and stuff' (Patel, 2015), ABC's 'Downscaling to a tiny house to find big happiness' (Shields, 2014), 'This Tiny Home doesn't have a toilet, but it might hold the key to happiness' (Dyas, 2014) from The Huffington Post, and The Globe and Mail's 'Smaller homes could make us happier' (Hague, 2019). Such headlines promote a positive view of the THL as something which offers self-reliant and hardworking individuals an empowering mode by which to reduce financial burdens and achieve a different way of life. Furthermore, notions of debt avoidance and not succumbing to risky debt culture are prevalent in THL discourses (Mitchell, 2018; Anson, 2014). Indeed, monthly expenses are reduced as rental/mortgage payments are minimal and utility costs low due to the smaller space. However, loan opportunities are sparse due to legal ambiguities as most do not meet minimum habitable dwelling requirements, and their high potential for loss in value (Sisson, 2017). Certainly, significant financial capital is required to support such a project, such that the opportunity to participate in the THL may be more limited than promoted.

A Legally Ambiguous Choice?

The lifestyle is defined by legal hindrances, such as permit issues, zoning laws, and land availability, which act as barriers for many dwellers. Tiny homes have no fixed definition, which has resulted in uncertainty around how best to handle these structures within zoning and coding regulations. Most often, these homes are built on wheels to counter their uncertain legal status, allowing them to be categorised as trailers or mobile homes. Depending on locality, some tiny homes can be classified as accessory dwelling units and placed in the backyard of larger single-family homes. This means that most tiny homes are currently located on private land as legal issues have limited the establishment of tiny house communities (Olito, 2021; Anson, 2017). The legal ambiguity of these small houses is complicated and locality-dependent; each dweller is required to educate themselves on specific options, and they often live within a legal grey area. Tiny house advocates have pushed for legal shifts, and have been successful in some regard. For example, in 2017, an appendix was introduced in the International Residential Code that relaxes ceiling height and stairway requirements (Sisson, 2017).

An Innovative Choice for Millennials?

Millennials, characterised by high levels of education, high levels of student debt, and an uncertain job market, are delaying or putting off purchasing 'large ticket items' such as homes and cars due to financial impracticality (Bleemer et al., 2014; Xu et al., 2015). This is exemplified by the growing phenomenon of 'Generation Rent', or younger people remaining longer in the rental sector, largely in the United Kingdom, the United States, and Australia (McKee et al., 2017; Ronald and Kadi, 2017). Schenk (2015) argues that a shift in the way these individuals identify with and value home has occurred after witnessing the financial hardship many of their parents experienced, and thus may partly explain their pursuit of the THL. Others suggest that millennials have the desire to own a home but simply are not able to do so (Davidson, 2014; McKee et al., 2017), while some are happy to pay rent (Gallier, 2016). This is a vital area of exploration, as this generation of young people will define the future of housing consumption trends. An exploration of the intentions and motivations around adoption and experience of the THL for all dwellers has the potential to support understandings around this lifestyle superseding traditional housing for the long-term for some parts of society. This chapter presents the outcomes of such an investigation.

Methods

A two-phase qualitative methodological approach was used, relying on ethnographic observations and semi-structured interviews. Ethnographic observations took place at tiny house events in Colorado Springs, Colorado, and Washington, D.C., a tiny house community and one-off home sites located in Orlando, Florida, Staten Island, New York, and New Hampshire, while semi-structured interviews with 20 tiny households (24 dwellers) occurred via phone, Skype, and in-person. Dwellers ranged in age from early 20s to mid-60s: 46% were women, 11 were single, and three had children. I stayed in the community in Orlando, Florida, and was immersed in the small-space living experience.

The THL arose and exists at many points of contestation and provides an opportunity to break out of traditional housing and debt systems. Therefore, as presented, this research examined how these governing practices 'happen' around the THL and the extent to which dwellers have or have not been governed into this 'choice' by the neoliberal mentality of rule.

Results

Empirical evidence provided insight around governing practices involved in the adoption and lived experience of the THL lifestyle. This chapter gives particular focus to interrogating the significance of the post-recession rise in popularity to address the limitations of existing understandings around placing this 'choice' amongst a broader housing context and to consider the nuanced happenings at play. Of particular interest to this chapter is how the THL is positioned as a low-cost housing option, and one which claims to offer greater freedom and fulfilment.

Motivations for Adopting Tiny Living

Motivations for adoption of the THL were investigated in order to understand the points from which dwellers entered this housing option. An exploration of the extent to which dwellers 'chose' this lifestyle was included. This allowed for consideration of underlying governing mechanisms that may have steered dwellers' expressions around their adoption, as subjectivities are developed and (re)constructed within this process of taking responsibility over one's housing and conforming to expectations of an optimal and aspirational way to be (Raco, 2009, 2011; Flint and Rowlands, 2003; McKee et al., 2017; McKee, 2011a; Flint, 2002, 2003).

Most dwellers were primarily driven by financial freedom to adopt the THL, while all expressed some form of financial freedom found via the THL. These themes arose organically, in a bottom-up, unprompted way. In an attempt to explore these expressions of freedom and thus the motivation for adoption of this lifestyle, two distinct resident types were developed in relation to traditional homeownership and the debt market.

Detractors

Ranging in age from mid-30s to 60s, this cohort includes those who are rejecting the contemporary American dream of traditional homeownership and resultant mortgage encumbrance. Two households interviewed are single mothers with teen children, three are couples, and the remainder are single (three women and three men). Two households are retired, while one couple left their jobs to establish a tiny house community. Career type includes retired investment banker, former engineer and tax and finance specialist, digital consultant for a bank, project manager for a consulting firm, IT consultant, director of psychological health for a military instalment, nurse, former lawyer, insurance adjuster, building design consultant, and professor of architecture. Detractors reside in the following states: Washington, Texas, Georgia, Massachusetts, Oklahoma, New York, New Hampshire, Virginia, California, and North Carolina.

Detractors were driven by unsatisfying experiences with and distrust of traditional housing, mortgage reliance, and debt, and working too much to support this normalised lifestyle resulting in being exhausted and unhappy. As opposed to Compromisers, Detractors were not constrained into the THL, but have adopted this lifestyle because it offers a feeling of choice outside of traditional institutions.

Detractors identified a sense of freedom in taking control over a housing market that has proven untrustworthy and dissatisfactory. Many dwellers emphasised the lack of contentment and fulfilment around prior traditional choices due to the need to afford this normalised lifestyle in order to not be considered a 'flawed' consumer of housing (Flint, 2003; McKee et al., 2017). Additionally, the burden of work in order to support the big house and accumulation of stuff became disillusioning:

> It got to the point that it felt like I was working so much that it felt like I couldn't even enjoy that great big house ... there wasn't time to enjoy this thing that I was working 60 hours a week to afford.
>
> (Kristin, mid-40s, female)

Detractors shifted their aspirations from traditional versions of the American dream to the THL dream. They expressed pride and freedom in abandoning this normalised version of success, as articulated by suggestions of traditional housing and related aspects being unsatisfying, burdensome, ridiculous, untrustworthy, and entrapping. However, as noted, the primary driver was the desire for financial freedom, and almost all dwellers adopted the THL after the 2008 housing crisis. Despite their ability to access the traditional market and claims of living outside of these institutions in order to obtain freedom, all Detractors were in pursuit of financial security on some level.

Compromisers

Compromisers are those pursuing an adapted version of the contemporary American dream (i.e. homeownership) as a result of being constrained. This cohort of individuals, those in their 20s and 30s, have been priced out of traditional homeownership. Four households are couples, one with a small child (age two), and the remainder are single (two women and three men). Career type includes manager for a roofing company, waitress, professional magician, aesthetician, founders of an animal rescue non-profit, student, marketing coordinator for a non-governmental organisation (NGO), project manager for a social justice NGO, and founder of a design/marketing company. Compromisers reside in the following states: Oklahoma, Texas, Minnesota, Florida, Oregon, Wyoming, and Massachusetts.

These dwellers, unable to follow the traditional path, are attempting an alternative and self-reliant approach to homeownership under the stronghold of a restrictive and unaffordable housing market. Many of these dwellers adopted the THL to enable them to access traditional homeownership in the future as they are currently unable to do so. These dwellers have been constrained into this 'choice' as part of their compromised and adapted American dreams. The Compromisers are recognised in scholarship that emphasises the continuation of the pursuit of homeownership despite fading opportunity in the current neoliberal era (Harvey, 2005, 2012; Aalbers, 2015; Chomsky, 2017). This type is also supported by scholarship that highlights the growing phenomenon of 'Generation Rent', or younger people remaining longer in the rental sector, largely in the United Kingdom, the United States, and Australia (McIntyre and McKee 2012; McKee et al., 2017; Ronald and Kadi, 2017; Wood and Ong, 2012).

Compromisers were largely motivated by an unaffordable and undesirable rental market, desire to save for the future, opportunity to live a cheaper life, opportunity to avoid a mortgage, and a housing stock shortage. Dwellers pointed to tiny living as providing a freedom from rental reliance, yet their accounts highlight the wider affordable housing crisis. Many dwellers recounted the extreme expense of renting, accounting a housing market, both homeownership and rental, that has become burdensome for so many (Ronald and Kadi, 2017). This was particularly so for the Compromisers who are unable to access traditional homeownership, yet also find the rental market and availability of housing options restricted. However, at the same time, participants saw renting as an inferior and financially irresponsible option, a 'flawed' way to consume house.

Further, several Compromisers expressed desire to avoid the traditional mortgage market. For instance, Cara (mid-20s, female) detailed being motivated by a desire to live cheaply and avoid being tied to a mortgage:

> I didn't want to be tied down to work my life away, essentially, my mom owns her own business and I watched her kill herself with work, and I didn't want to do that myself ... I also want to experience life so keeping my expenses down was a big part, I also didn't want to be tied to a mortgage for 30 years.

These two distinct dweller types were exposed through their divergent relationship to the traditional housing market that resulted in entering the THL from different points. The variance in life course between each type was evident and revealed the difference in attachment to the THL.

While empirical evidence suggests that dwellers are primarily adopting this lifestyle for financial reasons to find stability in unstable times, dwellers attached notions of freedom, being free from/free to, and self-determination to other aspects of the THL. Therefore, it is necessary to position these identifications of freedom amidst the context from which this lifestyle arose.

A Freeing Housing Experience

The following freedoms of the THL, explained as benefits, were identified by dweller accounts, from most to least discussed: (1) freeing up time and energy: simplification; (2) self-build and self-expression; (3) freedom of mobility; (4) freedom to work less; and (5) freedom from utilities and regulation. Table 8.1 presents empirical evidence to support these freedoms

Table 8.1 Implications of expressed freedoms/benefits

Freedom/benefit of the THL	*Dweller example*	*Implications, words used*
Freeing up time and energy: simplification	'I think the thing I most enjoy is the freedom of my time and my energy, and being able to direct that into places I want to see it go, instead of waking up and feeling you have all these pressures to pay these bills so you can have all these things. It's really a sense of freedom when you can scale everything down.' (Cameron, early 40s, male, Detractor)	Trade-off, easier life, more enjoyment, emotional benefits, priorities, 'focus on things I feel are important', 'anxiety off my shoulders'
Self-build and self-expression	'I liked building it, I liked the sense of freedom, the sense of empowerment from building the house, living in this way that was more on my terms.' (Ben, mid-30s, male, Compromiser)	Pride, empowerment, ownership, meeting needs, meaningfulness, 'extension of me'
Freedom of mobility	'I wanted the freedom to move my life in whatever direction it took me.' (Cara, mid-20s, female, Compromiser)	Flexibility, not being trapped to a location, movement, options
Freedom to work less	'I've got a tiny house that's paid off. I've got a car that's paid off. Why do I need to work full time? I don't have a mortgage. I mean that's what people work for, right? To pay things off, I'm debt free.' (Bill, early 60s, male, Detractor)	Enjoyment, control, more time, priorities, easier life, align with values, don't have to work 'a regular job', work from home
Freedom from utilities and regulation	'Being off grid I feel more free and independent of whatever else may be happening.' (Alice, late 20s, female, Compromiser)	Avoid restrictive system, control, on my terms

and the implications of these accounts. The restrictive nature of the THL and things sacrificed are presented around articulated freedoms. These arose when inquiring directly in semi-structured interviews, in contrast to the ways in which freedom claims arose without prompting.

Restriction and Sacrifices

Despite the freedoms explained by many dwellers, several expressed restrictions and sacrifices that can be attached to these suggested freedoms, including privacy, living on wheels, confined and restrictive space, legal issues, and issues with moving the home, to name a few.

Privacy: The issue of privacy arose for all three dwellers who had children, and was a greater concern for two dwellers who are single mothers of teenage daughters, thus highlighting potential areas of conflict if these younger single or coupled dwellers have the desire to grow their families. For example, the 17-year-old daughter of Debbie (early 50s, female, Detractor) stated her dissatisfaction in not having privacy and space to hang out with friends:

> It's just hard to have my friends over, cause it's just like, my mom is here and like we can't talk about anything because my mom is here. It's awkward.

Debbie is looking to address this issue by building her daughter a small tiny house of her own.

Oscar (mid-20s, male, Compromiser) attributed the minimal space and lack of privacy to his divorce; giving advice on how to avoid this, he stated:

> I recommend living in a tiny house alone for a while before inviting someone in or being very comfortable with a significant other … There's no space in a tiny home, so you need to be very prepared and comfortable with them. A lot of divorces are happening over tiny homes.

Living on Wheels: While tiny houses can be self-built on foundations, as was done by one Detractor at a cost of US$145,000, building on wheels allows for a more affordable self-build opportunity and a way to 'get around' legal issues that many face. However, a few dwellers explained that being on wheels felt less grounded and secure:

> Psychologically the fact that it was up off the ground, not on a solid foundation, and moveable, it somehow felt different. I felt less grounded and rooted in the world. Not the most pleasant feeling to have from one's home.
>
> (Ben, mid-30s, male, Compromiser, who abandoned his home)

Spatial/Layout Issues: Most tiny houses have lofted sleeping spaces. Manoeuvring around these spaces, as well as the need to climb steep stairs to access them, was an annoyance for many. One Detractor broke her foot within the first weeks of living in their tiny house after falling from the stairs, while a Compromiser spoke of her dissatisfaction with the height of the loft and her desire to live in a bigger space in the future:

> I least enjoy having such a short bedroom where I can't stand up, so when we do eventually live on a property … I would love to have a bedroom I could stand up in.

Furthermore, a couple of dwellers explained their concerns with having to climb steep stairs as they age. These were all Detractors and identified that in order to continue with this lifestyle as they get older, this needed to be considered.

Mobility: Mobility was identified as a restriction for several dwellers, with most stating an assumption of more mobility prior to adoption of the TFL. Many, however, still acknowledged that the option to relocate with the home was a positive aspect, but that moving the home frequently was less feasible. Dwellers found the home bulky, heavy, and requiring professional help to move:

> I initially saw myself as you know just hitching up my house and moving it but now that I've built it … it's a little intimidating for me to move.
> (Jackie, early 50s, female, Detractor)

Legal: One quarter of dwellers were attempting to sell their homes, all of whom reported the reason as legal uncertainty; two of them were forced to relocate their homes when they were reported to the authorities.

These articulations of issues with aspects of the THL could significantly impact the potential for this housing option to offer a long-term solution. These restrictions are representative of the ways in which expressions of freedom and choice around the THL are not as clear-cut as suggested by dwellers.

Discussion

The main motivation for dwellers to adopt the THL was financial, and this supports the argument that the THL was ignited by an affordable housing crisis. Yet participants expressed a range of benefits, identified as freedoms, offered by this alternative housing option. These provide insight into the extent to which dwellers are made subjects to neoliberal self-governing mechanisms and the ways in which they are being governed by the notion of freedom. Arguably, these individuals have been governed into understanding the THL as 'more free' than what is provided by traditional housing, rather than the result of a constraining neoliberal mentality of rule. The fact that the primary driver is low-cost housing and living, while neoliberal policies have created an affordable housing crisis, brings autonomy and choice around adoption and expressions of freedoms into question. Participants felt freedom, choice, and individuality in these many aspects that were also attached to burden or restriction. These observations highlight how the contemporary neoliberal regime operates through making people 'feel free', as presented in Rose's 'Power of Freedom' (1999a), and uncover the embedded nature of self-governing tactics. Arguably, dwellers' articulations of freedom and choice should be understood in the context of being governed by the desire to be deemed competent, self-reliant, and successful individuals, as the contemporary neoliberal 'personalisation agenda' suggests that 'competent personhood' happens through the 'continual exercise of freedom' and should be understood 'in terms of one's success or failure acquiring the skills and choice to actualize oneself' (Rose, 1999a, pp. 87). At the same time, individuals were found to be active within this process as they took the opportunity to redirect and choose how they were steered. Each resident type acted from differing places of agency – whereby Detractors were critiquing institutions in which they have taken part, or intentionally avoided, and Compromisers adapted their life courses due to a constraining housing and economic situation, and thus were not outright active in the 'choice' of dissent. Yet the findings in this chapter uncovered how dwellers crafted themselves to interrupt governing forces by adopting a more affordable lifestyle to remove themselves from restrictive traditional housing. These empirical findings contribute to scholarship on resistance and activated agency enacted around housing (see McKee, 2011b, 2016; Flint, 2003) and adds to scholarship on the agency/structure interface relevant to housing 'choice' (see McKee et al. 2017).

This research also revealed how Millennials understand and approach housing in the contemporary neoliberal era. Much of this scholarship, using qualitative methods to give a voice to these individuals, has focused on the UK context, referring to this cohort as 'Generation Rent' (see, for example, Hoolachan et al., 2017; McKee et al., 2017; Cole et al., 2016). Scholarship in the United States largely using quantitative analysis has reviewed the impact of student debt, labour market changes, the affordable housing crisis, and the impact of the Great Recession on access to and rates of homeownership by young people (e.g. Dickerson, 2016; Bleemer et al., 2014; Xu et al., 2015; Clark, 2018). Findings from such literature have revealed that Millennials are staying at home longer with their parents and/or avoiding homeownership due to financial instability. This research provides an examination of how some young people are using the THL to circumvent these barriers and gives a glimpse into this process through the lived experiences of tiny house dwellers. It is important to acknowledge that this opportunity is one of privilege as the upfront costs of the THL are significant and most Compromisers used loans or parents for assistance. Arguably, this younger cohort is acting with more caution around entering traditional homeownership and accruing traditional debt than older generations. It is uncertain how future housing aspirations will come to fruition; however, this research contributes to exposing one way this cohort is approaching and developing their housing trajectories.

Conclusion

The THL gained popularity in the wake of the global economic crisis of 2007–2008, whereby the United States real estate investment bubble collapsed, devastating housing markets, resulting in mass repossessions and evictions (Desmond, 2017). This research highlighted how tiny homes, a small and affordable housing option, have gained popularity amongst middle- and upper income individuals. Their prolific growth can be witnessed in the booming tiny house industry, while small legal successes in recent years point to overcoming this barrier in some localities, perhaps allowing for more security in adoption. The implications of the growth of the THL are significant as this alternative housing response has the potential to shift housing trajectories, especially for Millenials. This cohort has entered the housing market at a point of caution and uncertainty, developing subjectivities and aspirations accordingly. Therefore, underscored by memories of the Great Recession and with unstable housing markets and the predictions of the economic downturn from COVID-19, the potential for such alternative forms of housing to continue to shape housing trajectories remains. The approach taken by this research allowed for a substantive probing into the actualities of such a housing alternative.

References

Aalbers, M. (2015) 'The great moderation, the great excess and the global housing crisis', *International Journal of Housing Policy*, 15(1), pp. 43–60.

Anson, A. (2014) 'The World is my Backyard: Romanticization, Thoreauvian Rhetoric, and Constructive Confrontation in the Tiny House Movement', in Holt, W. (ed.), *From Sustainable to Resilient Cities: Global Concerns and Urban Efforts (Research in Urban Sociology, Vol. 14)*. Bingley: Emerald Group Publishing Limited, pp. 289–313.

Anson, A. (2017) 'The Patron Saint of Tiny Houses', in Finley, J.S., (ed.), *Henry David Thoreau in Context*. Cambridge: Cambridge University Press, pp. 331–341.

Belmonte, L. (2020) 'Tiny Houses on the East Coast are the latest Canadian Real Estate Trend for 2020'. *Narcity Halifax*, 7 August [online]. Available from: www.narcity.com/halifax/tiny-homes-in-canada-are-such-a-real-estate-trend-this-year-on-the-east-coast

Bleemer, Z., Brown M., Lee, D. and Van der Klaauw, W. (2014) 'Debt, jobs, or housing: What's keeping millennials at home?'. *FRB of New York Staff Report*, (700), New York, NY. Available from: www.newyorkfed.org/medialibrary/media/research/staff_reports/sr700.pdf

Chang, B. (2020) 'More than half of Americans said they would consider living in a tiny home in a new survey as the lifestyle increases in popularity amid the pandemic'. *Insider*, 12 December [online]. Available from: www.businessinsider.com/survey-reveals-why-tiny-homes-have-become-so-popular-2020-12

Chomsky, N. (2017) *Requiem for the American Dream*. New York, NY: Seven Stories Press.

Clark, W. (2018) 'Millennials in the housing market: The transition to ownership in challenging contexts', *Housing, Theory, and Society*, 36(2)., pp. 206–227.

Cole, I., Powell, R., and Sanderson, E. (2016) 'Putting the squeeze on "Generation Rent": Housing benefit claimants in the private rented sector – transitions, marginality and stigmatisation', *Sociological Research Online*, 21(2), pp. 1–14.

Davidson, J. (2014) 'What everyone gets wrong about millennials and home buying', *Time*, 12 November [online]. Available from: http://time.com/money/3551773/millennials-home-buying-marriage/ [Accessed 17th of April, 2018]

Desmond, M. (2017) *Evicted: Poverty and Profit in the American City*. New York, NY: Crown Publishing.

Dickerson, A. (2016) 'Millennials, affordable housing, and the future of homeownership', *Journal of Affordable Housing*, 24(3), pp. 435–465.

Dyas, B. (2014) 'This tiny home doesn't have a toilet, but it might hold the key to happiness', *The Huffington Post*, 15 July [online]. Available from: www.huffingtonpost.co.uk/entry/tiny-home-no-toilet_n_5589049 [Accessed the 14 March, 2018]

Flint, J. (2002) 'Social housing agencies and the governance of anti-social behaviour', *Housing Studies*, 17(4), pp. 619–637.

Flint, J. (2003) 'Housing and ethopolitics: Constructing identities of active consumption and responsible community', *Economy and Society*, 32(3), pp. 449–466.

Flint, J. and Rowlands, R. (2003) 'Commodification, normalisation and intervention: cultural, social and symbolic capital in housing consumption and governance', *Journal of Housing and the Built Environment*, 18(3), pp. 213–232.

Foucault, M. (1988) 'Technologies of the self', in Martin, L., Gutman, H., and Hutton, P. (eds.), *Technologies of the Self: A Seminar with Michel Foucault*. London: Tavistock, pp. 16–49.

Gallier, T. (2016) 'Millennial like me don't actually want to own our homes – with proper changes, renting could be the future', *The Independent*, 3 August [online]. Available from: www.independent.co.uk/voices/millennials-like-me-dont-actually-want-to-own-our-homes-with-proper-changes-renting-could-be-the-a7169631.html

Hague, M. (2019) 'Smaller homes could make us happier', *The Globe and Mail*, 26 August [online]. Available from: www.theglobeandmail.com/life/home-and-design/article-smaller-homes-could-make-us-happier/

Harvey, D. (2005) *A Brief History of Neoliberalism*. Oxford: Oxford University Press.

Harvey, D. (2012) *Rebel Cities: From the Right to the City and to the Urban Revolution*. London: Verson.

Hoolachan, J., McKee, K., Moore, T., and Soaita, A.M. (2017) '"Generation rent" and the ability to "settle down": economic and geographical variation in young people's housing transitions', *Journal of Youth Studies*, 20(1), pp. 63–78.

Lemke, T. (2001) 'The birth of bio-politics: Michel Foucault's lecture at the Collège de France on neoliberal governmentality', *Economy and Society*, 30(2), pp. 190–207.

McIntyre, Z. and McKee, K. (2012) 'Creating sustainable communities through tenure-mix: The responsibilization of marginal homeowners in Scotland', *Geojournal*, 77(2), pp. 235–47.

McKee, K. (2011a) 'Challenging the norm? The 'ethopolitics' of low cost homeownership in Scotland', *Urban Studies,* 48(16), pp. 3397–411.

McKee, K. (2011b) 'Skeptical, disorderly and paradoxical subjects: Problematizing the "will to empower" in social housing governance', *Housing, Theory and Society,* 28(1), pp. 1–18.

McKee, K. (2016) 'Social housing and the "new localism": A strategy of governance for austere times', in Bevir, M. (ed.), *Governmentality after Neoliberalism.* Abington: Routledge, pp. 111–34.

McKee, K., Moore, T., Soaita, A., and Crawford, J. (2017) '"Generation Rent" and the Fallacy of Choice', *International Journal of Urban and Regional Research,* 41(2), pp. 318–33.

Mitchell, R. (2014) *Tiny House Living: Ideas for Building and Living Well in Less than 400 Square Feet.* Blue Ash, OH: Betterway Home Books.

Mitchell, R. (2018) 'What is the tiny house movement?', *The Tiny Life* [online]. Available from: https://thetinylife.com/what-is-the-tiny-house-movement/

Olito, F. (2021) 'Tiny-house owners are facing evictions or living under the radar because their homes are considered illegal in most parts of the US', *Insider*, 14 December [online]. Available from: www.insider.com/tiny-house-owners-zoning-laws-2020-12

Patel, N. (2015) 'Tiny House, big benefits: Freedom from a mortgage and worries – and stuff', *The Washington Post*, 25 June [online]. Available from: www.washingtonpost.com/lifestyle/magazine/tiny-house-big-benefitsfreedom-from-a-mortgage--and-stuff/2015/06/23/f8f706f0-0acc-11e5-9e39-0db921c47b93_story.html?utm_term=.e0905f059ca2

Raco, M. (2009) 'From expectations to aspirations: State modernisation, urban policy, and the existential politics of Welfare in the UK', *Political Geography,* 28(7), pp. 436–44.

Raco, M. (2011) 'Neoliberal urban policy, aspirational citizenship and the uses of cultural distinction', in Tasan-Kok, T. and Baeten, G. (eds.), *Contradictions of Neoliberal Planning.* Dordrecht: Springer, pp. 43–59.

Ronald, R. and Kadi, J. (2017) 'The revival of private landlords in Britain's post homeownership society', *New Political Economy,* 23(6), pp. 1–18.

Rose,N.(1999a) *PowersofFreedom:ReframingPoliticalought.*Cambridge:Cambridge University Press.

Rose, N. (1999b) *Governing the Soul: The Shaping of the Private Self.* 2nd edn. London: Free Association Books.

Schenk, K. (2015) 'Flex House: Prefabricating the Tiny House Movement', Master of Architecture, University of Cincinnati, Cincinnati, OH. Available from: https://etd.ohiolink.edu/!etd.send_file?accession=ucin1428652984&disposition=inline

Shafer, J. (2010) *The Small House Book.* 2nd edn. Sonoma, CA: Tumbleweed Tiny House Company.

Shields, J. (2014) 'Downscaling to a tiny house to find big happiness', *ABC*, 30 April [online]. Available from: www.abc.net.au/radionational/programs/lifematters/dee-williams-and-the-big-tiny-house/5421452

Sisson, P. (2017) 'Tiny houses: Big future, or big hype?', *Curbed*, 18 July [online]. Available from: www.curbed.com/2017/7/18/15986818/tiny-house-zoning-adu-affordable-housing

United States Census Bureau. (2019) 'Characteristics of New Housing'. Last revised 1 June 2020 [online]. Available from: www.census.gov/construction/chars/highlights.html

Wilson, Alice Elizabeth. (2020) 'Why more people want to live in tiny houses', The *Independent*, 15 May [online]. Available from: www.independent.co.uk/life-style/why-living-tiny-houses-sustainable-minimalist-a9499866.html

Wood, G. and Ong, R. (2012) 'Sustaining home ownership in the 21st century: emerging policy concerns', *Australian Housing and Urban Research Institute Limited Final Report,* No. 187. Available from: www.ahuri.edu.au/research/final-reports/187

Xu, Y., Johnson, C., Bartholomae, S., O'Neill., B., and Gutter, M.S. (2015) 'Homeownership among millennials: The deferred American dream?', *Family and Consumer Sciences Research Journal,* 44(20), pp. 201–212.

Zhuang, B. (2020) 'Tiny Homes Carnival: 'An affordable option to put on land that you've already got', *The Guardian*, 9 March [online]. Available from: www.theguardian.com/lifeandstyle/2020/mar/10/tiny-homes-carnival-an-affordable-option-to-put-on-land-that-youve-already-got

9 Understanding Tiny House Sustainabilities through the Lens of Frictions

Hilton Penfold, Gordon Waitt & Pauline McGuirk

Introduction

A sustainability discourse has become the dominant portrayal of tiny houses in various social media platforms (Ford and Gomez-Lanier 2017; Penfold et al. 2018) and academic literature (Wotton et al. 2018; Shearer and Burton 2021). This literature purports that 'size matters', in which diminished resource consumption is equated with smaller houses, for both construction (Wilson and Boehland 2005) and everyday operation (Boeckermann et al. 2019; Crawford and Stephan 2020). We draw on Urban Political Ecology (UPE) to critique this emphasis on the physical dimensions of housing by appreciating the way in which our consumption choices are always embedded in how social and economic relations materialise flows of resources, including water, energy, and food (Kaika 2005; Lane and Gorman-Murray 2012). In this chapter, we focus on the social and economic relations that materialise flows of water in tiny houses in Australia. A UPE approach to sustainable tiny house living argues for the need to focus on flows of water as an expression of multi-scalar political economic relationships (Kaika 2005).

In what follows, we draw on Tsing's (2005) notion of friction as both enabling and constraining flows of water. After outlining the methodological design of the wider project from which this chapter is drawn, we work with two in-depth portraits which illustrate four emergent analytical themes – tenure, infrastructure, finance, and time – focussing on the households' toilet systems. We conclude by offering an important nuanced account of how sustainability is undermined and facilitated by frictions that shape flows of materials in and out of tiny houses – including water, food, and energy.

Urban Political Ecology

A key focus of UPE is on conceptualising cities as ecologies supported by large-scale infrastructures that sustain flows of water, energy, and food. These ecologies are conceived as driven by capitalist modes of sourcing

DOI: 10.4324/9781003173052-13

and disposing of materials (Robbins 2012). UPE scholars studying western cities critique the way urban infrastructure design can render political economic processes 'invisible' (Heynan et al. 2006). In everyday practice, the way infrastructural design operates to allow resource flows to be taken-for-granted is reinforced by the ease of turning on a tap to connect to mains water infrastructure (Kaika 2005).

The work of Loftus et al. (2019) illustrates the opportunities afforded by UPE to explore the shift from state management of drinking water as a public good, to a commodity managed by utility companies that prioritise profit-making. In this context of the centralised decision-making power of 'big water', some commentators have argued that constraints on individual power have led people to relocate to a region where mainstream infrastructures align with their political values (Vannini and Taggart 2014) or to disconnect from mains water and retrofit houses with off-grid technologies including 'small water' rainwater catchment and grey water recycling (Cousins 2017).

Household-scale 'off-grid' technologies and practices expose users to finite rather than seemingly unlimited quantities of material flows, which encourages people to align everyday practices with the local availability of material flows (Vannini and Taggart 2014; Shearer and Burton 2021). While UPE has focused attention on the political economic structures that present both barriers and opportunities for the material flow of domestic water, to date it has not done so in the context of tiny houses.

Tsing's (2005) concept of 'friction' offers an important lens to follow the flow of water in, through and out of tiny houses. Here, we follow Tsing (2005) in defining friction as a force that is simultaneously productive and inhibitive. She draws on the metaphor of transport infrastructure to help us understand the concept: "(a) wheel turns because of its encounter with the surface of the road; spinning in the air it goes nowhere" (Tsing 2005: 5). She further adds:

> (r)oads are a good image for conceptualising how friction works: Roads create pathways that make motion easier and more efficient, but in doing so they limit where we go. The ease of travel they facilitate is also a structure of confinement.

The concept of friction encapsulates how political economic processes generate 'structures of confinement', but avoids deterministic notions of 'path dependency' (Tsing 2005). We suggest that Tsing's (2005) concept of friction aligns with the "utility of Marxist notions of structure as a force constraining or enabling human behavior [sic]" (Glassman 2003: 684). Simply put, frictions allow us to consider how structures produce both barriers and opportunities for accessing 'big' and 'small' water systems. We argue that how political economic structures enable or constrain households to reduce material flows, or not, plays a key role in understanding the relationship between tiny houses and sustainability.

Methods and Analytical Themes

This chapter uses empirical material from a broader study of everyday tiny house living. The methodology combined semi-structured interviews, video diaries, and follow-up interviews. Empirical data were sourced between August 2019 and March 2020. Conducting interviews in and around tiny houses enabled participants to 'show and tell' their water, energy, and food systems and practices. Follow-up questions expand on the political economic structures shaping their decision making and everyday practices.

Thirteen tiny households consented to participate. All participants privately owned either mobile or permanently fixed tiny houses and were permanent residents, yet only two privately owned the land on which their tiny house was situated. All participants held strong environmental values and aspired to produce, reduce, or recycle the material flows connected to their homes. All were involved in the design and furnishing of their tiny house through custom professional builds, self-builds, or a combination of both.

Participants were recruited from across Eastern NSW, Australia, clustered primarily in metropolitan Sydney and the Northern Rivers region. These participant clusters differ significantly in terms of political economic structures that influence household water, energy, and food politics, including the provision of infrastructures, employment opportunities, housing affordability, and tiny house regulation. Households located in metropolitan Sydney were highly embedded in capitalist market relations for sourcing land, tiny houses, water, energy, and food, whereas households in the Northern Rivers were predominantly reliant on alternative and non-market economic relations. To ensure privacy, tiny houses are located regionally. Participants are given pseudonyms.

Analytical coding revealed four emergent thematic structures that both enabled and constrained how water flowed through tiny houses: tenure, infrastructure, finance, and time. Tenure security is key to understanding household sustainability (Crabtree 2006). Here we conceptualise tenure security as a friction that shapes how tiny households source, use, and dispose of water. Mee et al. (2014) explained how tenure insecurity in the private rental market functions as a barrier for adopting water-saving practices and technologies. In a similar fashion, Davison (2016) argued that homeownership enables households to engage in particular 'household sustainability initiatives' that have limited impact on urban sustainability due to the "disempowerment of the growing proportion of people excluded from home ownership" (111). Yet tiny houses differ from conventional housing tenure relations in that houses may be privately owned but land may be privately rented. As previously discussed, all participants in this research privately owned their tiny house.

Access to water infrastructures is a key friction discussed by UPE scholars. The UPE literature outlines how a connection to commoditised 'big water' infrastructure makes it possible for households to engage in water-intensive practices, such as watering lawns (Robbins 2012) and using flushing toilets (Ormerod 2019). Millington (2018: 28) argued that "[i]nfrastructures act in the world in ways that both co-produce the operation of power while also opening up space for material contestation." However, little is currently known about whether tiny houses are connecting to mains infrastructure to source water and dispose of sewage. We argue that tiny houses stand to provide crucial insights regarding how access to infrastructure produces friction that can work with and against environmental values and aspirations to reduce water usage.

Finance is a central tenant of UPE scholarship. Financial constraints may result in low socio-economic households reducing commoditised material flows including water and energy (Heynan et al. 2006). At the same time, tiny houses are often positioned as an affordable form of housing by reducing financial debt associated with expensive mortgages and rental payments (Ford and Gomez-Lanier 2017). Yet little is known about whether tiny households invest financial savings into small water systems or pay for commoditised big water services.

Finally, time is centrally important. Research suggests that household sustainability practices entail unpaid labour, which necessitates access to time spent outside of wage labour or 'free-time' (Gibson et al. 2013). However, free-time is not equally accessible. Some households rely on wage labour more than others to pay for commoditised essential needs. Exploring practices of 'voluntary simplicity', Dennis et al. (2005) demonstrated how employment in wage labour can increase reliance on commoditised food chains by limiting the time required for food gardens. Similarly, Wheeler and Glucksmann (2016: 110) uncover time as a friction shaping rubbish disposal practices. They explain:

> [S]orting [household rubbish] takes time and ... it is more difficult for people ... working full time to manage recycling consumption work alongside childcare and other domestic tasks.

Ford and Gomez-Lanier (2017) argue that, through their size and affordability, tiny houses drastically reduce waged and unpaid labour time involved in maintaining a large suburban house. Yet no research currently exists to substantiate or refute claims that the time alleviated by the cost savings and reduced household maintenance is being used to lift household sustainability. Further, many water-saving practices are time and labour-intensive. But little is currently understood about structures that limit tiny households' access to the time and unpaid labour required to engage in water-saving practices.

To advance our argument, we adopt a portrait approach to follow water in, through, and out of the toilet systems. This approach enabled us to offer a nuanced interpretation of the socio-economic relations that materialise flows of water in the tiny house. While both households evoked strong environmental ideals and sustainability commitments, they differed in terms of the political economic relations. The first householder (Jane) is situated in rural New South Wales, lives alone, and relies on a rainwater tank. Jane thinks of herself as a committed environmentalist and draws on tiny house narratives informed by an ethos of 'living simply' and a desire to be as self-sufficient as possible. Jane illustrates the frictions of political economic structures that made possible the small water infrastructure of the rainwater tank and compositing toilet.

The second householder (Penny) is situated in suburban Sydney, and lives with her partner and young family. Her tiny house is connected to the mains water supply. The tiny house is integral both to Penny's identity as a dedicated mother, who recently resigned from paid work to spend more time with her children, whilst maintaining the comforts expected of the contemporary family home without the same overheads. The contrasting portraits shed light on how diverse entailments in political economic relations, mediated by frictions associated with tenure, infrastructure, finance, and time, complicate straightforward association between tiny house living and sustainability gains. Penny offers insights into the frictions of political economic structures that are locked in commoditised big water infrastructure and the flush toilet.

Empirical Analysis: Toileting Frictions

To illustrate how frictions shape material flows of water in tiny houses, we draw on the example of toileting to explore how different frictions were negotiated in the decision to install a toileting system: composting or flushing. Drawing on a UPE framework, Ormerod (2019: 649) described toilets as "critically important infrastructures that facilitate environmental change". Kilman (2016: 6) identifies that in San Francisco "[m]ost tiny houses contain some form of a "humanure" system, where human waste is composted rather than flushed into a sewer or septic system." Most tiny households involved in this study were using composting toilets, with a minority having flushing toilets.[1] Before turning to two examples of how tiny households negotiate frictions that encourage the decision to use, respectively, a flush or a compost toilet, we provide some background on each form of toileting system.

Composting toilets transform human faeces into a dry humus soil through mixing dry organic matter into a ventilated compost chamber (Dimpfl and Moran 2014). The composting toilet requires users to empty the humus to a secondary composting chamber, using their own bodily 'unpaid' labour. Composting toilets are a technology that provides opportunities for the nutrients contained in faeces and urine to be recirculated into the household through food production. However, research participants in this study who had installed composting toilets were disposing of humus in a range of locations, including the base of trees, a hole in the ground, a municipal 'green waste' bin, a biogas digester, and a secondary compost facility. Diverted urine was being used as a liquid fertiliser for trees, poured onto the land or down a drain. The absence of water means that composting toilets are a key practice that can enable households to remain self-sufficient within a rainwater catchment without having to 'truck in' potable water, use shared water facilities, or buy bottled water (Jensen et al. 2014). The only way that tiny households were recirculating humus into their household food chain was through fruit trees, and all households explained that they would not consider using it on vegetables. This is because f humus being recirculated into the household's food supply chain often predicated land security for households to be ableto deposit humus onto fruit trees.

Flushing toilets transform bodily waste into sewage using water as a disposal medium. The flushing toilet enables users to dispose of bodily waste at the press of a button: "flush and forget" (Jensen et al. 2014). Low maintenance comes at the cost of large volumes of water needed to transport faeces without congesting or blocking urban sewage infrastructure (Marvin and Medd 2006). The process of transforming sewage is outsourced to treatment plants. Large amounts of material technologies and energy are required to remove contaminants that transform sewage into usable materials, such as biofuels and clean water (Miller-Robbie et al. 2017).

Composting Toilet: Jane

Jane is a single woman in her 30s with no children or pets who moved to Australia from Italy as an adult. She is employed part-time at a local health food store in Byron Bay and lives below the poverty line. The tiny house allows her to escape homelessness. Prior to building her tiny house, Jane was living in a poorly insulated caravan and relied on shared water and food facilities. She had saved 30,000 Australian dollars but still could not afford to mortgage land in the Northern Rivers where she lives and works. For Jane, the tiny house was her only opportunity to achieve homeownership and avoid the unaffordable private rental market.

Jane lives in a mobile tiny house that she designed herself and built with assistance from a professional builder she described as "out of the box". Her tiny house (see Figure 9.1) is constructed on a second-hand flat-bed trailer and is regulated as an unregistered caravan. She used many recycled materials in the house construction, and her walls are made from a biocomposite render composed of materials like hemp fibre that sequester more carbon than they release (Shanmugam et al. 2021). The materialities of Jane's tiny house reflect the diverse economies that went into its construction and into her small water system.

Figure 9.1 Jane's bathroom.

Jane's tiny house is located on a small section of a large rural property that she is renting in the Northern Rivers, a region renowned for its "countercultural past" and continued abundance of alternative subcultures. As Gibson (2002: 339) explained, this includes "social groups, from permaculture enthusiasts to surfing subcultures, artists, musicians, large numbers of unemployed young people and 'travellers' ". Her tiny house is a 30-minute drive from the regional centre of Lismore and provides panoramic views of a series of hills and jagged mountains. The area where she lives is not connected to council-owned water infrastructure and relies solely on 'small water' systems for everyday household practices.

The property is owned by an elderly friend of hers to whom she is paying a small amount of rent, and who allowed her to install a water tank and composting toilet on the property. Jane and her friend have an informal agreement that she can remain on the land until the property owner passes.

Jane's strong environmental values inspire the materialities of her composting toilet (see Figure 9.2) and produce aspirations to 'live simply' by reducing the ecological impact of material flows passing through her tiny house. Jane's aspirations aligned with a counter-cultural set of environmental values that prioritise reuse over the need for a home composed of new materials. When asking Jane if she would hypothetically connect to mains infrastructure, she replied "no, no, no, no, no, no, no, no, no". Hence, barriers to accessing mains water were an enabling friction for Jane whose 'live simply' ethos produced a desire to be self-sufficient in household water

Figure 9.2 Jane's composting toilet.

consumption. For Jane, the structural forces of absent mains water supply enabled rather than constrained her life choice.

The composting toilet fit within Jane's environmental politics and aligned with a non-capitalist political economic structure. Accordingly, Jane had not even considered the prospect of a flushing toilet. The following conversation highlights this:

HILTON. I'm interested why you decided to get a composting toilet for the tiny house.

JANE. Instead of like what? Not having a toilet.

HILTON. Is that the only other alternative do you think? [Pause] Do you think there are any other alternatives?

JANE. Than a composting toilet? The flushing toilet? I am so against the flushing toilet. It would be extremely expensive to build the whole structure and the land is not mine, and I don't like flushing, it's dry.

Figure 9.3 highlights how the frictions in Jane's life limited her capacity to install a flushing toilet and connect to 'big water' infrastructure. Hence, the non-capitalist political economic structures in which Jane's tiny house was embedded evoked frictions that facilitated living sustainably by using a 'small water' system and the composting toilet. For Jane, the frictions pushing her towards the composting toilet were productive rather than inhibitive and were in unison with her environmental values. For Jane, it was not the

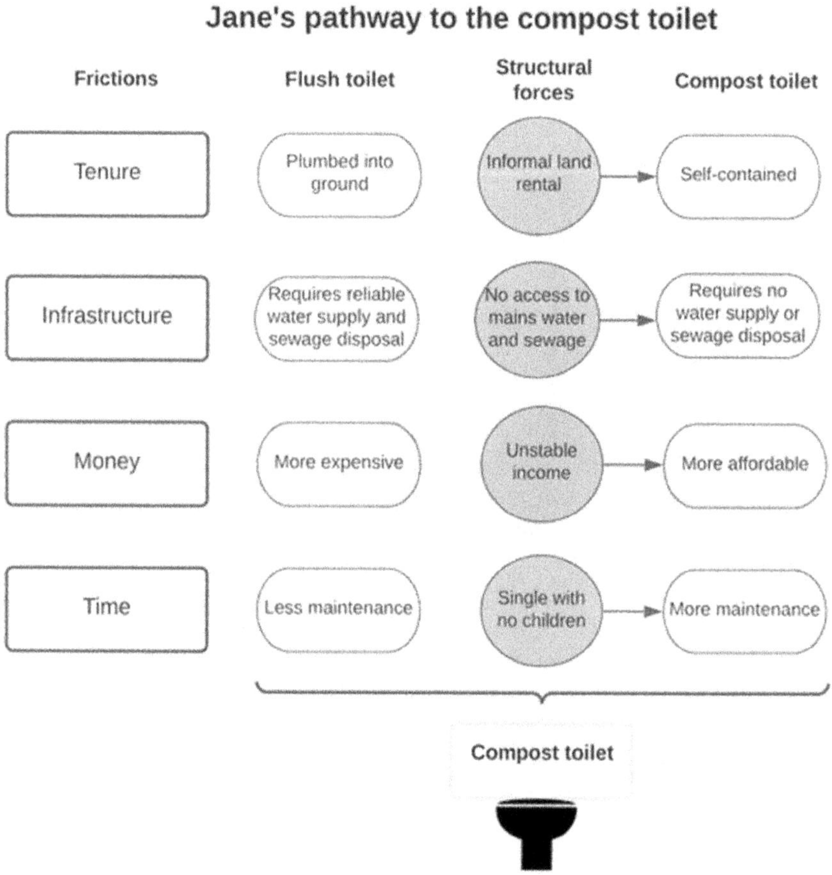

Figure 9.3 Mind map of the frictions shaping Jane's toileting decision.

shrinking domestic sphere that shaped the material flow of water, but rather the set of frictions that simultaneously constrained her from connecting to big water and enabled her to invest in a small water system.

Tenure

Irrespective of Jane's aversion to flushing toilets, structural barriers also prevented its instalment: first, her informal land rental agreement with her friend and, second, the regulation of her tiny house as a caravan. Caravans are not legally recognised as a permanent dwelling in NSW, and most local councils only allow flushing toilets to be 'permanently' connected to in-built black water tanks emptied at 'dump points' (Caldicott et al. 2014).

Further, a plumbed connection to sewage can provide leverage for councils to order the removal of tiny houses under section 4 of the EPA Act that factors sewage connections into the definition of a "structure" (Tamworth and Tamworth 2021).

These findings push beyond Crabtree's (2006) argument that tenure insecurity is a political economic structure that shapes households' capacity to adopt 'sustainable' technologies and practices. As she demonstrated, "(a) lack of affordability implies lack of long-term tenure or choice, undermining social diversity and equity or the ability to commit to place, hence undermining sustainability" (Crabtree 2006: 522). In Jane's case, tenure insecurity enabled her to source, use, and dispose of water via her small water system in ways that align with her environmental values. Mee et al's. (2014) exploration of the relationship between tenure security and political ecologies of water uncovered how rental insecurity functions as a barrier to households accessing resources for adapting to climate change. As they explain, "tenants' relationships to urban ecologies such as gardens, water, and energy are mediated by lease contracts, legislation, and relationships with landlords and/or property managers" (Mee et al. 2014: 336). However, Jane's friend and landlord enabled her to build an extension onto her mobile tiny house for her bathroom and composting toilet. Hence, informally renting land through a friend with whom she has close social bonds produced enabling frictions that allowed her to use a composting toilet and recirculate humanure into the land and her household food supply chain.

Infrastructure

A key part of Jane's 'small water' system is her small, second-hand intermediate bulk container water tank that stores rainwater collected from the roof of her tiny house. An intermediate bulk container is a semi-mobile water tank designed like a shipping container to be transported and stacked for industrial use. Jane's environmental values were so engrained that she had not investigated whether 'big water' infrastructures run through her street or not:

> I don't even know if they run pipes up here. It's pretty remote its 20kms from Lismore.

Indeed, a breadth of household sustainability literature discusses how, in rural areas, barriers to accessing water infrastructure can lead to water saving practices via the use of small water systems (Maller et al. 2012; Head et al. 2013). Jane's construction of a DIY bucket compost toilet in the absence of access to water or sewage infrastructure is a notable example of a water saving practice borne from her reliance on small water.

Finance

Jane offers insights into negotiating, in a one-person household, the frictions created by the 'structures of confinement' (Tsing 2005) of living sustainably below the poverty line. Jane negotiated the financial friction of working part-time in a low-income job by buying her small water technologies second-hand and DIY building as much as she could, including her waterless composting toilet. She used a large portion of purchased and found second-hand materials to build the composting toilet. Helping to negate the frictions of poverty included social norms in the Northern Rivers surrounding the practice of accumulating second-hand materials, the absence of the pressure of timelines surrounding the build of the compost toilet, and large rural blocks providing ample storage space.

Time

Furthermore, Jane negotiated the frictions created by the 'structures of confinement' by taking advantage of how part-time employment allowed her to maintain and empty the compost without sacrificing her leisure time. Indeed, maintaining the composting toilet fulfilled her aspirations to live sustainably. Jane was burying the humanure in the land near her tiny house and marking it to plant a fruit tree in 6 months.

Jane was able to engage in a range of alternative and non-capitalist economic relations by building a mobile tiny house and informally renting land privately owned by her friend. Additionally, being single and without children meant she had few temporal and financial commitments and relished spending her money and time in producing 'off-grid' water, energy, and food systems. Crucially, it was Jane's environmental ideology of living simply that meant that the barriers to accessing capitalist water, energy, and food systems were experienced as enabling rather than constraining frictions.

Flushing Toilet: Penny

Penny is a stay-at-home mother of two daughters, and her husband is employed in full-time waged labour. Their tiny house is in the outer suburbs of Sydney, around 40 minutes from the Central Business District. Penny explained that their decision to build a tiny house was driven by a desire to raise her two daughters while 'slowing down' through reducing her labour practices. Unlike most of the participants, Penny and her husband are paying off a mortgage for the land and suburban house at the front of the property, which they are letting.

Their tiny house is connected to big water infrastructure. Penny aspires to transition towards living more sustainably and 'simply', while also being a full-time carer. She articulated a version of 'living simply' that is highly

Figure 9.4 Side profile of Penny's tiny house and pool.

embedded in capitalist economies. In our broader conversation, Penny explained that she would rather pay for sustainable products and services than put "extra pressure on ourselves", noting that "if someone else is doing it [making sustainable products] locally I would love to support them." Penny's embeddedness in capitalist relations meant that her environmental values aligned with notions of eco-efficiency and ethical consumption principles. Furthermore, her idea of living simply is infused with middle-class ideas of home. For example, Penny's tiny house includes a vegetable garden and swimming pool, topped-up by rainwater collected from the roof of the primary dwelling at the front of the property (see Figure 9.4). Penny aspires to invest in a small water system and a composting toilet at some point in the future. She explained that her decision to install a flushing toilet (see Figure 9.5) was predominantly based around her life course stage as a young mother embedded in property relations.

For Penny, a flushing toilet connected to mains water and sewage enabled her to achieve her social aspirations of having a family and being a 'good mother' (Dowling and Power 2012). Her household's embeddedness in property relations meant that paying a small fee for commoditised big water was more financially viable than investing a large sum of money to purchase a small water system. A connection to big water supported the flushing toilet due to its low maintenance and cheap running costs. Figure 9.6

Figure 9.5 Penny's bathroom and flush toilet.

highlights how the structures produced by institutions that control mortgage repayments and 'clean' water supply produce frictions that militate against installing a compost toilet.

Tenure

As the owner of a suburban block, Penny's tiny house is regulated by council and building codes and legally required to be connected to big water and sewage infrastructure under public health regulations. Her tiny house is regulated as a 'granny flat', so its design and construction attain development approval. The flush toilet is a legal requirement for rental properties in NSW, and in NSW, secondary dwellings (granny flats) are regulated as a form of rental housing under the '*State Environmental Planning Policy (Affordable Rental Housing) 2009*' (NSW Government 2020). The NSW Government (2020) recently amended the regulation of flush toilets in line with eco-efficiency, and "from 23 March 2025, toilets are dual flush and have a minimum 3-star WELS rating." The land tenure arrangement on which Penny's house is built works to produce frictions that maintain the flush toilet.

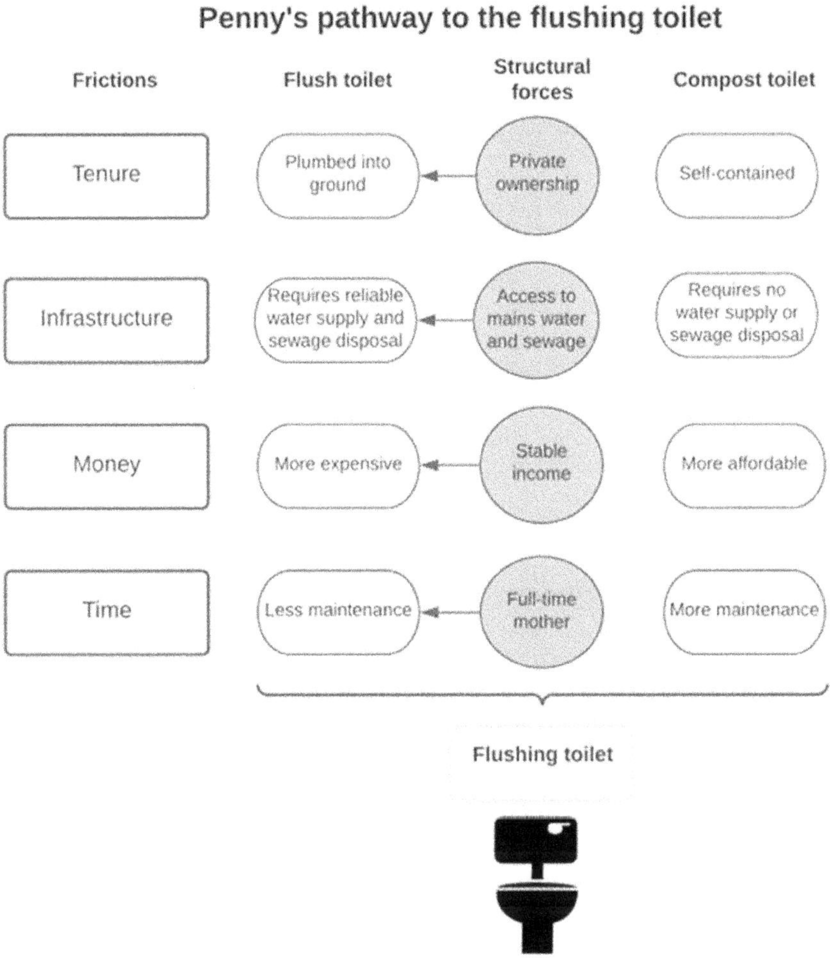

Figure 9.6 Mind map of the frictions shaping Penny's toileting decisions

Infrastructure

The mains water and sewage infrastructure may be conceived as a friction that sustains flows of water carrying sewage. Penny admits that they could have improved the sustainability of their water use, as she said:

> I think potentially we could have done more. My parents live in rural place and live off tank water for drinking and everything so we probably could have done more. I maybe would have done more, um, yeah I guess at the time resources, space, money, yeah.

Paying for infrastructure that sustains the culturally specific flush toilet works against investment in a compost toilet. Penny illustrates how, in a capitalist society where time is understood as money, she would rather pay for water infrastructure that maintains the flush toilet to help support her parental childcare role, which she said is a full time job.

Finance

Penny's wealth is tied up in the property, and the income generated from letting the front house is being used to repay their mortgage. Penny had spent a large amount of finance on the construction of their tiny house. She explained that rather than invest in a small water system during the build, they prioritised a pool, a large food garden, high-quality insulation, and new furnishings and household technologies. Today, Penny's household is left with little disposable wealth to invest in a 'small water' system after paying for groceries, school fees, bills, and other living expenses.

Time

Maintaining the composting toilet is labour-intensive compared to the flushing toilet. Labour equates to time commitment. Currently, the labour involved did not align with Penny's aspirations to slow down to focus on motherhood and vegetable gardening. Big water allowed Penny to achieve these aspirations, notably her large food garden. Penny explained that she wanted a garden to educate her daughters about where food comes from. Connection to big water at once inhibited Penny's aspiration to 'live simply' yet enabled her to teach her children about vegetable gardening and food sustainability.

Penny is embedded in capitalist economic relations stemming primarily from mortgaging land, building a tiny house with new, high-spec materials, and through her employment history. These capitalist relations produced a range of frictions that encourage the use of a flushing toilet connected to mains water and sewage. Crucially, it is Penny's aspiration to slow down that meant that barriers to accessing alternative and non-capitalist water systems were experienced as enabling frictions.

Conclusion

This chapter aimed to better understand consumption practices associated with the shrinking domesticities of tiny homes through drawing on UPE, and specifically Tsing's (2005) concept of friction. Examining household consumption practices, conceived in terms of the frictions of political economic structures, provides nuanced insight into how household water systems are shaped differentially by inter-related structures related to tenure, infrastructure, finance, and time. The chapter extends a conceptualisation of the shrinking domestic sphere of tiny houses, insisting on its connection to multi-scalar processes and complicating existing narratives of tiny house sustainabilities as necessarily reducing material flows.

The portraits of Jane's and Penny's households provide useful examples to trouble the presumption that tiny houses always produce more sustainable water consumption practices. Frictions around political economic structures can enable and constrain households and shape everyday practices that can both align and misalign with environmental values. This was illustrated via differences around engagement with water infrastructure shaped by political economic structures. For example, Jane's local council does not provide access to big water infrastructure whereas Penny was legally required to connect to big water. The current regulation of mobile tiny houses as caravans is shown to entwine households with frictions that encourage the use of small water systems and composting toilets. In contrast, the current regulation of permanently fixed tiny houses as granny flats produces frictions that encourage a connection to big water systems and flush toilets. Penny's household provides a useful example of how permanently fixed tiny houses that depend on private land ownership remain embedded in more 'conventional' financial and labour relations, such as repaying a mortgage, paying bills, raising children, and working full-time in wage labour.

These findings build on Davison's (2016) insistence that the modern household's embeddedness in property relations is the root cause of dependence on outsourcing commoditised materials via infrastructures. We reiterate his argument in the context of tiny houses:

> The desire of urban households to actively participate in the management, production and conservation of the resources on which they depend has potentially profound implications for public policy, planning and design for urban sustainability, as well as for the activation of participatory civil society.
>
> (111)

If tiny households' desires to actively participate in water politics is to be taken seriously as an opportunity for urban sustainability, as Davison (2016) suggests, then more work is needed by governments to foster political economic structures that enable rather than constrain this participation. The findings of this chapter confirm existing research claims that tiny houses may reduce material consumption. However, instead of focusing on dwelling size, we suggest that greater attention should be given to the role of political economic structures in shaping household sustainability decisions and practices.

Note

1 We cannot claim this small sample group is representative of tiny houses throughout Eastern NSW.

References

Boeckermann, L.M., Kaczynski, A.T. and King, S.B., 2019. Dreaming big and living small: examining motivations and satisfaction in tiny house living. *Journal of Housing and the Built Environment*, 34(1), pp.61–71.

Caldicott, R., Scherrer, P. and Jenkins, J., 2014. Freedom camping in Australia: current status, key stakeholders and political debate. *Annals of Leisure Research*, 17(4), pp.417–442.

Cousins, J.J., 2017. Volume control: Stormwater and the politics of urban metabolism. *Geoforum*, 85, pp.368–380.

Crabtree, L., 2006. Sustainability begins at home? An ecological exploration of sub/urban Australian community-focused housing initiatives. *Geoforum*, 37(4), pp.519–535.

Crawford, R.H. and Stephan, A., 2020. Tiny house, tiny footprint? The potential for tiny houses to reduce residential greenhouse gas emissions. *IOP Conference Series: Earth and Environmental Science*, 588 (2), pp.1–4.

Davison, A., 2016. Secure in the privacy of your own nature. In Cook, N., Davison, A., and Crabtree, L., eds. *Housing and home unbound: Intersections in economics, environment and politics in Australia*. Abingdon: Routledge, pp.99–115.

Dennis, C., Harris, L., Bekin, C., Carrigan, M. and Szmigin, I., 2005. Defying marketing sovereignty: Voluntary simplicity at new consumption communities. *Qualitative Market Research: An International Journal*, 8(4), pp.413–429.

Dimpfl, M. and Moran, S., 2014. Waste matters: Compost, domestic practice, and the transformation of alternative toilet cultures around Skaneateles Lake, New York. *Environment and Planning D: Society and Space*, 32(4), pp.721–738.

Dowling, R. and Power, E., 2012. Sizing home, doing family in Sydney, Australia. *Housing Studies*, 27(5), pp.605–619.

Ford, J. and Gomez-Lanier, L., 2017. Are tiny homes here to stay? A review of literature on the tiny house movement. *Family and Consumer Sciences Research Journal*, 45(4), pp.394–405.

Gibson, C., 2002. Rural transformation and cultural industries: Popular music on the New South Wales Far North Coast. *Australian Geographical Studies*, 40(3), pp.337–356.

Gibson, C., Farbotko, C., Gill, N., Head, L. and Waitt, G. 2013. *Household sustainability: Challenges and dilemmas in everyday life*. Cheltenham: Edward Elgar.

Glassman, J., 2003. Rethinking overdetermination, structural power, and social change: A critique of Gibson-Graham, Resnick, and Wolff. *Antipode*, 35(4), pp.678–698.

Head, L., Farbotko, C., Gibson, C., Gill, N. and Waitt, G., 2013. Zones of friction, zones of traction: The connected household in climate change and sustainability policy. *Australasian Journal of Environmental Management*, 20(4), pp.351–362.

Heynan, N., Kaika, M. and Swyngedouw, E., 2006. *In the nature of cities: Urban political ecology and the politics of urban metabolism*. Oxford: Oxford University Press.

Jensen, V.B., Darby, J.L., Seidel, C. and Gorman, C., 2014. Nitrate in potable water supplies: Alternative management strategies. *Critical Reviews in Environmental Science and Technology*, 44(20), pp.2203–2286.

Kaika, M., 2005. *City of flows: Modernity, nature, and the city*. New York: Routledge.

Kilman, C., 2016. Small house, big impact: The effect of tiny houses on community and environment. *Undergraduate Journal of Humanistic Studies*, 2, pp.1–12.

Lane, R. and Gorman-Murray, A., 2012. *Material geographies of household sustainability*. Farnham: Ashgate.

Loftus, A., March, H. and Purcell, T.F., 2019. The political economy of water infrastructure: An introduction to financialization. *Wiley Interdisciplinary Reviews: Water*, 6(1), pp.1–7.

Maller, C., Horne, R. and Dalton, T., 2012. Green renovations: Intersections of daily routines, housing aspirations and narratives of environmental sustainability. *Housing, Theory and Society*, 29(3), pp.255–275.

Marvin, S. and Medd, W., 2006. Metabolisms of Obe city: Flows of fat through bodies, cities, and sewers. *Environment and Planning A*, 38(2), pp.313–324.

Mee, K.J., Instone, L., Williams, M., Palmer, J. and Vaughan, N., 2014. Renting over troubled waters: An urban political ecology of rental housing. *Geographical Research*, 52(4), pp.365–376.

Miller-Robbie, L., Ramaswami, A. and Amerasinghe, P., 2017. Wastewater treatment and reuse in urban agriculture: Exploring the food, energy, water, and health nexus in Hyderabad, India. *Environmental Research Letters*, 12(7), pp.1–11.

Millington, N., 2018. Producing water scarcity in São Paulo, Brazil: The 2014–2015 water crisis and the binding politics of infrastructure. *Political Geography*, 65, pp.26–34.

NSW Government, 2020, Tenant Information Statement, *NSW Government March 2020*, Online at: www.fairtrading.nsw.gov.au/__data/assets/pdf_file/0009/608382/Tenant-information-statement.pdf Accessed on 11/06/2021.

Ormerod, K.J., 2019. Toilet power: Potable water reuse and the situated meaning of sustainability in the southwestern United States. *Journal of Political Ecology*, 26(1), pp.633–651.

Penfold, H., Waitt, G. and McGuirk, P., 2018. Portrayals of the tiny house in electronic media: Challenging or reproducing the Australian dream home. *Australian Planner*, 55(3–4), pp.164–173.

Robbins, P., 2012. *Lawn people: How grasses, weeds, and chemicals make us who we are*. Philadelphia, PA: Temple University Press.

Shanmugam, V., Mensah, R.A., Försth, M., Sas, G., Restás, Á., Addy, C., Xu, Q., Jiang, L., Neisiany, R.E., Singha, S. and George, G., 2021. Circular economy in biocomposite development: State-of-the-art, challenges and emerging trends. *Composites Part C: Open Access*, 5, pp. 1–16.

Shearer, H. and Burton, P., 2021. Tiny houses: movement or moment? *Housing Studies*, pp.1–23, doi:10.1080/02673037.2021.1884203

Tamworth, A. F. and Tamworth, K. B. 2021. Could the council force a home owner to remove a caravan from her land? Which case won? *Stacks Law Firm*. Online at: www.stacklaw.com.au/wcw/could-the-council-force-a-home-owner-to-remove-a-caravan-from-her-land-which-case-won/ Accessed on 11/06/2021

Tsing, A., 2005. *Friction: An ethnography of global connections*. Oxford: Princeton University Press.

Vannini, P. and Taggart, J., 2014. *Off the grid: Re-assembling domestic life*. New York: Routledge.

Wheeler, K. and Glucksmann, M., 2016. *Household recycling and consumption work: social and moral economies*. London: Springer.
Wilson, A. and Boehland, J., 2005. Small is beautiful US house size, resource use, and the environment. *Journal of Industrial Ecology*, 9(1–2), pp.277–287.
Wotton, J., Skates, H. and Shutter, L., 2018. Tiny House–when size matters. *Australian Planner*, 55(3–4), pp.209–220.

10 Meshing with Your Home

Seeking Trouble in Sharing Dwelled Spaces

Lauren Wagner & Clemens Driessen

Guests of Guests

This paper started on an airplane. On the way to the Association of American Geographers annual meeting in Chicago, in addition to being sandwiched together in a middle and aisle seat, Clemens and Lauren were enmeshed in some problems of temporary housing. Clemens was paying for part of a shared Airbnb, but only starting the following night; Lauren was paying for part of a shared Airbnb, but some of the other sharers were not arriving until the following night. The question arose of where Clemens would be sleeping that night (as well as what address he would put on his arrival card). And so we began to consider the negotiations and tensions of sharing dwelling space.

We first wondered who in fact 'owns' the housing space available in Lauren's shared Airbnb that night – the owner of the house, who might seem to have a right to know who is staying there, or the designated user in their Airbnb sharing group, whose arrival a day later left 'his' room open for this night? What about the other sharers in the Airbnb rental – do they own the use of that room as much as Lauren or the designated user? If Clemens were to be invited to stay – if Lauren were to invite him – whose permission should be sought? Obviously Clemens' occupation would not be limited to that room only. He would be present in other shared spaces, like the bathroom and the kitchen. His presence would be materially manifest: he would eat food, take a shower, sleep on the sheets, and leave all the normal traces of a human animal in a dwelling space. We wondered how extending a gesture of hospitality to Clemens, by offering this space to sleep which would otherwise be empty, is also an act of invasion and encroachment into the comforts, habits, and microbiomes of dwelling afforded by a home. We wondered how the intimacies of dwelling are becoming an exchangeable commodity, itself a complex of social and material ways that individuals take up space in housing, alongside the ways that housing is becoming segmented for exchange.

As we sat battling over 'personal space' in our overnight airline chairs, we thought this kind of battle is playing out at (slightly) larger scales – or

DOI: 10.4324/9781003173052-14

at the same scale but in ever growing variety and numbers of instances – through home-sharing platforms like Airbnb. Such platforms enable us to compartmentalize a 'home' into shareable and non-shareable housing space, based on the premise that those spaces can be commodities for temporary use by others. Yet when it comes to genuinely sharing housing space, this premise of treating housing as a commodity pitches the sharers, perhaps unknowingly, into negotiations of the many tentacles and footprints of dwelling. They throw into relief the tension between a house as a network of objects, with discrete purposes and actions of use, and as a meshwork of things, assembled and embodied with users and activities of dwelling (Knappett, 2011). In recognizing how we were struggling ourselves to tease apart dominion over things in a dwelling meshwork which we had not yet even entered, we decided to experiment with this problem together.

In the following sections, we elaborate on the 'experiments' we conducted in sharing dwelling space. For a series of work-related trips, we chose offerings from a home-sharing platform that involved sharing domestic space with the owners or with other renters. We reported back to each other on our experiences and the interactions we had with the owners and other occupants, and particularly our own discomforts and the instinctive limits we reached – and occasionally crossed – in meshing with the social and material dwellings of others. By pushing these limits, ethnomethodologically, we aim to probe the intimacies of dwelling that are presumed to be segmented and compartmentalized alongside the subunits of housing offered for hire. While many critical responses to the rise of home-sharing seem to affirm taken-for-granted notions of the home imbued with practices of privacy, ownership, and control of space and stuff, we take this as an occasion to probe assumptions of domesticity and how it borders. Building on Knappett's (2011) and Ingold's (2007) sense of meshwork, we are exploring how dwelling intimacies ebb and flow, expand and shrink, and are especially visible as such in the brief overlapping encounters between home-sharing guests and hosts. Thinking of domesticities as meshing or meshed means getting away from the domestic as a discrete ('personal') space with a certain dimension, but as something produced in materially mediated relations and affective practices. In this sense, we are considering not only how the economics of Airbnb shrinks home into commodifiable elements, but also how all kinds of actors – social and material – expand, contract, and enmesh with each other in the practice of sharing.

Units of Domesticity

"Home is where dependencies within and among species reach their most stifling" (Tsing, 2012:141). From nomadic shared mobile dwellings to neolithic longhouses, people have long lived in groups under the same roof (Fortunato, 2017). Modes of sharing dwelling space therefore not only predate but also persist after the arrival of the single 'nuclear' family house.

That discrete domestic form arguably emerged in early modern times in Western Europe (Stone 1975), though shifts in the character and composition of (extended) family and household structures have been debated (Smith, 1993; cf Braudel, 1981, p. 280). Domesticity could be unpacked as a particular "combination of the features of separation of living space from that of work, and its valuation of privacy, comfort and family-centredness" (Morley, 2000, p. 60). As such, assumptions about domesticity as 'private comfort' of a nuclear family is arguably a "specifically modern phenomenon, a product of the influence of capitalist economics, breakthroughs in technology and enlightenment notions of individuality" (Reed, 1996, p. 7, cited in Morley, 2000, p. 60) together with associated 20th-century gender roles and tasks in suburban nuclear family dwellings (Schwarz-Cowan, 1983).

That said, home-sharing platforms are often discussed from an assumed foundation of domesticity as something essentially private and non-commercial, which can – or, following some ideals, cannot – be segmented to 'share' in a neoliberal economy (Gibson-Graham, 2008). While we could question whether single-person, couple, or nuclear family households should be understood as a given or 'natural' unit defined by a strictly bounded private sphere, instead we allow this as a premise of what about the domestic house is considered 'under threat' from neoliberal intrusion and commodification. If domesticity has come to mean something about the intimacies of dwelling among a (nuclear) family, then our interest is in the frictions produced at the 'unruly edges' (Tsing, 2012) of that intimacy in home-sharing.

Whereas hotel rooms, at least historically, are purpose-built for the non-domesticating, transient dweller (van Lennep, 1987), home shares are, in principle, already-dwelled spaces, made specially available to welcome the guest seeking a temporary place to call home (Molz, 2012). Staying in a hotel room makes no requirements for social or material cohabitation with other dwellers or for revealing one's 'private' life – the raw needs of eating, sleeping, and shitting – with unknown others. Staying in an Airbnb – especially those where hosts are also resident – does demand this. So beyond the fulfilment of basic dwelling needs, the 'unit' being exchanged in home sharing is arguably the *process of sharing*: the alternating acts of hospitality and appreciation, the delineations of access and allowable behaviour, the allowance for private or 'personal space' behaviour, and the development of mutual understanding and friendliness (or not) that facilitate cohabitation.

It seems to be no accident that these elements are highly regulated and surveilled by Airbnb through the training and monitoring of hosts (Roelofsen & Minca, 2018), and that the regulation thereof is part of what makes it a successful platform (Gallagher, 2017). In a sense, hosts are asked to de-personalize through commodified personalization; they have to 'shrink' their own practices of dwelling to the service of the home product they are offering. For example, hosts – who presumably are owners and occupants of these already-dwelled-but-available spaces – are encouraged to produce a House Manual to guide guests on how to function in their new home (Airbnb, 2020), which makes that home accessible to any possible user. Starting with the Wi-Fi password (recommended as a first item to share), these instructions become necessary as a quick introduction to how to function in one's new home, which may be both familiar – containing recognizable features like a bed, a light switch, a trash can – and challenging. How does the hot water work? Where is the coffee maker? Which floorboard creaks badly? All the rough edges that would be quietly humming in the background in familiar homespaces as idiosyncrasies that our bodies have grown accustomed to become a feature to learn in the new environment. Likewise, the problems of living with the host and struggling over the footprint of one's 'personal' space becomes explicit and immediate. Whereas in other kinds of communal or cohabitational households, the understandings and dynamics of relationships between members would be worked out over time (Jarvis, 2011), here instructions for how the resources of the home are to be shared can be prescribed.

This practical work of sharing a home can be understood as a problem of stranger intimacy. Koch and Miles (2020) propose this framework as characteristic of digital technologies that facilitate encounter, especially those involving exchange of personal intimacies, like sex or friendship, or of resources like housing accommodation or a car. Through these exchanges, moments of potentially profound and intense intimacy – including openness of self, body, and property – can be produced as relationships are created, whether temporarily or durably, through matching preferences on a platform. Inevitably, these moments come with risk and vulnerability, and often the platforms involved mediate by building trust and promising security. This stranger intimacy is crucial in the process of home-shared dwelling, as it involves not only the host producing a space that is open to other selves and bodies, but also the guests adapting themselves to (temporarily) mesh into dwelling it.

The particular economy that produces, commodifies, and feeds on this process of meshing, in which personal relations and sociable encounters are part of the exchange of access to spaces and objects, could be thought to resonate with the accounts of the intricacies involved in alternative or diverse economies (Gibson-Graham, 2008). This arguably encompasses practices and relations that move beyond those strictly defined by capital and private ownership and as performed by neoliberal subjects that work on themselves to be the most value adding hosts (Roelofsen & Minca, 2018). What happens in commercial home-sharing practices then may not just be a matter of alienating people from their own pure zone of domesticity, as something produced in a supposedly non-labour environment of the domestic – something long contested in debates over gendered inequities and issues of unpaid housework. Domesticity is indeed something that, through platform capitalism, can be found to have surplus value that can be marketed and exchanged – but in the process there may also emerge more broadly positive, creative, and mutually meaningful forms of sociality. Focusing on the details of such processes could help move away from the assumption of private spaces as strictly bound, individualist, inherently colliding, and either expanding or shrinking, in favour of more complex and nuanced interminglings of practicing domesticity.

The paradox of sharing intimacies with strangers overlaps with the tension between objects and things: a stranger becomes intimate through accessing networked objects – such as a car, or a bedroom – as things, meshworked in a confluence of materiality and activity along with other bodies and entities (Knappett, 2011: 45–6). Though the product offered may seem spatially and temporally borderable and discrete – a 'home' or a 'room' in a home, for a fixed period of time – the structures for making that function as an economic exchange are meshworks full of ambiguous and interwoven overlaps, along trajectories of intersecting lifestories (Ingold, 2007: 80). These enmeshings may be temporary, but become encoded and adapted to by the species and the stuff that are involved, as part of the vibrancy of matter (Bennett, 2010) and the productive unruliness of edges that generates new possibilities at the margins of practice (Tsing, 2012).

These dwelling meshworks become especially visible through the use, arrangement, repair, and avoidance of stuff in our examples below. We were struck by the ways that stuff – like closets, tools, trinkets, and appliances – were repeatedly a site for working out the edges of sharing, and beyond that to weave and adjust ways of being in domestic spaces and its endlessly entangled sociomaterial character. This extended beyond just the access to storage or control of certain objects and the affordances that these may offer – the use of a saucepan, the leaving of clutter. What we found was also the vibrancy of objects as 'things' through the role they played in making houses sites where dwelling intimacies enmeshed as loaded with meaning, sense of self, relations with a variety of others, and being at home. The three narratives below show, in their own ways, how our tanglings over stuff included both moments of shrinking and compacting practices of dwelling and moments of enmeshing and expansive dwelling, making a home at once owned and shared.

Empirical Entrance: Experimenting with Sharing

Our autoethnographic 'experiments' (Latham & Wagner, 2021), in probing this process of meshing, form the empirical basis for this chapter. Starting from our initial experience in Chicago, when we noticed the trouble we were having in separating out our respective positions as dwellers and sharers, we decided to use further opportunities of Airbnb stays to explore how we ourselves engaged in these positionings.

Our approach to what we observed is both ethnographic and ethnomethodological. Related to the former, we are cognisant of our embodied positioning and perspectives in the global cultural empire of Airbnb: we are reasonably 'desirable' guests who are white, educated, and middle class, with (mostly) good reviews for our cleanliness and friendliness. With respect to the latter, we are treating the whole construct of home sharing as a set of social norms that can be ruffled. With these observations, we hope to bring attention to the unspoken rules and understandings that enable Airbnb transactions to take place, and especially to the unruly edges that emerge through them. Ethnomethodologically, we consider these edges as signs of 'trouble' (Greiffenhagen et al., 2015), or the telling disruptive interactional moments that reveal implicit social norms, through how they manifest as friction in our recounting of them in the vignettes below. Furthermore, in both of these traditions, we are attending to human and more-than-human elements as agents in vibrant assemblage (Bennett, 2010) – that is, as both ourselves and our hosts, but also stuff, pets, and affects that play into these dynamics.

To that end, we organized ourselves to be faced with troublesome encounters in shared homespaces. We reported to each other before and after work-related trips about our plans and intentions, sometimes also asking the other to evaluate options or choose the Airbnb, to disallow ourselves choosing only 'comfortable' accommodation without obligations to share. We tried to select accommodations that involved sharing space with the owner themselves, or which were normally inhabited by an owner and vacated for the purpose of home sharing, rather than homes dedicated exclusively to Airbnb rental, though this is not always possible to determine based on the information on the platform. The trips were usually oriented around conferences, though included accompanying family members or leisure time.

What follows is a series of vignettes, each showing a brief version of our experiences in different Airbnb encounters. They are narratively written and edited to focus on moments that evoke the evolving meshworks we made with different owners during some of the trips. We are not able to include all trips due to space, but have chosen ones that particularly illustrate how intimacies of dwelling evolved between ourselves and our hosts. Each vignette shows some elements of our own expectations about a kind of dwelling we anticipated in the home, along with how that sense of one's 'own' domestic space was challenged, perturbed, opened up and/or sometimes violated by hosts. In some cases, we were also the ones doing the 'violating' of meshed edges, whether purposefully or accidentally. Through meshwork, we do not seek to define private spaces with clear boundaries, rather to emphasize the productive frictions resulting from the impossibilities of clear boundaries.

Eventually, after our elaborate discussions on the plane, we resolved our qualms about who 'owned' the vacant-for-one-night bedroom, and Clemens did stay in Lauren's shared housing. The following day, he moved into his own Airbnb-to-be-shared.

Clemens in Chicago: Weirdly Personal Stuff

I was first to do the handover with the owner. On arriving, the owner lady asked me to repair her toilet paper holder, so within five minutes I was on the floor with tools next to her toilet, while she was walking around and we were making small talk.

And then she just strangely wouldn't leave for a full hour. She kept on explaining in ever more exquisite detail the rules of the house, repeatedly asking whether I wanted the leftover food in the fridge from the previous guests, how to operate every appliance from the TV, DVD player, to the bath, etc., not held back by my interjections that I really had no intention of using any of these.

When she finally left, I fell asleep on the sofa, to be woken up by Lauren and her buddies, together with the lady coming back in – she was still in the area and felt she had to bring more toilet paper.

Lauren in Los Angeles: Feeling Violated

Jody's two-bedroom apartment has two Airbnb listings: one for the independent second bedroom and another for a sort of mattress/daybed situated, as I discovered upon my arrival, on one end of the living room/office/central room of the apartment. That was the bed I had rented for 37 US dollars a night.

She let me bring my folding bike into the kitchen, barring against possible theft outside, and complimented my dedication to bring the bike transatlantically (she complimented this on her Airbnb review as well). I settled in, so to speak, even though there was no real space for me to settle into: this central living working space consisted of two long tables on one side of the room with her computer workstation; a large armchair, covered in dog hair and often occupied by her large companion dog; and the daybed, occupying a sort of corridor between the entry from the front door and the kitchen, and the back hallway towards the bathroom and bedrooms. There was nowhere to stow my stuff next to that bed that would not be in the way, so I started caching my things on the opposite end of the long table from her computer, next to the dog's chair. She suggested I take a shower (probably because of the hour of biking), and we could go out to eat. In order to do so, I rummaged through my bag to try to extract the necessary soaps and changes of clothes without exploding everything onto the workspace. Even that felt invasive.

We walked down the street to the closest branch of a local fast-food chain, and she carefully ordered and paid for herself separately from me, though we shared one of the laminate cafeteria tables. I found myself entering into some personal topics within the first hour of meeting Jody. Starting from being carless in Los Angeles, we went into husbands, boyfriends, and partners; careers, aspirations, and frustrations; philosophies of life and semi-spirituality. When we got home, she sort of cut off the conversation to get to work on something. I felt vaguely like I had been violated, convinced by a sweet-talker to reveal intimate information in exchange for staying in her living room. I forgot that I was also paying for it.

Over the next two days, I was hanging out in Los Angeles and staying in Jody's living-and-working room, though not staying there much during the day as that was one of her conditions for people renting this space. I continued to struggle with where to store my belongings. She had instructed me to keep my bag in that place next to the dog's dedicated chair, but when I left late one morning having opened it and arranged some items on the table, I came back later to find them rearranged. She had shown me a spot in the kitchen where I could store some of the food I had purchased at the supermarket she recommended; again, I found them moved around when I came home, and started gathering them together again, trying to make sure nothing had gone missing. Was she tidying my stuff for me? Or tidying her areas from my invasion of stuff? These rearrangements again felt like a violation that I had implicitly allowed by renting a bed in her apartment, but which emphasized my discomfort at occupying this semi-public space. I had no door to close, no cabinet to shut, no key to lock that could prevent her from fully exploring my travel bag and its precious contents when I left the house. I felt like I needed to carry my passport and cash around for safe keeping.

When I came home at night, I discovered the daybed turned down and ready for me.

Before I left, there were a couple of hours I found myself alone in the house. I took a nap on top of the duvet in the private bedroom, since it was between tenants – a chance for a little privacy. I took a shower and carefully hung her towels. I peeked into her bedroom where the dog was sleeping on her bed, and noted how she had decorated her personal space, now the only remaining space in the house that she did not share.

Clemens in Paris: Presence of Absent Owners

When we arrived to receive the key and instructions for living in the home for the next five days, the owner was on a little stepladder wiping the windows; he was deep cleaning his home. We were actually a few hours early, we had agreed that it was OK to drop off our baggage, but now our young daughter had to use the bathroom so we asked if it was OK for the two of us to already enter the home briefly for that.

In this way, we entered the space that was being prepared for the transition towards being our apartment.

The owner was very friendly, but there was also a bit of a sense of intrusion, an awkwardness of seeing our 'landlord' in his own home, in his 'cleaning attire' holding a mop. It was clearly an 'actual home' that this man normally lived in with his family. He was wiping away the fingerprints of his children from the windows, as a ritual perhaps to make the space more neutral, as part of cleanliness standards that Airbnb would survey us on after our stay. But also to generate privacy of sorts: our children were going to sleep in the beds of his children, with their trinkets, their posters.

We walked around, and after receiving instructions on how to use the kitchen, where the plates and pans were, there was a solemn final instruction. In the living room, there were various cupboards containing things we could use: board games, wine glasses. "But do not open this closet please", the man said, gesturing to two relatively large doors a bit higher up than the others.

I looked at these doors for the next five days and didn't open them. Throughout our stay, we were aware of being in the space of another family, gradually getting used to the appliances and furniture, making it our own. And we were inevitably curious about its 'real', actual residents now absent.

One evening, entering the apartment I bumped against a wooden structure on the wall with little carved birds. One small bird broke off, from what appeared as a personal and unique item. I felt very bad and decided to mention it on the 'check out phone call'. I was quite relieved when the man said it was not a problem.

Before leaving, we had ample time to clean – and I thought it was our turn to do some deep cleaning. Their dishwasher happened to be the same as ours. There was a switch inside that got stuck, so I managed to repair it. Then I got into deep cleaning it, going behind rubbers and in corners. I was really proud then, it felt like reparation and a contribution to the household which we were about to leave behind again.

Discussion

We want to bring attention to a few threads that connect these vignettes of our experiences in terms of our engagement with stranger intimacy through household stuff. By exploring moments of 'trouble', or where our narratives show discomfort and irritation in how we were interacting with the host and home through stuff, we notice how these meshworks of dwelling are produced in home sharing. Drawing together the three narratives, as well as other examples which space has not allowed us to share here, there are recurring questions that emerge in how our presence in the home meshed with its sharer: through our own intrusion into their space; through their encroachment into our sense of domestic intimacy; and through how our presence made traces on household things.

Our feelings of being intruders become most apparent in Clemens' entrance to the Paris apartment and Lauren's occupancy of the Los Angeles living room. We are both viscerally conscious of how we are taking up space in the 'wrong' places or at the 'wrong' times. Clemens arrives 'too early', interrupting the backstage work of clearing traces of the house's normal occupants; Lauren struggles with finding a place to leave her stuff in the host's workspace. The normal routines of the household – like the innate domestic privilege of leaving unwiped smudges on windows or of using the desk as a platform for work – become moments where we notice how our meshing into the household is taking place through the permission and active adaptation of someone else. These intrusions may be the most common story of home-sharing experiences in the unintended or sometimes unwanted intimacy of encountering the deeply personal domestic scenes of others. Airbnb's advice to personalize home space without being too personal (Airbnb, 2021) and to keep certain spaces of deeply personal items – like Clemens' unopened closet – inaccessible to visitors, is perhaps there to reduce that sense of over-intrusiveness.

Yet we also felt our own domestic intimacies encroached upon, and the pressure of shrinking one's own practices and things into what others might allow, or expanding into what others expected of us. Clemens' adventure in bathroom repair contorted him into the most awkward place in the house, on the floor in the toilet, while requiring him to manifest a home repair skill which he may reserve, in his own proficiencies and shortcomings, for his own family. Lauren, more strongly, felt 'violated' by the intimacy of the conversation instigated by her host, but carefully constructed to take place outside the home and without sharing other aspects of the experience, like the restaurant bill. The back-and-forth rearrangements of her things, like food and toiletries, generated some inexplicable panic of vulnerability through her stuff as a meshed extension of her 'space' and its tendency to be repositioned from where she had last left it. Clemens, on the other hand, was drawn into an intimate project of home repair, which meshed him into the background hum of the household more quickly than he was prepared for. In these moments, something about entanglements between home and bodies becomes visible in what we were expected to perform and to allow, in that we may become involved – comfortably or uncomfortably – in how the household works.

In recording and telling each other these experiences, we also became more aware of having left a mark on these households, and on ourselves, by engaging through stuff. For Clemens, the dishwasher provided a sense of familiarity and – paradoxically perhaps – giving it a thorough cleaning left a mark in him by encouraging him to commit to making a mark in the house. Lauren left a more transgressive and less permanent mark, as the imprint of a body on the top of a duvet and a towel moist after a shower. Clemens felt the effect of breaking an object more intensely than the owner seemed to; Lauren found herself surprised by a 'turn-down service' of preparing the daybed for sleep, as a material gesture towards her stuff-based comfort while she struggled in all other corners to find space. As much as this stuff 'belongs' to the sharing host, we came to occupy it, and inhabit that occupation in ways that resonate beyond the moment of contact.

What this discussion demonstrates is how we experienced moments seeming to revolve around binary oppositions with clear demarcations that produce a home: the personal idiosyncratic trinket is perceived as dusty clutter; the curiosity of a host sensed as an invasion of privacy; objects showing traces of use and amateur maintenance perceived as homely by some or as dirty, unhygienic, or impractical by others. But simultaneously, familiarity and interaction – both with people and everyday objects – generate different ways in which stuff starts to grow into you, accruing meaning through a brief and bounded interval of familiarity and use, and connecting to intimate knowledges a dishwasher or a decorative item has for those occupying the place at other times. Domesticity becomes an experience and a set of relations that does not just expand or shrink as a border zone between dwellers (as minimally simulated by Airbnb entrepreneurs), but is something that generates new meshworks of being at home with the traces of others.

Conclusion

Undoubtedly, these privileged, pre-Covid domestic mobilities reflect no more than a slice of what goes on in the messy dynamics of home-sharing. We have not had space to do justice to discussions on diverse economies and the problematic role that home-sharing occupies in neoliberal commodification of not just neighbourhoods but also homes and previously non-professional hospitality. Nevertheless, we propose that these experiments do offer some insight into how home-sharing and norms of domesticity – starting from a modern assumption of home as a private space that can shrink for sharing – are evolving as we learn to practice different modes of dwelling.

By drawing attention to the paradox of stranger intimacy and the process of sharing as the central functions under investigation, we aim to demonstrate how home-sharing – no matter which platform mediates it (Molz, 2012) – may hold the potential of opening up a seemingly simple liberal sense of the private home that can be shrunk or expanded, towards more complex types of relations, gestures of care, and sociability. In mundane everyday practices around dwelled spaces that caused us 'trouble', we see relations as meshing rather than occupying, encroaching, or even necessarily shrinking. That is, we see that while an individualist sense of one's 'personal space' may seem encroached upon, there is some potential in understanding the expansion of a sense of the home and what it means to (co)dwell with familiar and unfamiliar others through enmeshed, vibrant, material relations created by stepping on each other's toes. To that extent, we bracket the term 'personal space' because of its presumed boundedness, while we have attempted to recognize how it seeps in and gets rearranged and reconfigured through things and stuff.

To conclude, what we try to show here is how objects become things through the process of sharing, and how dwellers' things are in danger of being used merely as objects by guests. Through this engagement through stuff, precarious tensions multiply in shared homes, where relations between materiality and the conviviality of homes continuously risk falling apart through the intimacies being created between strangers who may feel intruded and encroached upon while trying to expand into dwelling. For that it is important to understand the home as meshworks – precarious assemblages of objects and affects and things with meanings and instrumental objects – to see the intricacies of the process of maintaining the value and meaning of dwelling.

References

Airbnb. (2020). "House Manual: Help Guests Get Comfortable in Your Space – Resource Center." November 18, 2020. www.Airbnb.com/resources/hosting-homes/a/house-manual-help-guests-get-comfortable-in-your-space-22

Airbnb. (2021). "Tips from Airbnb Plus Hosts: Design Your Space for Comfort – Resource Center." April 21, 2021. www.Airbnb.com/resources/hosting-homes/a/tips-from-Airbnb-plus-hosts-design-your-space-for-comfort-105

Bennett, J. (2010). *Vibrant matter*. Durham, NC: Duke University Press.

Braudel, F. (1981). *Civilization and capitalism 15th-18th Century, vol. 1. The structures of everyday life*. London: Collins.

Fortunato, L. (2017). Insights from evolutionary anthropology on the (pre) history of the nuclear family. *Cross-Cultural Research*, 51(2), 92–116.

Gallagher, L. (2017). *The Airbnb story: How three guys disrupted an industry, made billions of dollars ... and plenty of enemies*. New York: Random House.

Gibson-Graham, J. K. (2008). Diverse economies: Performative practices for other worlds. *Progress in Human Geography*, 32(5), 613–632.

Greiffenhagen, C., M. Mair & W. Sharrock. 2015. Methodological troubles as problems and phenomena: Ethnomethodology and the question of 'method' in the social sciences. *British Journal of Sociology*, 66(3), 460–485. https://doi.org/10.1111/1468-4446.12136

Ingold, T. (2007). *Lines: A brief history*. London, New York: Routledge.

Jarvis, H. (2011). Saving space, sharing time: Integrated infrastructures of daily life in cohousing. *Environment and Planning A*, *43*(3), 560–577.

Knappett, C. (2011). Networks of objects, meshworks of things. In: Ingold, T. (Ed.), *Redrawing anthropology: Materials, movements, lines*. Farnham: Ashgate, 45–63.

Koch, R. & S. Miles. (2020). Inviting the stranger in: Intimacy, digital technology and new geographies of encounter. *Progress in Human Geography*, October, 0309132520961881. https://doi.org/10.1177/0309132520961881

Latham, A. & L. B. Wagner. (2021). Experiments in becoming: Corporeality, attunement and doing research. *Cultural Geographies*, September. https://doi.org/10.1177/1474474020949550

Lennep, D. J. Van. (1987). The hotel room. In: Kockelmans, J. J. (Ed.), *Phenomenological psychology*. Phaenomenologica, vol. 103. New York; Netherlands: Springer, 209–215. https://doi.org/10.1007/978-94-009-3589-1_10

Molz, J. G. (2012). CouchSurfing and network hospitality: 'It's not just about the furniture'. *Hospitality & Society*, 1(3), 215–225.

Morley, D. (2000). *Home Territories Media, Mobility and Identity*. Abingdon: Routledge.

Reed, C. (1996). *Not at home: The suppression of domesticity in modern art and architecture*. London: Thames & Hudson.

Roelofsen, M. & Minca, C. (2018). The superhost. Biopolitics, home and community in the Airbnb dream-world of global hospitality. *Geoforum*, 91, 170–181.
Schwarz-Cowan, R. (1983). *More work for mother*. New York: Basic Books.
Smith, D. S. (1993). The curious history of theorizing about the history of the Western nuclear family. *Social Science History*, 17(3), 325–353.
Stone, L. (1975). The rise of the nuclear family in early modern England: The patriarchal stage. In: Rosenberg, C.E. (Eds.), *The family in history*. Philadelphia: University of Pennsylvania Press, pp. 13–58.
Tsing, A. (2012). Unruly edges: Mushrooms as companion species for Donna Haraway. *Environmental Humanities*, 1(1), 141–154.

Part IV

Sustainable Shrinking Domesticities

11 Minimalist Lifestyles

Performance, Animism and Desire for Degrowth

Miriam Meissner

Introduction

This chapter is about minimalist lifestyles – lifestyles that have as their aim the reduction of material belongings, work-life stress, mental distraction and material waste. Specifically, it examines how practicing minimalists perform for and with the material world of their homes. The basic characteristics that, in my definition, unite minimalist lifestyles is that its advocates and practitioners lament a world of 'too much' (clutter, stress, distraction and waste), that they engage in targeted strategies for reducing 'too much' and that they claim to improve their subjective levels of well-being through this practice. In terms of geo-temporal coordinates, it is difficult to pinpoint minimalist lifestyles. Google Trends indicates that, from 2004 onward, worldwide searches for the term 'minimalism' were common but slightly increased in 2015, with a peak in 2017. Moreover, minimalism seems popular in a number of regions, with Singapore, the Philippines, Estonia and Sweden on top of the index. Given this diversity of minimalist lifestyles and the fact they are still evolving, it is hard to make representative statements about what minimalist lifestyles are.

My analysis focuses on what minimalist lifestyles might become. Specifically, I ask which elements of minimalist lifestyles align or mismatch with the eco-political agenda of promoting a societal transition toward *degrowth*. Degrowth describes an 'equitable downscaling of production and consumption that increases human wellbeing and enhances ecological conditions at the local and global level' (Schneider et al., 2010: 512). In particular for rich countries with high eco-footprints, this is urgently necessary. Environmental scientists emphasize that the effective tackling of global heating and biodiversity loss hinges on supplementing efficiency measures, which seek to decouple economic growth from its negative eco-impacts (e.g., through green energy or recycling) with sufficiency measures that strive for an overall reduction in material production and consumption (Parrique et al., 2019). Yet, degrowth is not a call for a recession. Instead, degrowthers advocate a radical change in political economy, ecology and socio-culture.

DOI: 10.4324/9781003173052-16

To that end, degrowth requires both policy and cultural changes. In terms of culture, researchers underline that alternative values, narratives and ideologies are needed. Susan Paulson argues for a shifting 'value and desire away from productivist achievements and consumption-based identities toward visions of good life variously characterized by health, harmony, pleasure and vitality among humans and ecosystems' (Paulson, 2017: 426). Kate Soper supports *alternative hedonism* – a 'self-interested disaffection with consumerism' (Soper, 2008: 567). Serge Latouche calls for a radical *decolonization of the imaginary* (Latouche, 2015). Samuel Alexander advocates a movement of *voluntary simplicity* (Alexander, 2013). My work on minimalist lifestyles seeks to contribute to this line of research on what I wish to define as the 'cultural politics of degrowth' – the 'tactical employment of cultural practices, values, narratives, and identities for the pursuit of a degrowth-oriented transformation of socio-culture and political economy' (Meissner, 2021: 513). In particular, it asks how lifestyles whose practices and values overlap yet are not congruent with degrowth ideals might be mobilized in the political struggle for a degrowth transition.

Minimalism is a good example of a lifestyle whose practices and values overlap with degrowth ideals. Degrowthers and minimalists both advocate reduced material consumption and, to a lesser degree, wage labor. Beyond that, both maintain that well-being under conditions of material sufficiency is possible and even desirable. The perhaps most crucial difference is that degrowth describes a collective political project while minimalism, in most cases, focuses on individual lifestyle change (see Meissner 2019). Another issue is that minimalist lifestyles are currently hyper-commodified. They are promoted by hip lifestyle-influencers, who market and sell minimalism via self-help books, blogs, films, podcasts, television shows, courses and so on. This raises the question whether a product whose profit-motif is implicated in the growth-economic logic can help overcome this logic.

Following the cultural theorist Caroline Levine, my assumption is that it can. Levine argues that the same cultural object or practice can both afford and collide with a specific political goal, such as degrowth. The task of the cultural critic, then, is to examine which organizing patterns in a given cultural object or practice pave, block or derail the path toward this goal. For me, this means seeking to understand which ideas, practices, perceptions and narratives in minimalist lifestyles resonate with elements of a degrowth agenda, and what blocks these latent potentials from becoming actualized. To that end, my research involves the analysis of minimalist lifestyle narratives – including books, blogs, podcasts, films and television shows – and conversations with practitioners. For the latter, I have posted open questions on minimalist lifestyle practice in selected Anglophone minimalist Facebook groups. In addition, I have conducted in-depth interviews with practicing minimalists, most of whom I recruited via Facebook. While the research is ongoing, I have so far analyzed 20 minimalist lifestyle narratives, received more than 350 answers to my questions on Facebook, and conducted 10 one-hour interviews with respondents from North America and Germany.

Through this, I learned that many (though not all) practicing minimalists discovered minimalism in response to specific life challenges such as: separation, divorce and abusive relationships; illness, depression, anxiety and burnout; demanding caring obligations; unemployment and precarious flex-work conditions; the loss of a loved one; and the experience of having to clear out a deceased family member's home. Moving and downscaling homes also came up frequently – both in conversations with practitioners and in minimalist lifestyle narratives. Minimalist author Dominique Loreau has dedicated an entire book to the topic of living happily in small spaces (Loreau, 2017). For Loreau, this is a lifestyle choice. In contrast, Kyle Chayka – author of *The Longing for Less* – argues that minimalist lifestyles are often involuntary responses to flex-work demands, which impose frequent moves, as well as raising real-estate prices in global cities.

Whatever the specific motivation, it is clear that there is a connection between minimalist lifestyles and shrinking individual homes. In what follows, I focus on the performative elements of this correlation. To that end, I first consider why minimalist lifestyles are performative. I then analyze the meanings minimalists ascribe to their performances with and for domestic spaces and objects. Finally, I argue that minimalist performances express a longing for connection with the material world and promote an *animist sensitivity*. Both, I suggest, could be fostered to create a broader societal desire for degrowth.

Minimalism Is Performative

Following Richard Schechner, I understand performances as enacted relationships between different – including nonhuman – actors. 'Performance isn't "in" anything' but "between"' (Schechner, 2013: 30). As minimalist practice involves intentional interactions with the material world of the home, it is performative in a general sense. In a second narrower sense, minimalist practices are performative because they are 'built from known bits of behavior' (Schechner, 2013: 29). An example of this is the first episode of popular minimalist Marie Kondo's Netflix reality television series *Tidying up with Marie Kondo*. In this episode, Kondo is summoned to help a couple with two children tidy their home. Before starting the process, Kondo is shown engaging the family in a ritual that is repeated throughout the series. Kondo calls it 'greeting the house' and invites her clients to join. She then proceeds to 'find a spot', walking back and forth, then kneeling down with her hands resting on her thighs. 'Close your eyes', she instructs. While viewers watch Kondo and her clients engaging in this moment of silence, quiet piano music sets in. After a few seconds, Kondo lifts her hands from her thighs and places them next to her legs on the ground – wrists and palms facing the viewer – and performs a few small bows while moving her lips, presumably whispering something. She then proclaims 'Okay we're finished'.

From a performance studies perspective, it is relevant that Kondo's performance evokes familiar behavior. Commentators have pointed out that Kondo's rituals are inspired by Shinto, a polytheistic Japanese religion (Dilloway, 2019; Doyle, 2019). Central to Shinto is the belief that spirits inhabit humans, nature and inanimate objects (Doyle, 2019). Of course, it is likely that not all Kondo's clients, viewers and followers are familiar with this cultural reference. Yet, to make sense of the performance, this is not necessary. The action of kneeling with eyes closed evokes familiar behaviors, such as praying or meditating. People of diverse cultural backgrounds are likely to relate to it. This is reflected in the reaction of Kondo's client family to the greeting act. While both children are portrayed as notably silent during the performance, the father remarks afterwards:

> You know, what's funny is I obviously have never done that or thought about doing that, and it is nice to go: 'Yeah this has been a very good home for us'. Then I also got a sense of 'Are we doing it justice?'

Meanwhile, his partner is shown wiping away a tear.

Kondo's act of greeting the house is also performative in that it involves a *speech act*. John Langshaw Austin famously argued that certain linguistic utterances are not about describing or speaking the truth about something. Instead, they perform an action, such as greeting or baptizing. When Kondo and her clients greet the house, they perform an act of recognition. Here, the conversation partner, however, is not another human. It is an object – the home and its interiors. This is relevant because it explains why minimalist

Figure 11.1 Marie Kondo greeting the house in *Tidying up with Marie Kondo* (2019).

practice is performative even if it does not involve more than one person, nor take place in front of an audience. If, inspired by Kondo, I greet my apartment, then I am performing. I am reenacting the show and performing for my home. The home becomes a conversation partner.

This treatment of material objects predisposes an animist attitude. Following Graham Harvey, I understand *animism* as a behavior that assumes 'the world is full of persons, only some of whom are human, and that life is always lived in relationship with others' (Harvey, 2005: xi). Some minimalist practices conform to these criteria. They do so not because they proclaim relationships with nonhuman actors, but because they mobilize embodiment, affect and experience to perform these relationships. In so doing, minimalist practices can be seen to exemplify *new animism*, which involves 'performative acts in which people engage with other species or with material things' (Harvey, 2013: 6).

In performing with and for their homes, minimalist practitioners cultivate a kind of *animist sensitivity* toward the material world. Central to this sensitivity is that it does not just cognitively recognize but emotively embodies the assertion that things are not just things. From a degrowth perspective, this is relevant, because degrowth is not just about changing economic policies and institutions. As Jason Hickel puts it, what is needed as well is a 'deep ontological shift, to restore a sense of connection to the rest of the living world' (Hickel, 2020a). Following Hickel, I argue that a successful cultural politics of degrowth hinges on performing – feeling and enacting – this sense of connection to the world, and that minimalist lifestyles prefigure ways of doing so, if only imperfectly.

Interactions that Spark Vitality

Kondo, with her rituals of greeting the home and thanking objects, is not the only minimalist advocating performances with and for the home. Loreau, the author of multiple minimalist lifestyle books, assumes that material objects have an agency. 'We do not possess things. We are possessed by things', she laments (2017: 14). She also maintains that 'The things we have around us speak to us' (2017:23). For Loreau, this implies that individual minimalists should not just be aware of their material environments but interact with them according to a certain ethics – a set of moral and aesthetic principles. 'Surround your objects with space and respect', Loreau recommends (2017: 40). This aesthetic advice to leave space around objects can also be found in minimalist author and consultant Francine Jay's *The Joy of Less*. Jay dedicates a whole subchapter of her book to clearing surfaces, which – are 'sticky' by nature (Jay, 2010: 70). As such, surfaces are a 'magnet for clutter' – 'you can almost feel the gravitational pull' (2010: 69). To encounter this agency, Jay recommends keeping surfaces clear at all times except when immersed in an activity. Central to Jay's practice is that it affords increased vitality – capacity to move and live without blockage.

From a degrowth perspective, this focus on movement and vitality points to a form of well-being emerging from material sufficiency. For Jay, Loreau and other minimalists, material accumulation ruins vitality. Minimalists explain this in both practical and affective terms. In practical terms, they highlight how accumulated things require cleaning, maintenance and storage facilities – all of which cost time and money. In terms of affect, they put forth a range of arguments – all of which assume an embodied relation between individuals and the material world. Loreau for instance writes that 'Living permanently with objects we dislike makes us apathetic and miserable. When objects irritate us (consciously or otherwise), they provoke toxic hormonal secretions' (2017: 35). While no evidence is provided for this statement, it is safe to assume that being irritated by objects counts as a mild form of environmentally induced stress. Many minimalists recognize this correlation. One interviewee, for example, described how clutter in another person's home tends to distract her:

> I'm very visual and when I go into a new person's home, and this is probably bad on my part, but instead of concentrating first on the person I have to really take in my surroundings so that I can be comfortable. And I've noticed in homes with too much stuff you'd never see it all. And your eye keeps being drawn away from the person to the things. And I don't want that. I want to concentrate on the person.

Excess materials are perceived as a visual disturbance – as something that dilutes clarity of perception and creates discomfort.

Minimalists pay extensive attention to how material environments influence experience and vice versa. The basic assumption of minimalist self-help is that individuals can influence their environments in a way that will positively impact them. 'People who live in clean, empty spaces feel in control of their lives. They are not "possessed", and feel greater satisfaction and comfort as result', Loreau asserts (2017: 18). To account for this, Loreau refers to the Chinese practice of Feng Shui, which assumes 'that consciously or unconsciously the things that we fill our everyday lives with have the power to delight or irritate us every day, all the time' (2017: 24). Loreau asserts:

> We ourselves have the capacity to influence the world around us, by our attitudes, and by the way we walk, talk and behave. Our vibrations and energy act upon living things, and can affect our material surroundings. We receive and transmit the life energy known as 'qui'. ... Qui is affected by the raw material and form of each object it passes. Dust and dirt are traps for stagnant qui, destroying the harmony and balance in your home. Fitted carpet or rugs are material 'anchors': they magnify basic, existential resources. Energy rises from the floor, hence every surface in the home, and your shoes, should be clean.
>
> (2017: 24–25)

Loreau has a precise vision of how certain objects – such as fitted carpets – influence the individual, and how the opposite is true as well. She advises aspiring minimalists to walk, talk and behave in a way that exchanges 'life energy' with 'living things' and 'material surroundings'. For Loreau, vitality emerges through the right kind of performance with the domestic material world.

What remains unspecified, however, is how precisely aspiring minimalists should perform. Loreau and Jay frequently reference the concepts of 'lightness', 'grace' and 'fluidity'. In addition, both assume that, once the objects in the home are reduced and ordered, a certain calm, light and fluid behavior emerges. Loreau for example advises her readers to aim for 'superfluidity' in their homes by freeing space from cumbersome clutter, such as decoration, electricity wires, heavy carpets et cetera (2017: 17). In addition, she advises her readers to harmonize colors and materials in the home by favoring quality living over synthetic materials (2017: 39), and monochrome over color (2017: 18). Similarly, Jay describes the process of decluttering and ordering the home as 'streamlining' (2010:51) – a process that allowed her to 'feel the physical weight being lifted from my shoulders' (2010: 52) and 'live lightly and gracefully, with only the objects I find functional and beautiful' (2010:54). This reference to lightness also recurs in Kondo's 'spark joy' formula. In her series, Kondo explains: 'When you touch the item that sparks joy for you, you feel "Ching!" All of your cells are rising'. While explaining, Kondo herself performs a gesture of rising. She lifts her hands as light fists toward her shoulders and rises up with her body.

Later on, she explains that the 'spark joy' feeling is warm and positive – comparable to holding a puppy. She admits viewers may not be familiar

Figure 11.2 Kondo performing the feeling when objects spark joy.

Figure 11.3 Kondo explaining and performing folding in *Tidying up with Marie Kondo* (2019).

with it yet, but that their 'sensitivity to joy' will be honed as they progress through the tidying process. As with Loreau and Jay, Kondo uses associations with lightness, energy and new life to describe an ideal interaction between individuals and the material world.

In addition, Kondo recommends love and care when interacting with things. Interesting, in this context, is that the combination of love and care merges the affective with the embodied and performative highlighted when Kondo teaches her client family to fold their clothes. She explains that:

> When folding, it's important to convey love to your clothes. From the palms of your hands. By doing this, you will start to love folding clothes. Folding is not just making your clothes smaller. It is actually an important opportunity to talk to your clothes and thank them. By repeating this, you learn to love folding.

While explaining, Kondo kneels on the floor, with her clients and translator close and a top stretched out in front. Underlining Kondo's advice that folding should convey love 'from the palms of your hands', the camera zooms in on Kondo's hands when she repeatedly smoothens the top in front of her. She appears to caress the garment.

Strikingly, *Tidying up with Marie Kondo* frequently shows Kondo's hands when dealing with material objects. In so doing, the series puts particular emphasis on Kondo's soft and gentle manner of touching and holding things – embodying an affectively charged relationship.

Overall, Kondo, Loreau and Jay adopt an embodied and relational stance to the material world. The material world is a performance partner – to be

Figure 11.4 Kondo explaining and performing folding in *Tidying up with Marie Kondo* (2019).

treated with care, respect and awareness for its respective agency. Minimalism emerges as an animist ethics of performing with and for this agent.

Animist Sensitivities

There are limits to the observation that minimalists engage in *animism*. In fact, some minimalist narratives argue precisely the opposite. In *Soulful Simplicity*, Courtney Carver writes: 'Once we start looking at our stuff without filtering it through the lens of our expectations and emotions, we can see it for what it really is. It's just stuff' (2017: 51). In proclaiming that 'stuff' is 'just stuff', Carver advises her readers to detach material objects from any surplus meanings that consumer culture has taught them to attach to commodities. Carver seeks to de-fetishize objects by inviting people not to conflate commodities with the lifestyles they stand for. Similarly, the US American duo, The Minimalists, Joshua Fields Millburn and Ryan Nicodemus, regularly use the slogan 'Love people, use things – because the opposite never works'. Interestingly, the Minimalists' slogan reads like a reformulation of Karl Marx's critique of *commodity fetishism*, which describes capitalist societies' tendency to conceive of relationships between people as relationships between things. Yet, in contrast to Marx, the Minimalists do not link their critique to a systemic analysis of capitalism, but instead blame 'consumerism'.

While the reasoning behind Carver's and the Minimalists' critiques of misguided, fetishist relationships to things are not that elaborate, their writings reveal an implicit controversy in minimalist narratives surrounding the ontology of material objects. On the one hand, minimalist influencers frame their lifestyle advice as a pathway toward treating objects in a de-fetishized and functional fashion, while on the other they frame material objects as not just things but as potent actors to come to terms with through performance.

This tension was reflected in my conversations with practicing minimalists. When I asked members of minimalist Facebook groups how they decided whether or not to buy something, many respondents emphasized pragmatic considerations such as usefulness, efforts required for cleaning and maintenance, durability and socio-environmental impact. In contrast, others emphasized affective values such as joy and 'instant love'. A frequent phrase that came up was that practitioners wanted to surround themselves only with things that they loved. One interviewee, for example, defined minimalism as 'surrounding yourself with the things you absolutely love ... and without overwhelming your senses'. Things, accordingly, can be sources of extreme positive affect, but they can also act to disturb the individual's quality of experience. Overall, some minimalists thus see things in terms of functionality and pragmatic cost–benefit considerations, while others emphasize affective and experiential relationships.

Another revealing moment in my research was when I asked minimalists if they engaged in decluttering rituals and what these rituals allowed them to feel or do. Some respondents answered with a clear 'no' and emphasized that they were trying to refrain from any 'sentimental' attachment to things. The phrase 'throwing things out like a bad ex' came up – without thanking or overthinking – if things cause more problems than benefits, they need to leave. Some explicitly distanced themselves from 'animist' or 'Shinto' beliefs. This may relate to the public debate regarding *Tidying up with Marie Kondo*. When the series was released in 2019, commentators mocked and criticized Kondo for her tidying rituals (Schofield, 2019), while others defended and explained its relationships to Shintoism (Dilloway, 2019; Doyle, 2019). Given this public controversy, it is understandable that some wished to distance themselves from Kondo's tidying practice. And yet, a range of respondents also happily admitted to performing rituals such as thanking objects or taking a moment of silence before letting go of them. Respondents reported thanking objects either loudly or in silence, that they held objects in their hands, or took pictures before letting go of them. Interestingly, some explained that their reason to thank objects (and teach this ritual to children) was to show gratitude for 'the earth that provides us with everything' or for the resources – including time, money and energy – that went into the objects. This shows consideration for the socio-ecological genealogy of everyday things.

Noteworthy in this context is that minimalism was associated with a change in affective sensitivity to things. One interviewee – a practicing minimalist who also works as decluttering consultant – told me how her engagement in minimalism was not motivated by environmental considerations but developed in response to a personal life challenge. Gradually, however, the practice increased her sensitivity toward material excess and its environmental impacts. This sensitivity showed in particular when she donated her decluttered belongings to a German social department store, where secondhand items can be purchased for low prices. She felt 'overwhelmed':

> There are things from I don't know how many generations. And it gets fuller and fuller. ... There were hundreds of vases in different sizes, forms, and in part so ugly! I believe they will never – they won't get away from there. I found this so terrible – all these things that someone has bought at some point in the past. And also what this means in terms of resources [that went into these objects] and sustainability. My heart was bleeding. I found it really terrible to bring stuff there and to know: All this is dead material.
>
> (my translation from German)

Like this participant, most minimalists I surveyed, interviewed or whose narratives I analyzed did not engage in minimalism for environmental reasons, but rather practical and experiential benefits. Yet, awareness of the environmental impacts of consumption sometimes emerged gradually in the course of the minimalist practice, and it frequently combines with sensitivity for the material constituency of things.

This goes in particular for 'zero-waste minimalists', whose motivation is to reduce their individual solid waste to the absolute minimum by consuming less and packaging-free, as well as reusing, self-recycling and self-composting materials in their homes. A key figure here is Bea Johnson, author of *Zero Waste Home*. Johnson's advice is minimalist because its primary strategies for avoiding waste are to refuse and reduce unnecessary commodities and packaging. This is rooted in a well-substantiated critique of recycling. Similar to aforementioned examples of minimalist practice, zero-waste minimalism encourages engagement with material objects. *Zero Waste Home* advises how to compost materials – from eggshells to bamboo toothbrushes – but also how to make eyeliner from burned almonds, or avoid toxic chemicals in cosmetics and detergents. This might suggest that zero-waste minimalism has little to do with performance; that it is about pragmatic health and eco-impact calculations. I wish to argue that it is not that simple.

A close-reading of *Zero Waste Home* reveals that, for Johnson, zero-waste minimalism also creates an alternative life-experience. 'My life has been transformed – it is based on experiences rather than stuff', Johnson writes (2013: 9). In this context, performances with things play a vital role. For instance, Johnson describes how cooking without unnecessary gadgets (sorbet makers, panini presses, etc.) has transformed her cooking experience. Johnson suggests that minimalist cooking affords a more direct and empowered engagement with food – an experience of closeness and self-efficacy. To illustrate this, she gives the example of hand chopping instead of using a food processor, which 'is not only faster (than cleaning a big apparatus) but also more sensuous. Connecting with the food as you cook makes the whole process pleasurable' (2013: 45). The focus here, it seems, is not on eco-impact (e.g., electricity savings), but on embodied relations with material objects.

Another key performative element of zero-waste minimalism is the trash jar. Johnson claims to have reduced the solid waste of her four-person household to the size of a quart jar per year (2013: 10). Within the zero waste movement, this 'trash jar' became a kind of fetish object – the concretization of a lifestyle much broader (Leahy, 2018). And yet there is also critique. Kathryn Kellogg, the author of *101 Ways to Go Zero Waste*, calls the trash jar 'bullshit' (Kellogg, 2017). Kellogg's critique de-fetishizes the jar, warning practitioners not to confuse the signifier, the jar, with the signified, overall waste reduction. However, it is worth asking why the jar gained such importance in zero waste minimalism. To understand this, the notion of self-efficacy is central. Self-efficacy is an important motivator for pro-environmental behavior (Feldman & Hart, 2016; O'Neill & Nicholson-Cole, 2009). While it is not possible for individual zero-waste minimalists to perceive the compound eco-impact of their zero-waste efforts, it is possible to see impact in the jar. Johnson reports having 'filled a sixty-four-gallon can of trash weekly' before her engagement in zero waste minimalism (2013: 1). Converting from that to an annual quart jar is a strong indicator

Figure 11.5 'This is the waste that my family of four collected in 2014', still from *Zero Waste with Bea Johnson* (CGNT-America, 2015.

of a reduction in eco-impact. It is therefore not surprising that zero waste minimalists elevated the trash jar to a fetish object.

I therefore argue that performance, animism and fetishism are what makes minimalism successful. My analysis indicates that, at least for some of its practitioners, minimalism is not just about practical advantages, but also about affect, experience and embodiment. Even zero-waste minimalists, who pursue the pragmatic goal of reducing eco-footprints, emphasize the perceptions and feelings that emerge from performing with the material world.

Mobilizing Minimalism for Degrowth

It is widely recognized that humans' tendency to reify the material world – propelled by Western 'Enlightenment' rationality – is what drives their ongoing destruction of planetary ecosystems (Descola, 2005; Latour, 2012). When degrowth advocates envision how modern subjects might reconnect to the material world, they often cite examples from ancient or Indigenous cultures. Hartmut Rosa for instance argues that 'pre- or non-modern worlds of ancient, animistic, and totemic cultures' assume that things are 'interwoven in a web of resonant relationship and references to ancestors, spirits, or gods' (2019: 226). Similarly, Hickel cites the Achuar, an Indigenous community inhabiting the borderland between Ecuador and Peru, and the Bedamuni people of New Guinea, communities that assume an ontological continuity between humans, animals and plants. According to Hickel, this is not about projecting human qualities on the material world, but it is 'deeply ecological' … 'it anticipates the core principles of ecological science … which can be boiled down into a single phrase: everything is intimately connected; behave accordingly' (2020b: 264). Rosa and Hickel's examples envision what a non-reifying ethics of interconnection with the material world might entail.

Yet, in terms of cultural politics, taking inspiration from ancient or Indigenous cultures has limits. The majority of modern subjects are hyper-alienated from the material world. The challenge, then, is about recovering a sense of connection in a state of disconnection. This – degrowthers have argued – cannot be achieved in the context of a growth-oriented economy and socio-culture, which relies on the accelerating exploitation and commodification of ecology for profit (Hickel, 2020b; Rosa, 2019). Instead, it requires building a degrowth society, which overcomes its dependence on ever-expanding material production and, in so doing, decelerates. This is a macro-endeavor, requiring both blunt policy changes and a wide-ranging transformation of cultural values, practices and ideologies (see D'Alisa et al., 2015).

What I wish to focus on here is how to mobilize minimalist performances to make this degrowth transition more popular. To that end, it is interesting that Rosa argues that

> what late modernity lacks is not a reform program or institutional plan for improving how it processes the world ... but rather a perceptible, palpable vision of a different kind of relationship to the world, a concept for its now nameless longing.
>
> (2019: 443)

For Rosa, transitioning to degrowth is not just about establishing the right policies. Needed as well is widespread desire for an alternative – and the concept of resonance should spark this desire. Rosa defines resonance as

> a specifically cognitive, affective, and bodily relationship to the world in which subjects are touched ... by certain segments of the world, but at the same time are also themselves 'responsively,' actively, and influentially related to the world and experience themselves as effective in it.
>
> (2019: 163)

Whilst Rosa's 554-page theory of resonance is inspiring, I wish to suggest that, in addition, *performative mobilization* is needed – something that speaks to embodied experience to stimulate desire for a more resonant world.

As part of a wider voluntary and involuntary trend toward shrinking homes, minimalist performances provide inspiration for that. Admittedly, they do so with considerable limits. Minimalist performances can be criticized for their focus on individual lifestyle and the private home, for the fact that its advocates are complicit with capitalist growth-imperatives, and for seeking to control rather than resonate with the material world. Critique withstanding however, minimalist performances also express longing for a better connection with the material world – a desire that could engage a wider public for a degrowth transition. In this context, it is relevant that minimalist practice cultivates practitioners' sensitivity toward the ecological repercussions of material production, consumption and wasting, and that this sensitivity is not just cognitive, but also embodied and affective. It involves holding objects to show gratitude for the earth, feeling terrible when confronting the dead remnants of mass consumption et cetera. Degrowthers can learn from and appeal to this.

My suggestion for a degrowth cultural politics, then, is that degrowthers appeal to minimalists' longing for resonance and to their animist sensitivities in order to mobilize them for collective degrowth politics – for instance by asking minimalist authors to reflect on the broader economic origins of excess clutter and waste; or by inviting minimalist practitioners to fight for regulations that limit and forbid reifying and extractivist relations to the material world. Ideally, this politics would strive for institutions that establish animist ethics and sensitivities beyond the individual home. The goal is to create an economy and socio-culture that treats the material world not as resource or externality but as an actor to respect and resonate with.

References

Alexander, S. (2013). Voluntary simplicity and the social reconstruction of law: Degrowth from the grassroots up. *Environmental Values*, 22(2), 287–308.

Carver, C. (2017). *Soulful simplicity: How living with less can lead to so much more.* New York: TarcherPerigree.

CGNT-America (2015). Zero waste with Bbea Jjohnson. Retrieved from https://www.youtube.com/watch?v=7YkbEp7Dz_o

D'Alisa, G., Demaria, F., & Kallis, G. (Eds.). (2015). *Degrowth: A vocabulary for a new era.* Oxon: Routledge

Descola, P. (2005). *Par-delà nature et culture.* Paris: Gallimard

Dilloway, M. (2019, 22 Jan.). What white, western audiences don't understand about marie kondo's 'tidying up'. *HuffPost.* Retrieved from www.huffpost.com/entry/marie-kondo-white-western-audineces_n_5c47859be4b025aa26bde77c

Doyle, M. (2019, 24 Jan.). Marie kondo credits this spiritual practice with helping her figure out her tidying philosophy. *Bustle.* Retrieved from www.bustle.com/p/how-shinto-influenced-marie-kondos-konmari-method-of-organizing-15861445

Feldman, L., & Hart, P. S. (2016). Using political efficacy messages to increase climate activism: The mediating role of emotions. *Science Communication*, *38*(1), 99–127.

Harvey, G. (2005). *Animism: Respecting the living world.* Adelaide, Australia: Wakefield Press.

Harvey, G. (2013). Introduction. In H. Graham (Ed.), *The routledge handbook of contemporary animism* (p. 1015). Oxon and New York: Routledge.

Hickel, J. (2020a) *International development and post-capitalism/Interviewer: D. Z. Duncan.* Upstream Podcast.

Hickel, J. (2020b). *Less is more: How degrowth will save the world.* London: Random House.

Jay, F. (2010). *The joy of less: A minimalist living guide: How to declutter, organize, and simplify your life.* Medford: Anja Press.

Johnson, B. (2013). *Zero waste home: The ultimate guide to simplifying your life by reducing your waste.* London: Penguin.

Kellogg, K. (2017). 3 reasons the trash jar is bullsh*t. Retrieved from www.goingzerowaste.com/blog/three-reasons-the-trash-jar-is-bullsht/

Latouche, S. (2015). Decolonization of the imaginary. In G. Kallis, G. D'Alisa, & F. Demaria (Eds.), *Degrowth: A vocabulary for a new era* (pp. 117–120). London: Routledge.

Latour, B. (2012). *We have never been modern.* Cambridge, MA: Harvard University Press.

Leahy, S. (2018, 18 May). How people make only a jar of trash a year. *National Geographic.* Retrieved from www.nationalgeographic.com/science/article/zero-waste-families-plastic-culture

Loreau, D. (2017). *L'art de la simplicité: How to live more with less.* London: Oreon Publishing Group.

Meissner, M. (2019). Against accumulation: lifestyle minimalism, de-growth and the present post-ecological condition. *Journal of Cultural Economy*, *12*(3), 185–200. DOI: 10.1080/17530350.2019.1570962

Meissner, M. (2021). Towards a cultural politics of degrowth: Prefiguration, popularization, pressure. *Journal of Cultural Economy*, *28*(1), 511–532.

O'Neill, S., & Nicholson-Cole, S. (2009). "Fear won't do it" promoting positive engagement with climate change through visual and iconic representations. *Science Communication*, *30*(3), 355–379.

Parrique, T., Barth, J., Briens, F., Kerschner, C., Kraus-Polk, A., Kuokkanen, A., & Spangenberg, J. (2019). Decoupling debunked: Evidence and arguments against green growth as a sole strategy for sustainability. A study edited by the European Environmental Bureau (EBB). Retrieved from https://eeb.org/library/decoupling-debunked/

Paulson, S. (2017). Degrowth: Culture, power and change. *Journal of Political Ecology*, *24*(1), 425–448.

Rosa, H. (2019). *Resonance: A sociology of our relationship to the world.* Cambridge: Polity Press.

Schechner, R. (2013). *Performance studies: An introduction* (3rd ed. ed.). London: Routledge.

Schneider, F., Kallis, G., & Martinez-Alier, J. (2010). Crisis or opportunity? Economic degrowth for social equity and ecological sustainability. Introduction to this special issue. *Journal of Cleaner Production*, *18*(6), 511–518.

Schofield, A. (2019, 7 Jan.). What we gain from keeping books – and why it doesn't need to be 'joy'. *The Guardian*. Retrieved from www.theguardian.com/books/2019/jan/07/what-we-gain-from-keeping-books-and-why-it-doesnt-need-to-be-joy-marie-kondo

Soper, K. (2008). Alternative hedonism, cultural theory and the role of aesthetic revisioning. *Cultural Studies*, *22*(5), 567–587.

12 Tiny Houses and the Economics of Sufficiency

How 'Shrinking Domesticities' Fit within the Degrowth Paradigm

Samuel Alexander & Heather Shearer

Introduction

In this chapter, we offer empirical and theoretical insights into the tiny house movement, by exploring how this nascent social movement is seeking and (re)learning how to practice an 'economics of sufficiency' (Princen, 2005; Ingleby and Randalls, 2018). An economics of sufficiency can be understood as an orientation to material culture in which people secure basic material needs for a good life as simply and directly as possible, but then direct energy and attention from limitless material pursuits to seek happiness and satisfaction in non-materialistic sources of well-being (Mangold and Zschau, 2019; Alexander, 2012). The 'sufficiency' of a tiny house will be presented as an example of this alternative economic paradigm. Sufficiency can be contrasted with conventional economics of growth and consumerism (Jackson, 2009), in which ongoing material advancement, including expanding house sizes, is assumed to be a precondition for individual and/or societal progress.

Our point of departure is to explore an interesting paradox in the theme of this book—namely, that the 'shrinking domesticities' of the tiny house movement can actually evoke an 'expanded domesticity' of increased self-sufficiency and home-based production, as well as increased senses of security, resilience, and liberation. The phrase 'less is more' speaks to this paradox (Hickel, 2020) and is evidently embraced by many in the tiny house movement (Alexander and Shearer, 2019). We see value in unpacking this paradox of shrinking domesticities and exploring how these smaller material footprints can provide the modest foothold for a genuinely progressive expanded domesticity, as more households seek to 'escape the market' and begin building new, household and community economies beyond the dictates of capitalism and its consumerist cultures of consumption (Gibson-Graham et al., 2013).

We frame our analysis of the tiny house movement in the context of the 'degrowth' paradigm, which calls for planned contraction of energy and resource demands as a necessary part of any just transition to a sustainable economy. We present tiny houses not as a sufficient driver of a degrowth

DOI: 10.4324/9781003173052-17

transition—more will obviously be needed to derail growth capitalism. Instead, we argue tiny houses are a counterculture practice consistent with the ethos of degrowth and an example of the plurality of practices contributing, however modestly, to a degrowth transition. We also explore critical perspectives and literature that suggest tiny houses are not always what they seem.

The Global Predicament

By a wide range of indicators, the global economy is exceeding the sustainable carrying capacity of the planet (Wiedmann et al., 2020). Climate change is perhaps the most prominent ecological transgression, but there is also biodiversity loss and species extinction, resource depletion, pollution, deforestation, topsoil erosion, and many other deeply unsustainable impacts (Bradshaw et al., 2021). Ecological footprint analysis indicates that humanity would need 1.7 planets if the existing global economy were sustained over the long term (Global Footprint Network, 2019). If the United States or Australian way of life were globalised to the world's population, humanity would need four or five planets worth of biocapacity, implying a need to reduce 'first world' impacts by 75% or more.

Despite the global economy being in this state of ecological overshoot, billions of people on the planet are, by any humane standard, under-consuming (Hickel, 2017). If those in poverty are to raise their living standards to some dignified level of material sufficiency, as they have every right to do, it is likely that this will place further burdens on already overburdened ecosystems. But if sufficiency is a noble and necessary goal to lift people out of poverty, globalising affluence is far more questionable. According to material footprint analysis, the average Australian relies on 35 tonnes of material flows each year, compared to 5 tonnes for an average Indian (Wiedmann et al., 2015). This suggests that if all Indians consumed at Australian levels of affluence, the Indian economy would need to expand 7-fold. This growth-orientated vision of 'development' is ridden with ecological contradictions. The idea of globalising affluence is demonstrably and dangerously incoherent as a paradigm of sustainable development (Wiedmann et al., 2020).

To make matters more challenging still, there are now 7.9 billion people on Earth, increasing by about 200,000 people every day. Mid-range projections from the United Nations suggest we are heading for around 9.7 billion by mid-century and 11 billion by 2100 (UN Dept of Economic and Social Affairs, 2019). All this calls radically into question the legitimacy of continuous economic expansion and rising material living standards in the already-rich nations. And yet, despite humanity already making grossly unsustainable demands on a finite biosphere, all nations—including or especially the richest nations—are seeking to grow their economies without apparent limit (Jackson, 2021).

The Myth of 'Green Growth' and the Emerging Case for Degrowth

The dominant response to the environmental predicament outlined above is to hold up 'green growth' as a form of sustainable development. Many reports and meta-reviews have shown this approach fails to achieve the 'green' outcomes promised (Hickel, 2019; Parrique et al., 2019; Stoknes and Rockström, 2018). In a growth-orientated economy, technological advances and efficiency gains in production and distribution tend to be reinvested in more growth and consumption, not reduced impacts (Wiedmann et al., 2020). The critical point is that the degree of 'decoupling' required to make ongoing growth 'sustainable' is simply too great.

This crisis of ecological overshoot also provides insight into genuinely sustainable alternatives. Broadly speaking, the implications are clear but radical: if the global economy is to operate within the sustainable carrying capacity of the planet, this requires (among other things) the richest nations to initiate a 'degrowth' process of planned economic contraction, on the path to a 'steady state' economy of stable and sustainable biophysical throughput (Hickel, 2020). The poorest nations also need to achieve some 'steady state' in time, but first their economic capacities must be developed in some appropriate form to ensure basic needs for all are met. Justice and sustainability, therefore, intersect in ways that strongly indicate that contemporary consumer lifestyles, including the tendency for house sizes to grow with expanding incomes, must be transcended through consumer downshifting and economic degrowth (Kallis et al., 2020).

It is this recalibration of economic goals away from consumerism and growth that has led us to frame our analysis of the tiny house movement in terms of an economics of sufficiency, where people seek 'enough' to live a good life but otherwise give up the pursuit of limitless material upscaling. Indeed, in overconsuming cultures, sufficiency would often imply people first embracing radical forms of material and energy downshifting in search of genuine sustainability beyond growth (Jackson, 2021). Degrowth does not mean hardship and deprivation, but on the contrary, meeting basic needs—such as housing—simply, with minimal impact and maintaining a high quality of life (Alexander, 2014).

Housing is a pertinent area to focus on degrowth and sufficiency. Access to safe shelter is a basic human right, and with other physiological needs such as food and water, is one of Maslow's (1981) fundamental universal human needs. Furthermore, Safe and Affordable Housing is part of the UN Sustainable Development Goal 11—Sustainable Cities and Communities (UN, 2021). SDG 11 states "By 2030, ensure access for all to adequate, safe and affordable housing and basic services and upgrade slums". Even high-income countries such as Australia, the USA, and the UK are largely failing to ensure access to affordable housing for all—indeed, these are some of the most unequal nations, as well as where private property rights are most deeply entrenched (Baumann et al., 2021). Without having space to examine the complexities of these issues, we note that both inequality and existing private property systems can put increased pressure on access to housing, thus contributing to the drive to explore 'alternative' housing arrangements such as the Tiny House on Wheels (THOW).

Tiny Houses in Historical Context

While small dwellings remain the norm in much of the world, in some countries, especially Anglophone ex-British colonies such as the USA, Australia, Canada, and New Zealand, a tendency for the 'middle-class' to build ever larger suburban houses has for some time been commonplace. In 1961 in Australia for example, the average size of a detached house was around 90 m^2, whereas in 2019/20, the average floor area of new houses (combined capital cities) was 248 m^2 (Wilson and Boehland, 2008; Cohen, 2020; ABS, 2020). This increase in house size was inversely correlated with household size, which has decreased from around 3.6 persons in 1961 to 2.55 persons in 2016 (Qu, 2020; .idcommunity, 2021). Thus, in 1961, each person had around 25 m^2 of space whereas in 2016, they had around 97 m^2 (approximately 4 times as much space per capita) (Cohen, 2020).

This increase in house size largely coincided with the global take-up of neoliberal economics, which escalated in the early 1980s under the Reagan presidency in the USA and the Thatcher regime in the UK (Harvey, 2007; Hickel, 2012). These governments began relaxing bank lending requirements, freeing up mortgage borrowing, and concurrently, the development and construction industry mass marketed the aspirational narrative of the 'great Australian (and American) Dream'—owning your own home—ideally a detached house with a backyard (McKinlay et al., 2019; Nelson, 2018). The movement towards ever bigger houses and 'free for all' bank lending was briefly halted during the Global Financial Crisis (GFC), but soon resumed, with ever increasing levels of household debt (Colombini, 2019). The Dodd-Frank Act, put into place in 2010 after the GFC, to curb predatory bank lending, was further eroded under the Trump presidency (Snider, 2020). As so eloquently stated by Colombini (2019, p.448) "We dwell uneasily in this moment of neoliberal capitalism, in short, and in the heavily mortgaged, increasingly outsized and expensive houses that are its motif".

While privileging a few to 'achieve' their aspirational housing 'dream' (albeit predicated on increasing debt), neoliberal capitalism has left many others stranded in precarious, overcrowded, and insecure housing. This has impacted society's most vulnerable; people of colour, older women, disabled people, lifelong renters, and migrants and refugees. Many such people are keenly interested in the tiny house movement, not necessarily to minimise capitalist consumption, but to secure a safe and affordable house in which to live.

Beginning in the 1960s, however, has been a concurrent trend towards smaller houses, albeit on a far smaller scale. Building on voluntary simplicity movements of earlier years, such as Thoreau in the 1850s, the 'hippies' of the 1960s embraced the concept of living lighter on the land and were precursors of the #vanlife movement of the 21st century (Alexander and Shearer, 2019; Jackson, 2016; Evans, 2018). These early pioneers of the principles of degrowth embraced some of the later ideals of the tiny house movement, questioning superfluous consumption and downshifting housing from the 'bigger is better' trajectory (Nelson and Schneider, 2018; Alexander and Shearer, 2019; Alexander, 2014).

It was only in the late 1990s however, that the contemporary tiny house movement, as epitomised by the THOW, began in the Pacific Northwest of the USA (Anson, 2014; Evans, 2017). Fuelled by rising house prices, restrictive planning legislation and desires for 'freedom', early precursors (mostly architects and designers) began building THOW. Building a house on wheels circumvented planning restrictions on house size, the necessity to purchase (expensive) land, and was a more sustainable way to live because it minimised resources for building, energy for heating, and space for superfluous accumulation of stuff (Anson, 2014; Evans, 2018). This microeconomic or household approach to sustainable consumption resonates clearly with the macroeconomics of degrowth, even if the perspectives differ. Both seek sufficiency or 'enough' for a good life, without exceeding planetary boundaries.

Since then, the tiny house movement has become a global phenomenon, albeit mostly in countries with very large and unaffordable houses, such as the USA, Australia, New Zealand (Shearer and Burton, 2019). The rise of the tiny house movement has also coincided with rises in social media use and are glamorised on Instagram, Facebook, and YouTube (Penfold et al., 2018). The concurrent contemporary movements of voluntary simplicity and minimalism—as espoused in podcasts, books, and streaming media by Marie Kondo, The Minimalists (Joshua Fields Millburn and Ryan Nicodemus) and others—have also buoyed the tiny house movement (Carras, 2019; Penfold et al., 2018).

Sufficiency in Practice: Gaining Empirical Insight into the Tiny House Movement

Despite the popularity of the movement, a specific definition of 'tiny housing' remains amorphous. An attempt was made by Shearer and Burton (2019) to define tiny houses using criteria including size, mobility, design, and a DIY ethos. This however did not address the inherent problems around definitions based on dwelling type—inter alia how to differentiate between a 'tiny house' and for example, a caravan or studio apartment. A more recent article by the same authors argued that instead of defining tiny houses by dwelling form, it is more relevant to explore it as a countercultural *movement* largely separate from the dwelling per se (Shearer and Burton, 2021b).

This repositioning of the phenomenon as defined by its advocates, rather than dwelling form, resulted from seven years of empirical research into the Australian tiny house movement. Four surveys as well as extensive qualitative research identified that tiny house advocates are strongly motivated by the desire to live **sustainably** in some sort of **community**, and are seeking **affordable housing** and **freedom** (from regulations and economic constraints and debt) (Shearer and Burton, 2021b; Shearer and Burton, 2021a). While the movement itself has grown substantively over this research period, the importance and ranking of these drivers has remained constant.

Despite this, there has been minimal growth in actual tiny house living (particularly THOW), at least in Australia, with fewer than 200 people reporting living in tiny houses (Shearer and Burton, 2021a). Those interested in tiny house living are predominantly single, female, and over 40, but those living in tiny houses are more diverse demographically, including couples with children. This disparity may indicate that older women are more cautious about investing their money in a house with insecure tenure. In Australia, the primary barrier to the take-up of tiny house living is perceived by those in the movement as restrictive local government planning regulations as, almost without exception, local governments consider THOW as 'caravans' with limited permissible periods of habitation. Insecurity of tenure is arguably the major reason that tiny house living in Australia remains stagnant (Shearer and Burton, 2021a). Similarly, in the USA, while it is estimated that 2000 tiny houses are built every year, these are often used as ancillary dwellings or short-term tourism such as Airbnb (Cohen, 2020).

In Australia, tiny house advocates express a preference to locate their tiny houses relatively close to urban areas, ideally renting space from a landowner. The most recent survey by Shearer (February 2021) showed that 44% of tiny house dwellers 'rented space on someone else's private property' and 21% on 'a friend or relative's property' (Shearer, 2021). Most (nearly two-thirds) were located in rural residential (39%) or rural/remote areas (27%). In Australia, peri-urban 'rural residential' suburbs with large lot sizes within an hour's drive of major cities have always been desirable places to live. Anecdotally, tiny house dwellers locate in rural areas less by choice than from restrictive local government planning regimes, as in denser urban areas, there is more likelihood of neighbour objections.

Another drawback to the take-up of tiny house living is, conversely, their cost. Tiny houses are frequently 'sold' as a 'solution' to the wicked problem of unaffordable housing (Shearer, 2014; Sebag-Montefiore, 2017). THOW are of course, cheaper than standard housing, purely because they do not require the purchase of land and use fewer materials. The actual construction, however, is approximately 3–5 times more expensive per square metre than a standard house (for a ready-built THOW). This is due to the requirement for road-legal trailers, and bespoke fixtures and fittings. Moreover, THOW are also depreciating assets, and it is impossible to get mortgage finance to buy one. Their purchase is dependent on paying cash or sourcing an expensive, short-term personal loan.

Most THOW are spatially constrained by having to adhere to road regulations (limited to 2.4 m width) but otherwise are constructed similarly to standard houses, although to take advantage of limited space, tend to be as high as permitted (around 4.2 m). While this allows for more space, loft bedrooms are accessed by steep stairs or a ladder, unsuitable for anyone with mobility issues, including older people (an important demographic in the tiny house movement). More recently however, some tiny house builders are using '5th wheeler' trailers, situating the main bed on the same level as the rest of the THOW. Others, assuming that the THOW will be moved rarely, remove the trails and move them by truck.

Limited research exists on the sustainability of tiny houses; although they are more materially sustainable purely due to their smaller size—even with a trailer, a 27 m^2 THOW uses far less construction material than a 250 m^2 house on a slab (Cohen, 2020). Many are also 'off-grid' with solar power, composting toilets, and passive heating and cooling. Saxton (2019) found that the ecological footprints of tiny house downsizers were approximately half that of the US national average. This is similar behaviour to inner-city apartment dwellers, who generally have fewer possessions and use public spaces more than detached house dwellers (Cohen, 2020). Again, these practices clearly support the economics of sufficiency of the degrowth paradigm, which calls for 'planned contraction' of energy and resource demands in over-consuming nations.

On the other hand, while tiny house dwellers report minimising possessions, as mentioned above, most Australian THOW are situated in rural areas, where their dwellers depend on private motor vehicles to access employment, services, education, and so on (Cohen, 2020). Some wish to live closer to the city, but live in rural areas because of cheaper land and/or lower likelihood of being reported to the council. This contradicts the assumption that the mobile and temporary nature of tiny houses gives people the 'freedom' to live in 'more desirable' areas which they otherwise could not afford (Colombini, 2019). That said, there is certainly a thread in the movement that seeks the closer connection to nature that rural living allows, a sentiment that can be traced at least as far back as Henry Thoreau's tiny house experiment on the shores of Walden Pond.

'Freedom' from work and from debt, and from regulations, are consistent themes in the tiny house literature and empirics (Alexander and Shearer, 2019; Bennett, 2019; Boeckermann et al., 2019; Anson, 2014). This also meshes with themes in the degrowth movement, where calls are made to exchange superfluous stuff for more free time. Tiny house living is seen to allow freedom from the neoliberal necessity to work long hours to pay for a large mortgage—allowing more time to engage in valuable activities such as travel, sport, and spending time with family and friends. People could (theoretically) work part-time, or even give up work, and explore personal hobbies for which they previously had insufficient time or money. On the other hand, many, particularly older people, want to live in tiny houses legally—in any location—others in the movement want to maintain the 'under the radar' status and strongly oppose regulation (Weetman, 2018).

This latter concept of freedom is perhaps more reflective of the origins of the contemporary tiny house movement, deeply rooted in the American libertarian tradition of autonomy, rebellion, and individualism, from Thoreau onwards (Mangold and Zschau, 2019; Anson, 2014; Alexander and Shearer, 2019). This type of freedom can at times be in tension with the desire for community. Furthermore, desire to spend money on experiences rather than things can be deeply individualistic and resource and energy-intensive (e.g., flying for travel), and as consumerist as building a McMansion.

The 'Shrinking Domesticities' of Tiny Houses: Theoretical and Empirical Offerings for How Degrowth in Home Design Can Inform a More Sustainable Society

While this chapter does not aim to unpack tiny houses with an architectural and design lens, it is nonetheless worthwhile to briefly explore how design contributes to the 'shrinking domesticity' of tiny houses, especially given the origins of the contemporary movement in the architecture and design community. Cohen's (2020) perspective on 'sufficiency' in housing explores three factors, position of a dwelling respective to its neighbours (density), geographic location (proximity to transit, employment, etc.), and overall house size. Sufficient house size (or space per capita) has been more often mandated in terms of minima rather than maxima, for example the International Construction Code requirements to reduce overcrowding and preserve public health (Cohen, 2020).

Although there are certain biophysical requirements that must be 'sufficiently' met before any individual can survive and flourish (e.g., food, water, air), beyond those needs lie other more 'socially constructed' material requirements, without which a person may feel they cannot fully participate in society without shame. Without entering into the complex theoretical intricacies of defining sufficiency, need, and 'how much is enough?'(Ingleby and Randalls, 2018), we proceed on the assumption that a tiny house, modest as it is in size, 'sufficiently' meets the material need for housing.

Far beyond sufficiency, the neoliberal concept of continual economic growth is mirrored in the trend towards supersizing suburban houses, adding media rooms, parents' retreats, and multiple living areas to increase 'saleability' (McKinlay et al., 2016; McKinlay et al., 2019). This contrasts the fundamental philosophical underpinnings of the tiny house movement, whereby THOW designers create multi-use rooms by analysing time spent in the various zones of a standard house and translating this to tiny houses by concentrating and combining areas with high foot 'traffic' and eliminating the remainder. Furniture is also multipurpose, or stored out of sight during the day. Many THOW designers deliberately attempt to combine the aesthetics of innovation with function (Colombini, 2019).

Tiny house designers also draw inspiration from established boat and caravan design industries, and Japanese housing. The similarities between tiny houses and similar very small and/or mobile dwellings such as studio apartments, boats, and caravans, go beyond dwelling size to the behaviour of those who live within. While scholarly research on the tiny house movement is still in its infancy, there is a plethora of studies into how urban apartment dwellers use urban spaces, (Cohen, 2020; Post, 2014; Saelens and Handy, 2008; Burnett et al., 2010). Apartment dwellers, for example, report increased use of public spaces, such as parks, libraries, and coffee shops, as well as more public transport use (Post, 2014).

For many, living in a tiny space forces reflection on personal possessions and consumerist culture. As one interview respondent stated:

> I support the ideas of tiny houses for conscious consuming. We all consume too much land. infrastructure and space for what we need. We then choose to fill up the spaces with more stuff and travel further to our destinations using more fuel to get there. It's a downward spiral which could be contained by more sensible accommodation choices and a more thoughtful attitude towards resources.
>
> (Shearer, 2017)

In contrast to the hyper-individualism marketed by purveyors of the suburban McMansion 'dream', with each family member having their own bedroom, bathroom, and even living area—some live in tiny houses with children. Participants of the same survey, a couple with three children, said proximity leads not to conflict, but to deeper connections:"...one positive is...the interaction with family in the change from a larger to smaller house...you can't be angry with someone forever, if you're interacting, so it completely changes the way you relate to each other".

In a similar analysis, Colombini (2019, p. 452) positions tiny houses as a countercultural movement in direct opposition to the neoliberal pressures behind larger homes, mandatory consumption (minimum room and house size and single residential zoning), the normalisation of high debt levels, and the 'entrepreneurial desire for capital'. She likens the assertion by Jay Shafer (2009) that tiny houses lead to a 'happy life' with the Aristotelian concept of 'eudaimonia'—especially the broader translation of "pursuit of virtue, excellence, and the best within us" (Huta and Waterman, 2014, p. 1426).

Likewise, Mangold and Zschau (2019) see the advocates of tiny houses seeking a eudemonic 'good' or 'better life' by means of reducing debt, minimising possessions, and questioning consumption. As with Thoreau, prior to embarking on their new tiny house life, some experienced an existential crisis, questioning the dominant capitalist narrative of working long hours to afford the 'Great Australian/American Dream' (Anson, 2014; Alexander and Shearer, 2019).

As was shown in the historical context of the tiny house movement, motivations for choosing to downsize mirror voluntary simplicity, minimalism, and more recently, the right to repair movement (Johnston, 2020). Increasing numbers are questioning the pressure to constantly consume goods—be it clothing, technology, or other possessions, as well as downsizing and reducing debt. Tiny house advocates often emphasise the desire to live more sustainably in a 'community', and to seek 'experiences rather than things' (Mangold and Zschau, 2019). Similarly, the concept of community in the tiny house movement is likely reflective of similar drivers to downsizing and minimalism—a general dissatisfaction with growth and consumption and instead, a search for meaningful relationships (Mangold and Zschau, 2019). Australian tiny house advocates defined community as sharing resources, such as communal vegetable gardens, community kitchens, and BBQ areas (Shearer and Burton, 2021b). None of these require large houses.

Finally, it is important to highlight that the tiny house movement is not merely about personal choice and freedom of living arrangements for some (privileged) people. In Australia, tiny houses are consistently popular with single women over 55, a demographic at increasing risk of homelessness (Shearer, 2017; Petersen and Parsell, 2014). This group are motivated less by existential questioning of the neoliberal status quo, and popular social media movements, but rather by lack of access to adequate, safe, and affordable housing. This group strongly desires regulation, to legitimise their dwellings and for secure tenure. Many such women live not in expensive, architect-built THOW but in converted caravans, busses, and even tents, mostly in isolated rural areas. Largely abandoned by neoliberal governments, with minimal pension savings, dependent on the private rental market, they turn to tiny houses for basic shelter. While trendy and expensive THOW are likely to be regulated in future as acceptable dwellings, their less aesthetically appealing shelters may continue to be relegated by NIMBY complaints to where they are 'out of sight and out of mind'.

For many, tiny houses are about making the best of insecure or even desperate socio-financial situations, rather than the romantic rural get-away often portrayed in social media. This again raises structural issues of inequality and the wealth-concentrating effects of advanced capitalist property systems. As with 'green growth' often being used to justify increased consumerism, degrowth of housing needs to be equitable and accessible to all demographics, not just overpriced bijou caravans deemed satisfactory by those privileged enough to own property.

The tiny house movement can be understood as a social phenomenon consistent with the frugal and minimalist material ethos of degrowth. However, it is clear that a deeper structural adjustment is also required if tiny houses are to be genuine expressions of freedom and simplicity as opposed to a way of managing the insecurities and precariousness of life under neoliberal states with hollowed out welfare states and marginalising land regimes (Baumann et al., 2021).

Conclusion

In closing, we suggest that the tiny house movement is consistent with the degrowth movement at the macroeconomic perspective, which argues planned contraction is needed for overgrown economies to move within sustainable limits. Tiny houses are, both physically and in ethical orientation, the opposite to the overgrown McMansions of late-stage capitalism. Tiny houses are also consistent with the degrowth movement at the micro-economic, personal/household level; advocates of both movements express desires to seek sufficiency and flourishing, motivated by the search for freedom, sustainability, happiness, and/or security in the face of today's overlapping crises.

We can see these two paradigms of sufficiency as offering complementary perspectives on sustainability. The tiny house movement, like degrowth, can be viewed as an embrace of sufficiency, a movement towards enough, and a creative exploration of whether 'less can be more'. Nevertheless, we have also raised various ways in which tiny houses for some people are less an expression of sustainable ethics or free choice, and instead the creative yet desperate response to harsh socio-economic situations. These divergent realities coexist, and any grounded understanding of tiny houses must recognise this.

Although we have not had an opportunity to link the tiny house movement to a theory of change, we wish to suggest in closing that it is part of the cultural shift that is needed to create the cultural conditions for a politics of degrowth to emerge (Alexander and Gleeson, 2020). There will never be a macro-economics of degrowth until there is a culture of sufficiency that sees sufficiency as empowering and liberating. Any social movement that embraces and practices an economics of sufficiency has the potential to advance sustainability transitions and build societal resilience in the face of forthcoming social, ecological, financial, or health crises (Holmgren, 2018). This suggests that those who choose to live in a tiny house in search of freedom and sustainable living, and those who are forced into tiny houses due to insecure socio-economic situations, might in time both contribute to creating the social conditions for political change, even though the motivations and pressures for practicing sufficiency are different.

References

ABS. 2020. Australians building houses on smaller blocks. *In: Statistics*, A. B. O. (ed.). Available: https://www.abs.gov.au/articles/australians-building-houses-smaller-blocks

Alexander, S. 2012. The Optimal Material Threshold: Toward an Economics of Sufficiency. *Real-World Economics Review*, 61, 2–21.

Alexander, S. 2014. Life in a 'Degrowth' Economy, and Why You Might Actually Enjoy It. *The Conversation.*

Alexander, S. & Gleeson, B. (2020). Urban Social Movements and the Degrowth Transition: Towards a Grassroots Theory of Change. *Journal of Australian Political Economy*, 86, 355–378.

Alexander, S. & Shearer, H. 2019. The Search for Freedom, Sustainability, and Economic Security: Henry David Thoreau as Tiny House Pioneer. *Ethical Perspectives*, 26, 559–582.

Anson, A. 2014. "the World Is My Backyard": Romanticization, Thoreauvian Rhetoric, and Constructive Confrontation in the Tiny House Movement. *From Sustainable to Resilient Cities: Global Concerns and Urban Efforts*, 14, 289–313.

Baumann, A., Alexander, S., & Burdon, P. 2021. Land Commodification as a Barrier to Political and Economic Agency: A Degrowth Perspective. *Journal of Australian Political Economy*, 86, 379–405.

Bennett, K. 2019. Freedom To, From, and for Whom: Analyzing Freedom Discourse in Tiny House Blogs.

Boeckermann, L. M., Kaczynski, A. T. & King, S. B. 2019. Dreaming Big and Living Small: Examining Motivations and Satisfaction in Tiny House Living. *Journal of Housing and the Built Environment*, 34, 61–71.

Bradshaw, C. J., Ehrlich, P. R., Beattie, A., Ceballos, G., Crist, E., Diamond, J., Dirzo, R., Ehrlich, A. H., Harte, J. & HARTE, M. E. 2021. Underestimating the Challenges of Avoiding a Ghastly Future. *Frontiers in Conservation Science*, 1, 9.

Burnett, K., Holt, E., Fisman, L. & Chang, G. 2010. *Research on factors relating to density and climate change.* National Association of Home Builders, Washington DC.

Carras, M. 2019. *'Tiny House, Big Impact?': An Investigation into the 'Rise'of the Tiny Home Lifestyle (THL) in the United States.* University of St Andrews.

Cohen, M. J. 2020. New Conceptions of Sufficient Home Size in High-Income Countries: Are We Approaching a Sustainable Consumption Transition? *Housing, Theory and Society*, 38(2), 1–31.

Colombini, C. 2019. The Rhetorical Resistance of Tiny Homes: Downsizing Neoliberal Capitalism. *Rhetoric Society Quarterly*, 49(5), 1–23.

Evans, K. 2017. *Integrating Tiny Houses into the American Urban Fabric: A Comparative Case Study of Land Use Policy Change in the Carolinas.* Clemson University.

Evans, K. 2018. Integrating Tiny and Small Homes into the Urban Landscape: History, Land Use Barriers and Potential Solutions. *Journal of Geography and Regional Planning*, 11, 34–45.

Gibson-Graham, J.-K., Cameron, J. & Healy, S. 2013. *Take Back the Economy: An Ethical Guide for Transforming Our Communities.* University of Minnesota Press.

Global Footprint Network. 2019. Earth Overshoot Day 2019, Living Beyond Nature's Limits. EU.

Harvey, D. 2007. *A Brief History of Neoliberalism.* Oxford University Press.

Hickel, J. 2012. A Short History of Neoliberalism (and how we can fix it). *New Left Project.*

Hickel, J. 2017. *The Divide: A Brief Guide to Global Inequality and its Solutions.* Random House.

Hickel, J. 2019. Degrowth: A Theory of Radical Abundance. *Real-world Economics Review*, 87, 54–68.
Hickel, J. 2020. *Less Is More: How Degrowth Will Save the World*. Random House.
Holmgren, D. 2018. *RetroSuburbia: The Downshifter's Guide to a Resilient Future*. Melliodora Publishing.
Huta, V. & Waterman, A. S. 2014. Eudaimonia and its Distinction from Hedonia: Developing a Classification and Terminology for Understanding Conceptual and Operational Definitions. *Journal of Happiness Studies*, 15, 1425–1456.
Idcommunity. 2021. *Australia: Household size (Community Profile)* [Online]. Available: https://profile.id.com.au/australia/household-size [Accessed 28 April 2021].
Ingleby, M. & Randalls, S. 2018. *Just Enough: The History, Culture and Politics of Sufficiency*. Springer.
Jackson, M. 2016. *The 'Tiny Houses' of the 20th Century* [Online]. Available: https://www.architectmagazine.com/design/culture/the-tiny-houses-of-the-20th-century
Jackson, T. 2009. *Prosperity without Growth?: The Transition to a Sustainable Economy*. Available: https://www.sd-commission.org.uk/data/files/publications/prosperity_without_growth_report.pdf
Jackson, T. 2021. *Post Growth: Life after Capitalism*. John Wiley & Sons.
Johnston, P. 2020. The "Right to Repair" Inquiry by the Productivity Commission Could Make Planned Obsolescence Obsolete. *The Fifth Estate*. [Online] Available: https://www.pc.gov.au/inquiries/completed/repair/report/repair.pdf
Kallis, G., Paulson, S., D'Alisa, G. & Demaria, F. 2020. *The Case for Degrowth*. John Wiley & Sons.
Mangold, S. & Zschau, T. 2019. In Search of the "Good Life": The Appeal of the Tiny House Lifestyle in the USA. *Social Sciences*, 8, 26.
Maslow, A. H. 1981. *Motivation and Personality*. Prabhat Prakashan.
Mckinlay, A., Baldwin, C. & Stevens, N. J. 2016. *Influences on dwelling size in Australia. 22nd PRRES conference*. PRRES Sunshine Coast, 17–20.
Mckinlay, A., Baldwin, C. & Stevens, N. J. 2019. Size Matters: Dwelling Size as a Critical Factor for Sustainable Urban Development. *Urban Policy and Research*, 37, 135–150.
Nelson, A. 2018. Housing for Growth Narratives. *Housing for Degrowth: Principles, Models, Challenges and Opportunities*, 2, 3–14.
Nelson, A. & Schneider, F. 2018. *Housing for Degrowth: Principles, Models, Challenges and Opportunities*. Routledge.
Parrique, T., Barth, J., Briens, F., Kerschner, C., Kraus-polk, A., Kuokkanen, A. & Spangenberg, J. 2019. Decoupling Debunked. *Evidence and Arguments against Green Growth as a Sole Strategy for Sustainability. A study edited by the European Environment Bureau EEB*. European Environmental Bureau.
Penfold, H., Waitt, G. & Mcguirk, P. 2018. Portrayals of the Tiny House in Electronic Media: Challenging or Reproducing the Australian Dream Home. *Australian Planner*, 55, 164–173.
Petersen, M. & Parsell, C. 2014. Homeless for the First Time in Later Life: An Australian Study. *Housing Studies*, 30, 368–391.
Post, R. 2014. Are Tiny Houses and Micro-apartments the Future of Urban Homes. *The Guardian*.
Princen, T. 2005. *The Logic of Sufficiency*. Mit Press.

Qu, L. 2020. Families Then & Now: Households and Families. *In:* AIFW (ed.) *Australian Families Then and Now*. Australian Government.

Saelens, B. E. & Handy, S. L. 2008. Built Environment Correlates of Walking: A Review. *Medicine & Science in Sports & Exercise*, 40, S550–S566.

Saxton, M. W. 2019. *The Ecological Footprints of Tiny Home Downsizers: An Exploratory Study*. Virginia Tech.

Sebag-Montefiore, C. 2017. Could Tiny Houses Help Solve Australia's Affordable Housing Crisis? *The Guardian*.

Shafer, J. 2009. *The Small House Book*. Tumbleweed Tiny House Company.

Shearer, H. 2014. Move over McMansions, the Tiny House Movement Is Here. *The Conversation*.

Shearer, H. 2017. Interest in Tiny Houses Is Growing, So Who Wants Them and Why? *The Conversation*.

Shearer, H. & Burton, P. 2019. Towards a Typology of Tiny Houses. *Housing, Theory and Society*, 36, 298–318.

Shearer, H. & Burton, P. 2021a. Loving the Idea of Tiny House Living, Even If You Don't Live in One. *The Conversation*.

Shearer, H. & Burton, P. 2021b. Tiny Houses: Movement or Moment? *Housing Studies*, 1–23.

Snider, L. 2020. Beyond Trump: Neoliberal Capitalism and the Abolition of Corporate Crime. *Journal of White Collar and Corporate Crime*, 1, 86–94.

Stoknes, P. E. & Rockström, J. 2018. Redefining Green Growth within Planetary Boundaries. *Energy Research & Social Science*, 44, 41–49.

UN. 2021. *11: Sustainable Cities and Communities* [Online]. UN. Available: www.globalgoals.org/11-sustainable-cities-and-communities [Accessed 29 April 2021].

UN Department of Economic and Social Affairs. 2019. Population Facts. United Nations.

Weetman, V. M. 2018. Resistance is Fertile: Exploring Tiny House Practices in Australia. *Australian Planner*, 55, 232–240.

Wiedmann, T., Lenzen, M., Keyßer, L. T. & Steinberger, J. K. 2020. Scientists' Warning on Affluence. *Nature Communications*, 11, 1–10.

Wiedmann, T., Schandl, H., Lenzen, M., Moran, D., Suh, S., West, J. & Kanemoto, K. 2015. The Material Footprint of Nations. *Proceedings of the National Academy of Sciences*, 112, 6271–6276.

Wilson, A. & Boehland, J. 2008. Small Is Beautiful U.S. House Size, Resource Use, and the Environment. *Journal of Industrial Ecology*, 9, 277–287.

13 Tiny Living as an Everyday Practice of Sufficiency

Some Experiences of Tiny House Owners in Germany

Petra Lütke & Louisa Elbracht

Introduction

In the Global North, it is generally understood that "more is better." This is especially true for our built environment—the dwellings in which people live or want to live in the future. While in many parts of the Global North the average size of dwellings has been increasing, a recent movement is challenging the logic that bigger is supposedly better: the Tiny House movement. Numerous literatures on the Tiny House movement has positioned micro-living in debates on sustainability and degrowth (e.g., Anson 2014; Cristiano, 2020; Maile 2020; Harris and Nowicki 2020). This chapter explores tensions between the trend of an accelerating per-capita consumption of living space on the one hand and the growing popularity of tiny houses on the other. For this purpose, we asked people who live in or intend to live in tiny houses in Germany about their personal motivations to choose this lifestyle and about developments in society that promote this way of life, often described as a sustainable lifestyle.

Our conceptual framework on Tiny House movement consists of two strands. First, we adopt the perspective of interpreting sufficiency as a practice of everyday strategies of sustainable development. Second, we integrate the former with Pierre Bourdieu's theories of society and distinction of classes. By linking the concept of sufficiency with Bourdieu's social theory, we explore the question of whether a sufficiency-oriented lifestyle can contribute to social status and prestige and thus strengthens one's own position in the social arena. A little-researched topic in the context of Germany, qualitative interviews with individuals interested in and supporters of the Tiny House movement provide initial insights into the motivations of the movement, as well as the relationship between forms of living and social positioning.

The Tiny House movement in Germany is enjoying increasing popularity, with numerous blogs and online articles[1] emerging in recent years. Although no figures on quantities of the Tiny House movement in Germany are available, a growing trend has emerged, evidenced for example by the

DOI: 10.4324/9781003173052-18

fact that that around 125 per cent more bookings of tiny houses on Airbnb in Germany were recorded in 2018 than in the previous year (Statistisches Bundesamt 2018).

Sufficiency as a Strategy for Sustainable Development

Strategies of Consistency, Efficiency, and Sufficiency

Following sustainability discourses in the wake of the 1992 Rio Conference and Agenda 21 action plan, measures to improve cross-border cooperation to solve environmental problems have been addressed in very different ways; they can be divided into strategies of consistency, efficiency, and sufficiency (Hunsicker 2005: 1). **Consistency and efficiency strategies** were devised to continue tackling environmental challenges by way of economic–technical innovations, while sufficiency aims at voluntary self-restraint, thus directly affecting the lifestyle of individuals. **Efficiency strategies** refer to dematerialization trends that seek to reduce the amount of energy and materials needed to produce goods (Bittlingmayer 2000: 26) with the goal of maintaining the level of household consumption while simultaneously reducing environmental impact. **Consistency strategies** meanwhile aim to improve the quality of these material flows so that they can be used in a more ecologically sound manner. These types of strategies try to change existing structures not by reducing the amount of energy and materials used but rather by finding alternatives that use as few resources as possible. The two approaches both view sustainable development as an economic strategy "that wants to use nature rather than protect it" (Bittlingmayer 2000: 30; translated by the authors).

The **sufficiency strategy** to change current lifestyles can be traced back to the Agenda 21 action plan. The concept of sufficiency is largely based on the realization that current lifestyles, especially in industrialized countries, do not meet sustainable development goals (Bittlingmayer 2000: 33). In contrast to the previous two strategies, sufficiency does not aim at economic–technical change but focuses specifically on the social and cultural implications of sustainability discourse (Speck 2016). Sufficiency intends to "limit, rethink, change, and replace social practices and patterns of action that can be classified as environmentally- and resource-intensive" (Speck 2016: 7; translated by the authors). Transformation of everyday practices requires realignment of the prevailing logic of consumption as well as a change in the ways people use goods and services. There is thus no universal definition of sufficiency but rather a range of everyday choices that reflect the fluid nature of the transition from conventional to sufficiency approaches.

Sufficiency is not about doing without certain goods and services because of financial constraints; it is rather about making a voluntary commitment to criticize the excesses of a consumer society that seeks to quickly gratify through the consumption of material goods. Sufficiency thus targets one's own needs and beliefs with regard to personal consumption and has far-reaching normative implications. A commitment to sustainability is widely accepted and internalized as a social norm in modern societies (Hunsicker 2005: 29) and perhaps even expected in some parts of society.

To live a sustainable lifestyle in the spirit of sufficiency, however, ecological awareness must also be reflected at the behavioral level. This requires voluntarily limiting one's own consumption, both in terms of quantity and quality. A lifestyle of sufficiency therefore requires consuming less and selectively, that is, according to ecological criteria (Hunsicker 2005: 24). However, "a high level of environmental awareness does not automatically result in environmentally friendly behavior, i.e., there is not necessarily a significant link between high levels of environmental awareness and environmentally friendly consumption patterns" (Hunsicker 2005: 29; translated by the authors). It can thus be concluded that even if one assumes an individual is highly aware of environmental hazards, this in itself is "not a sufficient prerequisite for acting in an environmentally sound manner" (Hunsicker 2005: 35; translated by the authors). Although it can be assumed that a greater awareness of the environment correlates with behavior that is more sustainability-oriented, this correlation should not be overestimated.

Dimensions of Sufficiency

In order to empirically explore the various dimensions of sufficiency as an everyday practice, we apply the four dimensions of sufficiency according to Sachs (1993: 69ff.): **decluttering, decommercialization, decentralization,** and **deceleration.**

Decluttering refers to a responsible use of commodities by shifting focus from the importance of material to immaterial goods (Speck 2016: 9). The goal is not to do without all the conveniences of modernity but to use essential goods and services in a sensible way. The opposite of a simple, decluttered lifestyle is thus not the luxurious but the frayed lifestyle (Sachs 1993: 91f). The decluttered lifestyle does not require a life devoid of possessions but a deliberate and reflective approach to acquiring consumer products. **Decommercialization** intends to link employment, home-care work, self-employment, and communal work (Speck 2016: 9). This aspect of sufficiency focuses ultimately on the shift away from the rigid growth paradigm. **Decentralization** entails a stronger reconnection to geographically proximate spaces and demands to reflect more critically on the effects and consequences of globalized processes (Speck 2016: 9). As a dimension of sufficiency, **deceleration** seeks to oppose dominant logics of growth-oriented acceleration by deliberately searching for spaces to slow down and relax (Rosa 2005). Sufficiency thus aims at a change in the behavior and lifestyle and can be understood as a social practice.

Bourdieu and Sufficiency of Everyday Practices

Bourdieu shows that lifestyles and tastes, including consumer choices, are not based on free and individual decisions but are an expression of social class affiliation and a means of distinction. Recognizing class-specific lifestyle differences inevitably directs attention to the "fight for legitimizing a lifestyle [which is] also always a question of the convertibility of capital, in sum: a question of asserting power" (Heinritz-Fuchs et.al. 2014: 52f.; translated by the authors).

By further developing Bourdieu's insights, we may ask whether sufficiency practices can serve as a form of positional good that functions as a means of distinction. If lifestyle is not a voluntary, entirely independent choice but rather an expression of one's position in social space and class, then lifestyle and consumer choices can be used to symbolize class membership. Bourdieu's intention is not to describe differences in lifestyles but to find and explain their origins. He sees their origin in the fact that lifestyles shaped through the interaction of forms of practice and taste are clearly not individual nor freely chosen—they are, instead, a central feature of social class (Bourdieu 2018: 18). Particular, legitimate goods serve to symbolize an individual's class membership and social positioning, and to distinguish oneself from other classes or class fractions. This differentiation is of course mainly intended with respect to socially disadvantaged groups (Bourdieu 2018: 111). The issue is that class factions strive for the positional goods of the classes above them while simultaneously abandoning those that could be acquired by the classes below them. The classes above them however follow the same pattern thus creating a perpetual race for the definition of legitimate cultural goods.

At this point it is useful to link Bourdieu's approach to the theory of sufficiency. To preserve the distinctive function of positional goods, this perpetual race inevitably leads to a spiral of growth and expectations ("Wachstums-und Steigerungsspirale"), which, while perfectly compatible with the logics of capitalism, can barely meet the requirements of sustainable development. How can differentiation be maintained in societies in which almost all its members possess particular positional goods and adhere to shared norms? If basically everyone can own a car, the automobile of the ruling class would need to be faster, more efficient, more robust, and so on. But once the middle class is able to buy these faster, more efficient, more robust cars, the ruling class must in turn find ways to own even faster, more efficient, more robust ones. This argument could be taken further and applied to many other areas of consumption. The question is whether differentiation could also happen outside the spiral of expectations. If differentiation in economic terms is difficult, differentiation in cultural terms may be conceivable. This links to Bourdieu's approach because cultural capital is just as important an indicator of class membership as economic capital.

This is illustrated, for example, by the fact that not just the economically but also the culturally powerful—intelligentsia—belong to the ruling class. Bourdieu's theory of the space of lifestyles thus suggests cultural positional goods can be used to differentiate between classes. Sufficiency could perhaps be viewed as a positional good associated with cultural capital, meaning that a sufficiency-oriented lifestyle could enhance one's own cultural capital. Because this perspective is substantively comparable to the frugal lifestyle of some intellectuals, it is perhaps consistent with Bourdieu's thinking. Even though Bourdieu's research suggests that intellectuals practice this lifestyle primarily due to lack of financial resources, it nevertheless becomes apparent that deliberate and thoughtful consumption is associated with high levels of cultural capital. By combining the concept of sufficiency and Bourdieu's social theory, we ask: Can a sufficiency-oriented lifestyle contribute to social standing and prestige, and thus serve to strengthen or maintain one's own position in social space?

In the media the Tiny House movement in Germany is often associated with a lifestyle that is critical of consumption, often presented in the context of sustainable and innovative forms of living that deliberately oppose the growth logics of capitalist consumer society. The movement is also deemed to be activist in nature, setting an example of a more sustainable alternative to traditional housing. But do the lives and daily routines of its residents measure up to this high standard that society has set for the Tiny House movement? In the remainder of this chapter we consider whether tiny house living is indeed an everyday practice based on sufficiency and whether it can generate social recognition. It is important to understand how the movement perceives itself and what claim it makes about its actions, but also public perceptions of the movement, as well as possible discrepancies between how the movement perceives itself and how it is perceived by others. Another focus are the motivations for deciding to live in a tiny house. Finally, we discuss the role that sufficiency-related everyday practices play in differentiating the tiny house dwellers from practices in society at large.

Research Methodology of the Study

This study does not claim to be representative. Rather, it explores the motivations of the German Tiny House movement and contextualizes it in Bourdieu's social theory. Problem-centered interviews were selected to inform the research (see Table 13.1). Since it is a theory-driven empirical study, this form of data collection is suitable because its structured nature follows the study's theoretical framework. For this purpose, the interviews followed a general outline that pre-structured the conversations to match the research purpose whilst offering room for participants to emphasis what they saw as most relevant. Data analysis was done using MAXQDA, software for computer-aided qualitative data analysis.

Table 13.1 List of interviewees

Name of Interviewees	*Ajala*	*Simone*	*Yvonne*	*Jan & Fiona*	*Mimi & Florian*	*Sarah*	*Jenny & David*
Age	Early 40s	Early 50s	Mid 50s	Early 30s	Early 30s	Late 20s	Early 30s
Profession	Freelancer	Interior designer	Administrative assistant	Jan: Replacement teacher Fiona: Student	Both freelance yoga-teachers, sustainability consulting, Florian is also a PhD student	Used to work in the renewable sector, but is now a freelancer Tiny House consultant	Educators
Housing	Moves into her own Tiny House soon	Plans to live in a Tiny House with her life partner and his son	Single mother plans to live in a Tiny House with her youngest daughter	Jan lived in his Bulli for some years, Fiona lived in a shared apartment; they are living in their self-build Tiny House for 6 months now	Living in their self-build Tiny House for 6 months now	Living in her self-build Tiny House	Living now in a one-room apartment and plan to live in a Tiny House or another alternative housing

Discussion

The Tiny House as a Practice of Sufficiency

If sufficiency is understood to be a voluntary reduction of non-essential consumption (Stengel 2011, 140; Speck 2016, 8ff.) it would seem to suggest that a tiny house requires a sufficiency-oriented lifestyle because the smaller space requires critical examination of one's own consumption behavior. Life in the tiny house thus seems to reflect sufficiency in the sense of decluttering living space. It is however important to note that the decision to declutter is a voluntary one that does not necessarily mean giving up essential items. As one participant explained,

> Well, we have everything we need, so I mean if we notice that there is something we may need, we would find room for it and besides it's nice not to have so much stuff, although it's still so much [laughs] I don't feel like we have not enough stuff now,
>
> (Mimi and Florian)

To dispose of some material goods is thus not perceived as giving up something with regret but rather as an opportunity for a new experience. The participant added: "*I don't feel the need to buy anything new now [...], I'm more in the process of learning a lot and taking things in for myself, inside of me and there's even more space than in the tiny house* [laughs]" (Mimi and Florian).

By breaking free of material constraints, the goal is to live a free, independent life. Yvonne commented that

> I could live much more relaxed [...] I have to make less money for all this stuff that I have to pay for and then I can live in a more deliberate way and be more satisfied with less [...] [that's] like being a hamster in a wheel trying to generate electricity and at some point, you think, nope, I don't care, I'll stop running, I can't do it anymore [laughs].
>
> (Yvonne)

By living in a tiny house and not having to pay high rents, many owners hope to benefit financially and subsequently increase their quality of life by having more free time. Tiny house living thus raises the expectation of a sufficiency-based life in a sense of decelerating people's lives. Sarah pointed out however that the maintenance of tiny housing takes up more time than a conventional apartment:

> You just have to pay more attention [...] these are just things that you don't have to do with a regular house or with an apartment, so you

> inevitably have to deal a lot more with your living situation and that's of course very nice [...], but it takes time and you have to be aware of that.
>
> (Sarah)

The extra work involved in building and maintaining a tiny house can take up more time, increasing feelings of stress. On the one hand, life in a tiny house shows the potential of a decelerated life, on the other, it also ties up additional time and does not itself escape the acceleration logics of modernity. Whether and to what extent a tiny house contributes to decelerating people's lives depends on residents themselves—whether they perceive the additional time needed for construction and maintenance as stressful or as liberating.

The same applies in relation to decentralization and decommercialization. Participants indicated that they value the quality of consumer products over quantity. "For example, I'm part of a foodsharing-group, it has a lot in common with the idea of tiny houses, there is always the question about how much I really need and how can I sensibly use the finite resources" (Sarah). Living in tiny housing does not necessarily encourage the consumption of regional products. As far as this study is concerned, it can be said however that the participants themselves claim to strengthen local economies. It can thus be concluded that residents' claim of lifestyles based on sufficiency as far as decentralization is concerned exists, but it is not clear to what extent this claim can be borne out.

The same applies to the area of decommercialization. For the study participants, living in tiny housing goes hand in hand with desires for a self-sufficient life. From vegetable gardens to having their own power and water supply, all participants were trying to combat commercialization with some form of self-sufficiency:

> Sustainability in all aspects of life would be great! In a community not everyone needs to own a car, you can share it with the others, same with tools. We already decided to build a shed to put a drilling machine and other tools in there so they can be used by everyone, or a little library, just to share things like that. Or to produce our own electricity, composting toilets, stuff like that.
>
> (Jenny)

Due to its size and ownership type, tiny housing provides more opportunities for a self-sufficient utility supply system than a rental apartment. Similar to other dimensions of sufficiency, tiny housing does not necessarily generate these decommercialized practices, but rather encourages its occupants to adopt them. In summary, living in tiny housing can be described as a sufficiency-based practice. Participants' aspirations to make their everyday practices as sufficient as possible is evident in all interviews, and practices of sufficiency represent an ideal they want to live up to. While tiny housing holds great potential, it is not inherently sufficient and does not necessarily lead to sufficient practices by residents. What is important however is their reputation for producing sufficiency-based sustainable practices that their residents presumably practice. Tiny houses imply a sustainable, sufficiency-oriented lifestyle that can be transferred to their occupants. However, is this the reason why people decide to move into a tiny house, or are there other motivations?

Motivations ... for What?

The research identified two dominant categories of motivations that influence decisions to move into tiny housing. The following motivations can be assigned to the category of sustainability: deceleration, focus on essentials, closeness to nature, sustainability, and decluttering; while these motivations belong to the category of independence: adventure, freedom, and property. When deciding to move into tiny housing, several overlapping and intersecting motivations are often present. In terms of their primary motivation, participants fall however into one of the two categories. Interestingly there is a correlation between these categories and the age of respondents. While the younger respondents (Jan and Fiona, Mimi and Florian, Sarah, Jenny and David) can be allocated to the category of sustainability, the older interviewees (Anjala, Simone and Yvonne) belong to the category of independence. A closer look at the category of sustainability reveals that all interviewees indicated that their decision was influenced by the sustainable nature of this form of living. It cannot be ruled out, however, that the discursive linking of tiny houses and sustainability could have biased participants' statements in terms of an assumed social desirability It is therefore conceivable that some participants may have assigned more importance to aspects of sustainability during the interview than was actually the case in terms of their decision to purchase and move into a tiny house, due to wanting to benefit from the positive image of sustainability. For the interviewees who can be grouped into the main category of sustainability, it becomes apparent that in particular ecological sustainability plays an important role in many other areas of their lives such as nutrition and waste reduction. It can therefore be concluded that there is a general awareness of sustainability issues among those participants: "Sustainability is very important to us, we are `zero waste´ and are vegans" (Mimi and Florian).

Desire for sustainable development was a fundamental motivation for participants in their decision to live in tiny housing. This also coincides with media coverage and societal perceptions of the Tiny House movement. However, participants also said that their desire to own a home influenced their decision because they value the freedom and independence that comes with owning property. Tiny housing offers more advantages than a conventional house to many people—with a comparatively lower purchasing price. Owning property had positive connotations for participants as something to aspire to. Tiny housing seems attractive to younger participants because they would not have to carry debt for decades, while older people see it as security in their senior years, partly out of fear of old-age poverty:

> We both grew up in private homes and as a homeowner you have the freedom to do whatever you want [...] but we don´t want to get up in one´s ears in debt so that we would be forced to earn money just to pay back debts, we want to be free to try something new, without any big commitments.
>
> (Mimi and Florian)

One goal of tiny housing is to address the fear of rising rents in old age and to ease financial pressure. Some participants showed symptoms of exhaustion and a fear of sliding down the social ladder, both of which indicate "slipping slope syndrome" (Rosa 2005: 219). The constant pressure to meet the demands of an increasingly fast-paced society can be so overwhelming that those affected feel they have to escape such pressure. Yvonne explained that, "[t]he whole life [...] had become too much to handle, so I thought I'd get me a hut, move to the edge of the forest, and you all can kiss my ass" (Yvonne). Respondents feel pressure to satisfy all the requirements of their social positioning. At the same time, they feel society expects them to strive for more. This pressure contributes to increased instances of life events that effect socioeconomic status, like divorce and unemployment. This could also explain the correlation between the categories of motivation and age. While the younger respondents try to find their place in society, the older ones are at a turning point in their life, provoked by separation, occupational changes, or their children leaving home. The fear of losing social positioning has become a major cause of stress that increases the desire of dropping out of mainstream society.

Differentiation/Distinction

What is the difference between dropping out of mainstream society to live on the edge of the forest to live in a tiny house? In addition to legal aspects, outside perception and image certainly also play a role. For example, while for the parents of one interviewee the image of a construction trailer evokes ideas of a "slovenly lifestyle" (Jenny and David), tiny housing is a more accepted alternative form of living. It is designed for permanent living with all the essential components that make up a house—just on a smaller scale. Based on this premise, tiny housing does not have to compete with those alternative forms of living, but with small-scale conventional forms of living such as one-bedroom apartments. When asked about smaller conventional types of housing, participants often mentioned one-bedroom apartments in large residential buildings, which for them do not represent a true alternative to eco-friendly tiny houses. There are certainly other examples of small purpose-built housing units than those in residential blocks, but the mention of this alternative in particular shows that the participants try to draw a clear line of distinction between themselves, the Tiny House movement, and these large housing developments. Particularly those participants who see tiny housing as a retirement investment seem to want to protect themselves from the scenario of having to live in an "apartment block":

> I used to live in a cheap apartment, but it was a bad neighbourhood [...] I always expected burning dustbins around the corner [...] but I wanted my kids to grow up in a nice, maintained area, where educated people live who are cultivated and at least nice to each other [...] I made it one day, but €1,200 rent, that´s the price I pay [...]. Some people might not be able to pay such high rents when they retire. In a few years I will just receive a pension, I don´t have a partner, I need to take care of myself all by myself, that scares me a lot.
>
> (Yvonne)

Tiny housing can therefore be seen as to preventing loss of status in old age. The preservation or even enhancement of status can only succeed, however, if there is a clear cultural differentiation of tiny housing from apartment blocks. This requires a positive image of the Tiny House movement, which can be generated by linking it discursively with sustainability. By emphasizing the fact that residents give up some of their possessions voluntarily—as a prerequisite of sufficiency—a clear line of cultural differentiation can be drawn between the Tiny House movement and more conventional small-scale forms of living. While it is often assumed that these forms of housing need to be small-scale due to a lack of financial resources, the Tiny House movement focuses instead on the voluntary nature of reducing possessions not because of financial hardship but a deliberate decision to have a positive impact on the environment. As a result, tiny house occupants have the opportunity to gain the social recognition that comes with homeownership, despite spending a comparatively small amount of economic capital. They can simultaneously strengthen their cultural capital by associating themselves with the socially accepted ideal of sustainability. In relation to Bourdieu's space of lifestyles, there are significant similarities here to the frugal lifestyle of intellectuals. Potential shortfalls of economic capital can be masked by linking them to claims on cultural capital. The voluntary nature of giving up some possessions is loaded with cultural significance and explained as a deliberate decision in support of a higher purpose. This enables residents of tiny houses to secure their societal position while investing a relatively small amount of economic capital. In this way, reinforcing one's cultural capital enables a person to either climb up the social hierarchy or to secure their current position in the face of changing socioeconomic circumstances. Living in tiny housing and making claims of sufficiency can therefore secure or even enhance one's position in the space of lifestyles.

As long as the Tiny House movement is associated with sustainability and sufficiency, residents can benefit from its positive image. Therefore, the movement needs to be popular, whilst simultaneous preserving its uniqueness, to be authentic and credible. This is challenged by tiny housing that is used as a vacation home or secondary residence. It is becoming increasingly apparent that there is a fine line between increasing popularity and delegitimization of the Tiny House movement in terms of sustainability.

Conclusion

Whether life in tiny housing can be consistently characterized by sufficiency-oriented everyday practices depends heavily on the individual attitudes of its residents. All interviewees indicated that life in tiny housing holds great potential for sufficiency-based practices. The extent to which occupants tap into this potential however cannot be conclusively determined in this study. It is crucial for the movement that there is a certain level of expectation on the part of society regarding the sufficiency of everyday practices. This expectation can be used to derive positive outcomes for tiny house residents. By discursively linking the Tiny House movement to the concept of sustainability, occupants can take advantage of the positive image associated with a sustainable lifestyle. Sustainability, in this case in the shape of sufficiency, functions as a socially recognized cultural positional good through which prestige and recognition can be generated. Cultural capital can be enhanced by emphasizing the voluntary nature of giving up possessions in support of the higher purpose of sustainable development. As a result, one's position in social space is reinforced. This also means that residents must continue to promote the positive, sustainable image of the Tiny House movement and foster it through their actions. The question is therefore not whether their actions are actually sustainable or not, but rather whether tiny house residents are able to maintain the positive image of a sustainable, conscious life. This sustainable image itself can be used as a class-oriented virtue to ensure or improve social positioning, and to distance themselves from other forms of living. But these lines of distinction thus run not only along other forms of living but also inside their own community. There are potential lines of distinction between those who built their houses themselves and those who purchased their houses through a commercial homebuilder, as well as along the size of the house. The motto of the Tiny House movement, "the smaller the better" seems to highlight the movement's self-image and the idea of not using more space than necessary. The most important distinction, however, is the question of intended usage. As they become more popular, tiny houses being used a second homes or vacation cabins will certainly increase. Ironically, although the phenomenon of tiny housing aspires for sufficiency, it is also not able to escape the growth logics of the free market, despite its claim to the contrary. This means that the same mechanisms that make the tiny housing valued by society also undermine the basic idea of sufficiency.

Note

1 See for example: https://tiny-houses.de/blog/, www.kleinerleben.de/blog/, https://tinyhouse-wanderlust.com/.

References

Anson, April (2014): "The World is my Backyard": Romanticization, Thoreauvian Rhetoric, and Constructive Confrontation in the Tiny House movement", *From Sustainable to Resilient Cities: Global Concerns and Urban Efforts* (Research in Urban Sociology, Vol. 14), Bingley: Emerald Group Publishing, 289–313.

Bittlingmayer, Uwe H. (2000): *Askese in der Erlebnisgesellschaft? Eine kultursoziologische Untersuchung zum Konzept der "nachhaltigen Entwicklung" am Beispiel des Car-Sharing.* Wiesbaden: Westdeutscher Verlag.

Bourdieu, Pierre (2018): *Die feinen Unterschiede. Kritik der gesellschaftlichen Urteilskraft.* 26. Aufl. Frankfurt a.M.: Suhrkamp.

Cristiano, Silvio (2020). In: A. Nelson and F. Schneider (Eds.), *Housing for Degrowth: Principles, Models, Challenges, and Opportunities.* Routledge, 2019, p. 296, ISBN: 9780367358334. *Journal of Housing and the Built Environment*, 35. Doi: 10.1007/s10901-020-09746-4.

Harris, Ella; Nowicki, Melanie (2020): "Get smaller"? Emerging geographies of micro-living. *Area*, 52(3), S. 591–599.

Heinritz-Fuchs, Werner; König, Alexandra (2014): *Pierre Bourdieu. Eine Einführung.* 3. Aufl. Konstanz: UVK Verlagsgesellschaft.

Hunsicker, Stefan (2005): *Soziale Milieus und Ressourcenverbrauch. Zur Umsetzungsproblematik des Leitbildes einer nachhaltigen Entwicklung in der Erlebnisgesellschaft.* Berlin: Wissenschaftlicher Verlag Berlin.

Maile, Lisa (2020): *Tiny House movement: Eine kulturwissenschaftliche Betrachtung alternativer Wohn-und Lebensformen als Ausdruck einer Postwachstumsstrategie* (Vol. 32). utzverlag GmbH.

Rosa, Hartmut (2005): *Beschleunigung. Die Veränderung der Zeitstrukturen in der Moderne.* Frankfurt a.M.: Suhrkamp.

Sachs, Wolfgang (1993): Die vier E´s. Merkposten für einen maß-vollen Wirtschaftsstil. *Politische Ökonomie* 11(33), S. 69–72.

Speck, Melanie (2016): *Konsum und Suffizienz. Eine empirische Untersuchung privater Haushalte in Deutschland.* Wiesbaden: Springer VS.

Statistisches Bundesamt (2018): Beliebteste Unterkunftsarten auf Airbnb weltweit im Jahr 2018 nach Buchungswachstum im Vergleich zum Vorjahr. Online: https://de.statista.com/statistik/daten/studie/950151/umfrage/beliebteste-unterkunftsarten-auf-airbnb-nach-buchungswachstum/#statisticContainer (18.07.2021)

Stengel, Oliver (2011): Suffizienz. Die Konsumgesellschaft in der ökologischen Krise. München. Oekom Verlag. (Wuppertaler Schriften zur Forschung für eine nachhaltige Entwicklung Band 1.).

Part V

Alternative Shrinking Domesticities

14 The Tiny House Movement

Ecology, Survival, and Inequality

Jenny Pickerill, Adam Barker & Jingjing Wang

Introduction

The rising popularity of 'tiny homes', those homes which are purposefully small in size and are often smaller than national housing regulations' minimum size requirements, deserves critical analysis (Harris & Nowicki, 2020). These are perfect examples of shrinking domesticities. Small homes are, of course, not new. There are a wide range of possible dwellings that may be considered to fall 'in' or 'out' of the boundaries of the tiny house movement (Shearer & Burton, 2019):

> the iconic tiny house on a trailer, a tiny house on skids, a cottage, townhouse, apartment, granny cottage, extension, holiday house, converted shed, container house, caravan, beach shack, converted bus or truck, mining hut, tourist cabin, laneway dwelling, Japanese flats, yurts, fonzi flats, squats, tiny house villages, intentional communities, eco-housing, co-housing etc.
>
> (305, references removed from original)

There is clearly an established history of economic and social processes that have long restricted the size of many people's homes, a set of processes which result in a denial of home space, either completely (in homelessness) or partially (through the reduced size of home spaces), what Harris (2019) calls compensatory housing.

We are interested here in what tiny homes 'do' and what hope they offer for a world otherwise. Tiny homes can be understood as a vehicle for social change, a form of appropriate technology (Murphy, 2014). But they could just as easily be a continuation of existing capitalist extraction from, and accumulation via, housing – housing financialization, or an entrenchment of existing injustice and inequality. This chapter explores what tiny homes are, what they can be understood to do and achieve, and what they do not, and finally, therefore, what hope they might offer as alternative homes spaces, low carbon housing, affordable shelter, or political tactics.

DOI: 10.4324/9781003173052-20

Tiny homes, as a loosely defined genre of housing, emerged in the early 2000's, driven particularly by prototypes and advocates in the USA. Tiny homes are stand-alone structures, often purposefully built as private dwellings that contain cooking, sleeping, washing, and living space together in a very compact design. These homes are often off-grid. Initially this genre of tiny home was the preserve of those seeking to reduce their environmental impact, designed to enable living with less (stuff) (Salomon, 2006). Tiny homes were also a statement of liberation from gender norms. Salomon helped build two tiny homes at Lama Foundation, New Mexico, constructed by a women-only work group and constructed in silence (Figure 14.1). Their smaller size and simplicity reduced the need for previous construction expertise (Pickerill, 2015).

Although self-built, these homes were designed and constructed by those who had the social and economic capital to access land, materials, and expertise, and the mobility to locate in places that permitted such development. The possibilities that tiny homes offered were further realized by architects and builders in cities such as Portland, Oregon, where planning codes facilitated the subdivision of housing plots with existing dwellings and the subsequent construction of tiny homes without the need for further planning approval, under the stipulation of permissible 'accessory dwelling units' (Figure 14.2). This led to the growth of tiny homes in urban spaces, and relatedly growth in the design of tiny homes on wheels (in the British

Figure 14.1 Tiny home at Lama Foundation, New Mexico, USA.
Source: Pickerill.

Figure 14.2 Tiny home on a subdivided plot in urban Portland, Oregon, USA.
Source: Pickerill.

Shepherd Hut style), the legality of which were initially ambiguous in many places.

As Harris and Nowicki (2020) note, while emerging from an environmental ethos, the proliferation of tiny homes (particularly in cities) began to be articulated as a potential solution to the worldwide housing crisis. Although still tied to an environmental ethos of reducing consumption, in this context tiny homes get repurposed as an affordable 'solution' to housing inequality as the scale and problems of the contemporary failure of the housing market are revealed. This is despite many forms of micro-living demanding above market rents (Harris & Nowicki, 2020). As tiny homes' popularity grew so did the critique of their possibilities. These were two-fold; that their autonomy and off-grid potential were not as easy to achieve, or frequently practiced, as suggested and that the celebration of reduced home space ignored the reality of those who already lived in cramped inadequate housing (Milkman, 2016; Matthews, 2016). Articulating tiny homes as an affordable solution made visible how racial capitalism has already stripped many (predominantly marginalized and non-white) communities of choice and power in housing space.

The fundamental question we wish to consider in relation to these spaces is what makes them liveable and for whom? This is not a straightforward question: at times the purported benefits of 'small' and the realities of globalized capital, the exploitation of distanced labour, and normative assumptions about relations to property are in conflict. It requires understanding how these homes work financially, socially, emotionally, and ecologically.

Delimiting Tiny Homes

In their attempt to develop a typology of tiny homes as seen by the tiny house movement itself, Shearer and Burton (2019) note that both mobile (and semi-mobile) and permanent (or semi-permanent) dwellings can be and frequently are classified as tiny houses. Size is an important factor, but as Shearer and Burton also point out, it is an insufficient category on its own for understanding tiny houses – for one, there is an often-unspoken desire for tiny houses to be literally houses (Figure 14.2), recognizable as such despite changes to size, and generally detached from other dwellings. Their typology also notes that affordability is far and away the largest motivating factor for those involved in the tiny house movement, with the implication that tiny houses are more economically accessible. However, as Shearer and Burton rightly note, tiny houses can cost more per square foot than their larger counterparts, and while they may be cheaper overall, many cannot be built or purchased through mortgages, meaning the buyer/builder must have cash in hand (or the wherewithal to spend time and personal energy finding materials and building the dwelling). Sustainability and a sense of community are important for some folks, but not for all tiny house advocates, and there is equally a strong ethic of 'DIY' independence behind the desire to build and occupy a tiny house that may not be particularly rooted in sustainability but rather a frontier 'homesteading' claim to place (Willoughby, et al., 2020).

Building on Shearer and Burton's typology, we propose here a spectrum of small dwellings, some of which are clearly understood as part of the tiny house movement, some of which are debatable or grey areas of the movement and are perhaps best understood as micro-homes (Harris & Nowicki, 2020), and some of which illustrate the problems and shortcomings of the tiny house movement by dint of being excluded from it. The first category (Type 1) comprises the 'core' dwellings of the tiny house movement: 'jewel box' houses, mini-houses, and eco-cabins.

'Jewel Box' Houses

Small but luxurious dwellings – a miniature house made of very high-quality materials. Appeals to precarious middle class who wish to have class comfort and display in their home but cannot access luxury housing market (Figure 14.2). Portrayed as a superior alternative – all the luxury without all the added cost and unused space (Gamerman, 2019; Farmer, 2016; Patteson, 2009).

Mini-Houses

Full time dwellings, for individuals or families. Often attempts to have all the necessities of a 'normal house' in miniature. Not frequently mobile as they usually need connections to electricity and plumbing, yet many houses of this type are built on trailers (or are of a size that means they can be mounted on a trailer) in order to skirt building regulations (Figure 14.3). Frequently built on property of existing houses. Proponents cite cost and environmental impact, as well as aesthetic of 'less stuff' and 'a simplified lifestyle'' as reasons for living in these dwellings (Boeckermann et al., 2019, 61; see also: Murphy, 2014).

Eco-Cabins

Designed primarily to minimize resource use. Can be built from a pre-designed kit, but often self-built from reclaimed materials (Figure 14.4). Primary challenges are power and sanitation; clean water and issues around heating (Pickerill & Maxey, 2009; Pickerill, 2016). Usually owned by environmentalists and intended to be in situ most of the time.

Figure 14.3 Sketch of a mini-house trailer (artist: Diana Boyle).

Figure 14.4 Eco-cabin at Trelay, Cornwall, England.
Source: Pickerill.

The second category (Type 2) comprises types of tiny houses that are only contingently recognized as part of the larger 'movement' – transitional houses and mobile homes.

Transitional Houses

Ranging from well-designed to ramshackle and even failed structures, their primary purpose is as temporary dwellings for the unhoused and people on societal fringes. Likely organized together as part of a camp or squat that will share a number of facilities, from workshops to laundrettes to kitchens and social spaces. Their construction varies widely in composition, quality, and permanence. Considered a 'stepping stone' to more permanent housing, the primary benefits are in cost to construct and the dignity and self-sufficiency of residents who are otherwise poorly served by social support networks (Figure 14.5) (Priesnitz, 2014; Wyatt, 2016; Nesterak, 2021). The majority seem to be constructed on the Pacific coast in cities like Portland, Seattle, Los Angeles, and Oakland.

Mobile Homes

These are vacation vehicles converted into long-term dwellings. These are similar to historical and contemporary examples of Roma caravans and

Figure 14.5 Dignity village home.
Source: Pickerill.

house trailers/wagons. Environmental impact is rarely a concern – mobility is primary the motivation. Frequently used by workers who travel seasonally and by American seniors who cannot support themselves in retirement and so have sold their properties and travel looking for work (Figure 14.6).

These two types are interesting because of how they are included or excluded from the 'movement' category of tiny houses. There is clearly a great deal of classism at play. In addition to being stereotyped as 'poor', places like Dignity Village (Portland, Oregon) are built specifically to serve those who fall through the traditional social safety net. As Wyatt (2016) describes, this includes many convicts who are often excluded from both rental and shelter spaces by their criminal records. A similar class-based argument seems to apply to mobile homes and RVs. These people live a contemporary nomadic life, but with different aesthetics to Type 1 tiny homes.

The third category (Type 3) of micro homes is almost entirely disavowed within the tiny house movement – very small, frequently shared, living spaces necessitated by urban overcrowding and inequality. Whether credited as innovative responses to increasing pressure on housing in growing urban centres, especially in eastern Asia (China, Japan and South Korea), or portrayed as dystopian and dehumanizing 'cages' that cause moral outrage, these pod homes have several common points. First, the actual living space

Figure 14.6 RV home, Crestone, Colorado, USA.
Source: Pickerill.

is not just minimal – it is below what is necessary for survival. Many key features are shared, whether spaces for cooking, bathing, repair or craftwork, or recreation, if such spaces exist at all. If they do not, the residents of high-density pod homes must by necessity venture out into other spaces to access essential services, in contrast to the eco-cabins discussed above, in which going 'off grid' is seen as a positive choice rather than a necessity imposed by poverty. Second, pod homes are mostly the domain of workers and labourers, rather than mini-homes designed for families, eco-cabins for environmentalists, or RVs frequently used by retirees. There are differences in location here, as pod and cage homes in Hong Kong, for one example, include a large number of elderly poor – notably different than 'retirees' as many have not chosen to stop working but rather have endured on the fringes of poverty for long periods – while similar types of dwelling in the UK are targeted and intended almost exclusively for younger workers and labourers (Jones, 2018; Agbonlahor, 2018). These pod homes exist not to serve workers, but to serve capitalist elites by housing their workers close to their places of employment, conditioning workers to 'expect less' in terms of material rewards for their labour, and making it increasingly difficult for workers to enjoy leisure time or recreation in their own personal spaces.

While some pod homes are dressed up in high-technology, with shiny plastic, glass and metal surfaces, sleek design, and futuristic aesthetics, the majority are built to fairly minimal standards. They rely on existing technologies alongside the dehumanization of individuals under capital to provide a less-than-minimal shelter to workers who are increasingly encouraged to consider such dwellings as "a reworking of what constitutes ideal homes" (Harris & Nowicki, 2020, 592) These arguments are precisely why we consider pod homes as one of our three types here: on the surface, pod homes appear to have little in common with other forms of tiny houses, but extended examination reveals that they are not fundamentally different and share many features of structures in the other two categories (the core types, and transitional and mobile homes).

What Tiny Homes Do (and Don't)

Among these three categories of tiny homes, there are further axes of relative difference to be sketched. We propose analysis of: spatial strategy; material construction; mobility and accessibility; and autonomy and durability, in order to create a relational matrix that allows for more critical engagement with the different types – and possibilities – of tiny homes.

Spatial Strategies

Tiny homes are notable in part because they represent active intervention in taken-for-granted dwelling and domestic spaces. As such, different types of tiny homes can be described in part by their spatial strategy – how they seek to intervene in spatial systems, demonstrate the value of different spatial arrangements, and account for gaps in existing dwelling spaces. Type 1 tiny homes generally replicate the system of private property dwellings common in most urban and suburban environments. These homes are often intended to be occupied by relatively privileged and wealthy people, as conveyed in Patteson's laudatory article which asserts that "Tailored to the owners' way of life, smaller 'jewel box' homes suit a variety of demographic groups, including newlyweds, young professionals, empty-nesters and retirees – the last two a fast-growing segment of the population" (Patteson, 2009). The loss of space in these dwellings is not necessarily equated with a loss of privilege as the spatial strategy of these types of tiny homes relies on the minimization of home space through the elimination of 'unnecessary' luxuries – anything from extensive granite counter-tops to running water, depending on individual desires. It should be noted, however, that there is a clear divide between jewel-box type houses and both eco-cabins and trailer-mounted tiny homes: trailer-mounted and eco-cabin type homes often exist in a legal grey area. As Ford and Gomez-Lanier explain:

> If viewed strictly as a house, they often violate building codes regarding size, both in terms of overall size (many areas designate a minimum square footage for a space to be considered habitable). Furthermore,

> certain "green" features often employed by tiny house owners (for example, graywater or compostable toilets) may not be permissible.
>
> (Ford & Gomez-Lanier, 2017, 400)

Transitional and mobile homes also provide the necessities of life but in a form that is either unfixed, or not intended to be permanent (or more accurately, intended to be changed and changeable). Whether in the form of a well-constructed small transitional home which a person is intended to pass through, or an improvised dwelling which is unlikely to survive long-term, these are not long-term 'family homes'. For example, while Dignity Village is intended to be permanent as an overall site and community, individual dwellings may not be permanent – some degrade or were never truly fit for purpose and must be dismantled, even cannibalized for other structures. Individual homes are also often customized by the inhabitants who, given the transitional nature of the site, may change relatively frequently. Thus while the site remains, the dwellings themselves are in a state of flux and change. The inverse is essentially true for RVs, wherein residents may reside in the dwelling long term, but with particular 'migratory' patterns tailored to the lifestyle of the user:

> Sara and Matt Janssen spent nine months traveling more than 15,000 miles to 42 states in a 250-square-foot RV with their three-year-old daughter, Bella, as part of the Live Lightly Tour. They furnished the home-on-wheels with thrift-store finds and things from their previous house.
>
> (Bender, 2009)

In terms of square footage and the ability to live in the space for extended periods without deprivation of basic needs, RVs and similar spaces certainly deserve consideration alongside less mobile or stationary tiny homes.

Combining the permanence of Type 1 tiny homes with very high density construction, and the mobility of occupants primarily defined by conditions of precarity similar to those affecting many Type 2 occupants, Type 3 tiny homes are spatial containers, liminal storage for dehumanized labour. The prime example of these shoebox dwellings are the 'small-sized units' ('小户型' in Chinese) in urban China, typically between 50 and 90 m^2 or less. Driven by high land prices, nationally restricted family size, and a standardized, low cost and fast construction process, there is little individualization of residential buildings. These are not self-defined as 'tiny homes', rather these small units are considered as an adequate response to an acute housing problem. Landlords also further subdivide small apartments into multiple-occupancy homes, letting individual rooms with communal kitchens and bathrooms. Crucially residents, especially young people, migrant workers, and the elderly, are considered to have little alternative choice, and as soon as they are able, they move into bigger homes.

Material Construction

Most Type 1 homes are made of good quality materials, even if repurposed or self-designed. For the jewel-box type, luxury, high-quality, individual designs replicating the structure and functions of larger houses are common. For the popular trailer-mounted type of tiny home, the trailer itself acts as limiting agent for avoiding being registered as a structure – the house designed to otherwise approximate a normal dwelling but within the base confines of a trailer. Meanwhile, eco-cabins are usually comprised of a combination of designed 'green technology' (i.e., solar cells and batteries) and found or recycled materials, including repurposed materials not originally designed for building.

With respect to Type 2 tiny homes, there is a wide degree of variation regarding the material construction of transitional homes, as they are often made from found or repurposed materials, and can be heavily dependent on the availability of skills in the wider community for construction and repair. By contrast, mobile homes like RVs are almost always of a standard design – this is partly because they tend to be mass produced, but also because they must adhere to legal restrictions on size, speed, and safety which mean there is less possibility for variance. Regardless, in both cases the materials used in the construction tend to be of lower quality compared to the 'granite counter tops' of jewel box houses.

Shoebox units and pod homes rarely have any flexibility, and seldom are innovative technologies used to improve the liveability of these spaces. Unlike Type 1 tiny homes they do not have purpose-designed multifunctional or fold-away furniture, mezzanines, or smart applications. Though recently there has been more emphasis on learning from Japanese compact storage strategies to 'make small homes bigger', there is a common reliance on plain, shared features such as bathrooms and cooking and eating spaces, and materials are almost always mass produced and construction-grade with few, if any, amenities.

Mobility and Accessibility

As one would expect of dwellings that replicate private properties, Type 1 tiny homes are largely immobile. Jewel-box and eco-cabin type homes are almost certainly fixed in place, as many rely on immobile infrastructure, whether plumbing and connections to electrical grids for jewel-box homes, or in the case of eco-cabins, batteries and solar cells which are heavy and unwieldy or composting toilets which are not intended to be moved. While this might seem counter-intuitive, many trailer-mounted tiny homes are also fixed in place – trailers are often part of the design, largely to skirt legal regulations on permanent structures and/or to make a single initial move from construction to site occupation, after which the trailer becomes a foundation for the house. Residents are almost always long-term, and many devote considerable time to designing, building, and customizing these homes.

By contrast, transitional homes are deserving of this label not just because people 'transit' through them, but also because the dwellings themselves are often transitional: built with minimal financial investment and technical skill and intended to be abandoned, torn down, repurposed, or rebuilt as necessary. This is a key component of making these homes accessible to marginalized and unhoused urban populations: no upfront economic investment is required, therefore so long as a person can get to the area where the transitional housing is being created, they can conceivably have housing. The problem is that many of these sites, including Dignity Village, are not easily accessible given current infrastructure and services. For example, there are no bus lines that directly connect Dignity Village to other areas of the city. Similarly, unlike Type 1 tiny homes, mobile homes are intended to be *mobile*, rather than for long-term habitation. For one particular group of mobile home inhabitants, North Americans in their 50s and 60s, mobility is key to economic survival, and not just because a tiny home is cheaper than a suburban property. Rather, many Americans in this age group find themselves in financial trouble and, having sold off a family home to pay debts, now travel in their mobile home between low-paying seasonal jobs (Eisenberg, 2018). While moving from place to place is within the normal design of a mobile home, wear and tear can eventually immobilize homes – as little as a flat tire can be a fatal equipment failure. While the cost of mobile homes varies, used versions can be had cheaply (especially when this cost is often covered by the downward mobility of selling a property).

In contrast to the at times dubious potentials for mobility associated with Type 2 tiny homes, Type 3 tiny homes are often defined by a type of carcerality. In 2009, the Society for Community Organization (SCO), a registered charity working on behalf of better living conditions for the impoverished in Hong Kong, including workers whose jobs were lost to mechanization, changing policies, and neoliberal globalization, relocated a 'cage home' from the Tai Kok Tsui neighbourhood[1] to the centre of Hong Kong as part of an ArtWalk[2] display. The display, meant to underscore the inhumane living conditions, also showed pictures and provided descriptions of residents. Many of the residents found themselves living in cage homes or 'cubicle' dwellings because of economic pressures beyond their control. While cage and pod homes are often referred to in the English-language press with horror, similar types of arrangements in the UK and North America are treated as experiments holding great potential to ease urban housing pressure and provide low-cost dwellings to young professionals. In an article for the BBC by Winnie Agbonlahor (2018), shared accommodations in London which – other than perhaps in terms of aesthetic – are similar to many pod homes in Asia and are lauded as places to build community and flexible living environments for specific groups of younger people. While the tone of the article is qualified rather than laudatory – "I wouldn't like living there but I suppose it will work for some people" – it remains similar to, though orders of magnitude apart from, the dystopian descriptions of Asian pod homes.

Autonomy and Durability

Again, as one would expect of permanent dwellings replicating private property, Type 1 tiny homes are intended to be permanent and permanently inhabited – just like a normal house. With the exception of eco-cabins, they are usually linked into service grids either directly (registered electrical, water services, etc.) or indirectly (piggy-backing on existing services), and these links are often crucial to both the living standard within the dwelling and the maintenance of the structure itself – for example, many tiny homes need to be heated to avoid water lines freezing, just like a normal house. While some tiny homes skirt building codes, they are not generally seen as socially problematic by authorities.

Type 2 dwellings, transitional homes, and RVs exist as semi-autonomous and, as discussed above, somewhat transitory spaces. While transitional dwellings like those in Dignity Village may sit somewhat outside of the mainstream provision of services and legal rights to adequate housing that does not mean these places are without rules. As Anne Wyatt describes with respect to Dignity Village:

> Membership and residence in DV was of variable terms, contingent upon adherence to rules and a one-month trial residence period. In addition to pitching in for costs, DV residents, "members," were required to volunteer ten hours per week of community service and to follow a few rules: no violence, no theft, no constant disruptive behavior, and no alcohol or illegal drugs on-site or within a one block radius.
>
> (Wyatt, 2016, 41)

Likewise, as Wyatt goes on to note, despite the lack of formal systems of organization, "order and reciprocity is the norm" (44), implying a form of collective agreement around social norms and behaviours that also carries consequences when breached. By contrast, mobile home living is a much more individualized lifestyle. RV dwellers, like transitional housing dwellers in places not 'intended' for such use, (i.e., private property, unused or abandoned industrial sites, city parks, etc.) must find areas where they are able to set up, knowing that many areas specifically prohibit these actions. However, the solidarity and collective strength of transitional villages, as well as the at least nominal claims to be providing for social welfare, means that they are at times able to assert a more permanent foothold even when their construction is technically 'illegal'. By contrast, RV dwellers must find temporary respite but often with the knowledge that they will be required to relocate in the near future.

In contrast with the potential – if not always realized – for other types of tiny homes to improve the long-term living prospects of a variety of unhoused or precarious people, shoebox and pod homes are intended to limit the horizons of individuals to their labour and remove individuation. In a very real sense, the permanence of the structures speaks to the lack of autonomy of residents, who are far more transient than the buildings themselves (the inverse of transitional homes). In terms of what Type 3 tiny homes do, their spatial strategy is about reactive and needs-based survival, in conventionally constructed and static homes. Comparing this third type of tiny home with those discussed before makes visible the explicitly Anglo context in which many tiny homes are currently understood, while demonstrating the risks of fetishizing tiny homes without attending to social justice. There is little to substantially distinguish these small units in China from corporate co-housing projects in London and Dublin.

Conclusions

The assertion that tiny homes must have a lower environmental impact than larger homes needs critical interrogation. Homes that share common energy, water, and waste infrastructures and dense multiple-occupancy buildings with few external walls are the most efficient in terms of energy and material consumption (Pickerill, 2016). The 'less is more' ethic apparent in tiny homes implies an environmental consciousness, but this is not actually inherently environmentally friendly. Environmental impact can only be considered alongside the accessibility of the technology required. Many tiny homes of the types that replicate individual family dwellings on a smaller scale rely on technologies that are not affordable to many people who would be looking to downsize in order to reduce their personal financial commitments. This represents an enormous stumbling block to tiny houses having significant environmental benefits or standing in as housing solutions for the economically disadvantaged.

Central to the liveability of these tiny homes is often the connection to infrastructural support – be that energy provision, water, sewerage, or more diffuse notions of infrastructural systems in terms of food supplies, telephone communications, transport, et cetera. Early prototypes were off-grid and consequently required purposeful simplicity (e.g. limiting use of energy, heating), significant manual effort (e.g. collecting firewood) and disconnection from the connectivity and luxuries of contemporary life (e.g. lack of Wi-Fi). Yet some contemporary examples belie their connections and the use they make of infrastructural provisions, ignoring the privilege of using neighbours' Wi-Fi signals, or national power grids, most hypocritically when articulated as an ecological act. Suggesting therefore that tiny homes are a panacea to the housing crisis ignores that small homes that have long existed, erases the privilege that enables many advocates to choose the conditions in which they live, and ignores how they fit into existing systems (or not) of infrastructural connections.

Yet tiny homes retain some hopeful possibilities when they seek to reconfigure, rather than entrench, existing relations. These relations are not just to capitalism or to the environment, but also towards others (community), and the land. Tiny homes have been, and continue to be, used as a form of anti-homelessness activism, not by simply providing more dwellings, but rather by providing a community where homelessness is not stigmatized. A Better Tent City, a homeless tiny homes community in Kitchener, Canada, shares similarities with Dignity Village, reworking what 'shelter' means, particularly the need for private spaces that look and feel like homes. That these spaces are also often collectively governed by the residents themselves helps reconfigure notions of community control, belonging, and collectivity. This sense of legitimacy, of being in a place with some sense of stability, is vital for residents (Griffin, et al., 2021). In this way tiny homes might support often the most marginalized in society and might challenge or at least subvert elements of capitalism – albeit schemes are problematic in normalizing substandard housing provisions for the homeless. Similarly, but less driven by explicit homelessness, are homes built by the Canadian Mud Girls collective. The Mud Girls are an all-women's house building collective who build tiny homes from natural materials (Kenny and Murphy, 2018). Focusing on building with low-income communities and explicitly anti-capitalist, they articulate their home building as a form of activism which centres feminism, childcare, community, and collectivity. Finally, the Tiny House Warriors[3] are using the construction of tiny homes on unceded Secwepemc Territory in Canada, as a political tactic to prevent the building of the Trans Mountain oil pipeline. The homes provide housing while also being their protest strategy. It is in these examples, where tiny homes are tied to quests for social change, that they offer spaces of hope in remaking the world differently, more justly and more inclusively.

Notes

1 https://soco.org.hk/en/cage-home_exh/
2 The SCO refers to ArtWalk as "Hong Kong's biggest charity art event" (SCO 2009).
3 www.tinyhousewarriors.com

References

Agbonlahor, W. 2018. Co-living in London: Friendship, fines and frustration. *BBC News*, 24 April. www.bbc.co.uk/news/uk-england-london-43090849

Bender, K. 2009. Little Boxes: The new movement to seriously downsize our homes. *The Environmental Magazine*, 30 May. https://emagazine.com/little-boxes/.

Boeckermann, L., Kacynzski, A. & King, S. 2019. Dreaming big and living small: Examining motivations and satisfaction in tiny house living. *Journal of Housing and the Built Environment*, 34: 61–71.

Eisenberg, R. 2018. Many older Americans are living a desperate, nomadic life. *MarketWatch*, 24 November. www.marketwatch.com/story/many-older-americans-are-living-a-desperate-nomadic-life-2017-11-06

Farmer, R. (2016) Jewel-box homes. *Boomer* [online magazine], 7 February. www.boomermagazine.com

Ford, J. & Gomez-Lanier, L. 2017. Are tiny homes here to stay? A review of literature on the tiny house movement. *Family and Consumer Sciences Research Journal* 45(4): 394–405.

Gamerman, A. 2019. Luxury Homeowners put a ring on jewel-box homes. *Wall Street Journal* [online], 11 December. www.wsj.com/articles/luxury-homeowners-put-a-ring-on-jewel-box-homes-11576081060?mod=hp_lead_pos12

Griffin, E., McClymont, K. & Sheppard, A. 2021. A sense of legitimacy in low-impact developments: Experiences and perspectives of communities in South-West England. *International Journal of Housing Policy*, 22(1): 83–105.

Harris, E. 2019. Compensatory cultures: Post-2008 climate mechanisms for crisis times. *New Formations*, 99(99): 66–87.

Harris, E. & Nowicki, M. 2020. "GET SMALLER"? Emerging geographies of micro-living. *Area*, 52(3): 591–599.

Jones, R. 2018. Are these the worst new flats in Britain? *The Guardian*, 25 August.

Kenny, C. & Murphy, M. 2018. *Mudgirls Manifesto: Handbuilt homes handcrafted lives: the mudgirls natural building collective*. Gabroila Island: New Society Publishers.

Matthews, D. 2016. The case against tiny homes. *Vox*, The New New Economy Series. URL: www.vox.com/a/new-economy-future/tiny-houses

Milkman, A. 2016. The tiny house fantasy. *Jacobin*, 19 January. www.jacobinmag.com/2016/01/tiny-house-movement-nation-tumbleweed-environment-consumerism

Murphy, M. 2014. Tiny houses as appropriate technology. *Communities*, 176 (winter): 54–59.

Nesterak, M. 2021. Indoor tiny house village for homeless people set to open next month in Minneapolis. *Minneapolis Reformer* [online newspaper], 18 February. https://minnesotareformer.com/2021/02/18/indoor-tiny-house-village-for-homeless-people-set-to-open-next-month-minneapolis/

Patteson, J. (2009). "Jewel-box" houses are built smaller, smarter. *Seattle Times* [online], 3 July. www.seattletimes.com/business/real-estate/jewel-box-houses-are-built-smaller-smarter/

Pickerill, J. 2015. Bodies, building and bricks: Women architects and builders in eight eco-communities in Argentina, Britain, Spain, Thailand and USA. *Gender, Place and Culture*, 22(7): 901–919.

Pickerill, J. 2016. *Eco-homes: People, place and politics*. London: Zed Books.

Pickerill, J. & Maxey, L. 2009. Geographies of sustainability: Low Impact Developments and radical spaces of innovation. *Geography Compass*, 3(4): 1515–1539.

Priesnitz, W. 2014. Tiny houses, tiny neighborhoods. *Natural Life Magazine*, March/April. www.life.ca/naturallife/1404/tiny-houses-tiny-communities.htm

Salomon, S. 2006. *Little house on a small planet: Simple homes, cozy retreats and energy efficient possibilities*. Guilford, CT: The Lyons Press.

Shearer, H. & Burton, P. 2019. Towards a typology of tiny houses. *Housing, Theory and Society* 36(3): 298–318.

Society for Community Organization. 2009. Cage Home Exhibition. Available at: https://soco.org.hk/en/cage-home_exh/ (accessed 11 October 2022).

Willoughby, C., Mangold, S. & Zschau, T. 2020. Small houses, big community: Tiny housers' desire for more cohesive communities. *Social Science*, 9(16): 1–33.

Wyatt, A. 2016. Tiny houses: Niche or noteworthy? *American Planning Association: Planning Magazine*, 82(2), www.planning.org/planning/2016/feb/

15 Cluster Apartments

Living with Less as Model for Lived Solidarity?

Manuel Lutz

Introduction

In European and North American cities, living small has become (once again) a response to housing insecurity where affordable and adequate housing is out of reach for many especially the growing urban populations of single households. Specific to the 21st century, however, economic necessity as the main driver coincides with an ecological necessity for reducing human exploitation of natural resources, and a social necessity where new demands for living together find no adequate offers in standardized housing markets. On this background experiments to reinvent housing are necessary. This requires more than well-designed architectural solutions: whether imposed for profit or to achieve a smaller ecological footprint, reducing the size of housing is likely to intensify insecurity and precarity for those marginalized in the housing market already. The emergence of new forms of small living in micro apartments or co-living arrangements but also in non-commercial forms of collaborative housing therefore requires critical analysis of how much choice living small entails and what are the conditions for living well in small space?

To address these questions, the chapter examines so-called cluster apartments that have become popular among architects and housing providers in German-speaking countries where they are highlighted as one solution to the big question of how we can live together in more sustainable ways. Interrogating this promise of cluster apartments, I analyse how live-able this design solution for living well in small space is and for whom, that is, what kind of housing problems it solves.

Outline

The chapter first introduces and contextualizes cluster apartments in the context of other forms of shared housing. Following a brief overview on methodology and case studies, I propose to criticize the transformative potential of cluster apartments for solving housing problems by asking what

DOI: 10.4324/9781003173052-21

kind of solidarity these solutions exhibit. The comparison shows how non-profit and market housing developers have reduced living space, integrated social diversity of inhabitants and achieved affordable rents. I discuss these outcomes in relation to four strategies of project developers for balancing cost- and space-efficiency as well as individual and collective interests. Highlighting tensions, conflicts and trade-offs between these strategies to enable internal and external solidarity, the conclusion summarizes lessons from the experiment of cluster apartments for producing solidarity-based small living.

The Innovation of Cluster Apartments

The defining feature of cluster apartments is their distinct architectural design. Characteristic is a floor plan where individual units, consisting of one to three rooms with a bathroom and often an optional small kitchen, are clustered around common spaces including a shared kitchen. Cluster apartments do not simply minimize domestic space but seek to reconfigure functions and practices of housing. Unlike the typical flat share (Wohngemeinschaft) or commune, they offer more private space including private bathrooms. Unlike micro apartments or co-living spaces, that provide where common spaces but separately – e.g. at the end of a corridor, in cluster appartments common spaces are integral. Every resident enters immediately to the common areas that flow around the private units. This special design is cost-efficient as it eliminates the dead space of hallways, increases the rentable area and allows for locating cluster apartments in buildings with large depths, but it underlines primarily the strategic design purpose of facilitating shared community living.

Reminiscent to hotel living, this specific housing typology was "invented" in the early 2000s by Swiss cooperatives which sought to develop further their concepts of large communal households with more than 20 members. The aim was to allow more privacy for ageing members but also to provide spatial diversity for new household formations beyond the standard of the nuclear family (Hofer 2011). Interestingly, this housing innovation that originated in and learns from the lived realities of squatting and alternative housing projects has quickly become acceptable and even popular. Featured in numerous exhibitions, research talks, and media articles, cluster apartments are by now a shorthand for creating housing that is innovative, efficient and ecological, and contributes to liveable, resilient, and sustainable neighbourhoods (Kries and Ruby 2017). The aesthetics of cluster apartments surely enhance their popularity as a suitable housing option for single-households and those interested in but not fully convinced of CH: dispelling stereotypes and concerns, the images demonstrate that living with less and together does not need to result in barren micro-efficiency cubicles or cramped communes with no privacy.

Figure 15.1 Common space with shared kitchen in a cluster apartment; housing cooperative mehr als wohnen, Zurich.
Source: Prytula et al. (2019).

Analysing Small and Shared Housing as Struggle for Solidarity-Based Living

On what ground can we criticize such small living arrangements? Commonsense notions of how much space it takes to be housed well prove difficult to generalize. The acceptability or adequacy of small living is always shaped by its historical and temporal context, of plausibly available alternatives, and the hegemonic orientations of what housing is desirable. Following critical theorist Rahel Jaeggi (Jaeggi 2013), I thus propose to understand cluster apartments as socio-spatial experiments for a new form of life to solve problems. Accounting for changing normative orientations and expectations of housing, the critique then focuses on practices of collaboration as the central determinant of living together well – especially in small space.

This focus on living differently through collaborative practices is central to the emerging research on collaborative housing (CH) which offers additional conceptual guidance (Czischke et al. 2020; Lang et al 2018). Housing cooperatives are a typical example of CH that is characterized by the active agency of users who collaborate to balance individual autonomy and collective capacity to provide housing that fulfils their common aims such as user-driven design, affordable rents, ecological building, and alternative forms of community-oriented living. While CH typically emphasizes practices of sharing in common spaces to achieve social or ecological aims, increasingly sharing becomes also an economic strategy to lower housing costs (Ledent 2021; Lutz 2019, 2020).

Small living relates thus to the central values of CH: autonomy, participatory democracy, and solidarity (Sørvoll and Bengtsson 2019: 10). Highlighting solidarity, Sørvoll and Bengtsson argue that the main task for CH is to enable not only internal solidarity between members of the group to live together harmoniously but also external solidarity which opens the benefits of CH to others beyond the group. Other CH researchers similarly call for such external solidarity when they criticize the self-marginalization of CH as exclusive, "inward-looking residential enclaves" of a privileged middle class (Bossuyt 2021; Chiodelli 2015; LaFond et al. 2017). Realizing such solidarity, however, means to deal with the three main mechanisms that challenge CH: "the conflicting interests of different member categories", "welfare state cooptation", and "the dominant capitalist logic of competition and growth" (Sørvoll and Bengtsson 2019: 10). This mix of internal and external solidarity is crucial far beyond CH. Really sustainable urban development requires a radical shift in production and consumption that presupposes a shift in social, political values, and practices towards a quality of life that is not simply based on (individual) welfare and growth (WBGU 2016). Solidarity becomes here an umbrella term to capture the learning of new solidarity-based practices of living that fundamentally reorient social relations towards recognition and support for others without expecting direct return. This "great urban transformation" (ibid.) poses the difficult challenge of making reduced consumption liveable by not sacrificing individual hedonism entirely to ecological sufficiency or cost-efficiency.

This transformative perspective grounds a normative critique of housing including forms of small and shared living that assesses how they address existing and future problems of housing. Can cluster apartments be more than an economic necessity or a pragmatic trade-off to compromise some privacy for affordability? Can they nurture learning of more solidarity-based forms of life that recognize own interests and those of others including future users and the global ecology? Exploring this I will compare the material and social conditions of cluster apartments provided by housing cooperatives with those provided by market and state actors. While the latter are excluded from the definition of CH (Lutz 2021) this extended analysis allows to examine differences but also similarities in how cluster apartments by profit and non-profit developers work as problems-solving instances that succeed or fail to solve specific problems of living together on smaller space and of the larger intersecting problems of producing and consuming housing regulated by the market and private property. Within the contradictions of capitalism such experiments are necessarily contradictory, too, wherefore the benchmark of critique is how cluster apartments demonstrate and enable processes of learning from failures to develop more adequate housing solutions.

Research Methodology

The chapter is based on findings from a two-year research project conducted by a team of architects and planners from the University of Applied Sciences HTW Berlin and the University of Applied Sciences Potsdam. Funded by the German Ministry of the Interior and Building, the research assessed how cluster apartment contribute to urban resilience. Our multidisciplinary analysis includes architectural, sociological, and governance perspectives to examine how cluster apartments are planned, built, financed, managed, and lived. The case study analysis includes document analysis of reports, plans and budgets, field visits, ten interviews with project developers, and an online survey of users in which 51 of the 122 residents of the examined cluster apartments participated. The findings of this first comprehensive overview and comparative analysis of cluster apartments have been discussed publicly and published to stimulate the ongoing debate on this housing innovation (Prytula et al. 2019, 2020).

Case Studies

Cluster apartments are defined here by the specific architectural typology and the character of intentional, self-governed communities. Cluster apartments are an expanding niche phenomenon. The research identified 33 projects in Switzerland, Germany, and Austria with a total of 81 cluster apartments but since 2019 more have been built in various cities (ibid., STATTBAU 2019). The selected eight case studies represent the typical variation of cluster apartments in regards to ownership, location, and design features (Table 15.1). Typically realized as (small) part of larger and mixed housing projects, most cluster apartments are built by housing cooperatives which accordingly dominate the sample. Representative for so-called young housing cooperatives that have pioneered the experiment of cluster apartments, these cases range from small and medium to large projects with up to 1,300 residents. Municipal housing corporations and private developers make up only 15% each of all identified projects. While these housing providers are increasingly interested in realizing cluster apartments to attract new groups of tenants that may also stimulate community life thus increasing social acceptance of contested new developments, the limited number of cases represents the status quo. Included is one market case in Zurich, and one state case in Cologne, both of which are small projects.

Table 15.1 Case studies of cluster apartments in Switzerland and Germany

Project	*City*	*Year*	*Housing provider*	*Total living space in the project (size in m²)*	*No. of cluster apartments (size in m²)*
Spreefeld	Berlin, GER	2014	Housing cooperative	5.600	2 (400.907)
mehr als wohnen	Zurich, CH	2014	Housing cooperative	41.000	16 (312–399)
Neufrankengasse	Zurich, CH	2015	Private developer	1.011	2 (229)
wagnisART	Munich, GER	2016	Housing cooperative	9.565	8 (294–358)
Zwicky Süd	Dübendorf, CH	2016	Housing cooperative	12.750	2 (320.430)
inklusiv wohnen Köln	Cologne, GER	2017	Municipal housing association	1.400	2 (426.426)
StadtErle	Basel, CH	2017	Housing cooperative	2.940	1 (346)
Annagarten	Oranienburg, GER	2017	Housing cooperative	1.044	1 (276)

Findings on Solidarity-Based Living in Cluster Apartments

The following findings compare cluster apartments by cooperative, state, and market providers in regards to four outcomes: (a) the shrinking of private living space which indicates external ecological solidarity; (b) the resident´s practices of living together which indicates internal solidarity; (c) the social demographics of residents which indicates external solidarity as inclusivity; and (d) the affordability of housing costs which indicates both internal and external solidarity.

Shrinking Private Space

The cases reveal a fascinating diversity of floor plans (Figures 15.2 and 15.3). Inhabited by 5 to 23 persons most groups have between 7 and 10 members which on average use 39.40 m² of living space per person: this footprint

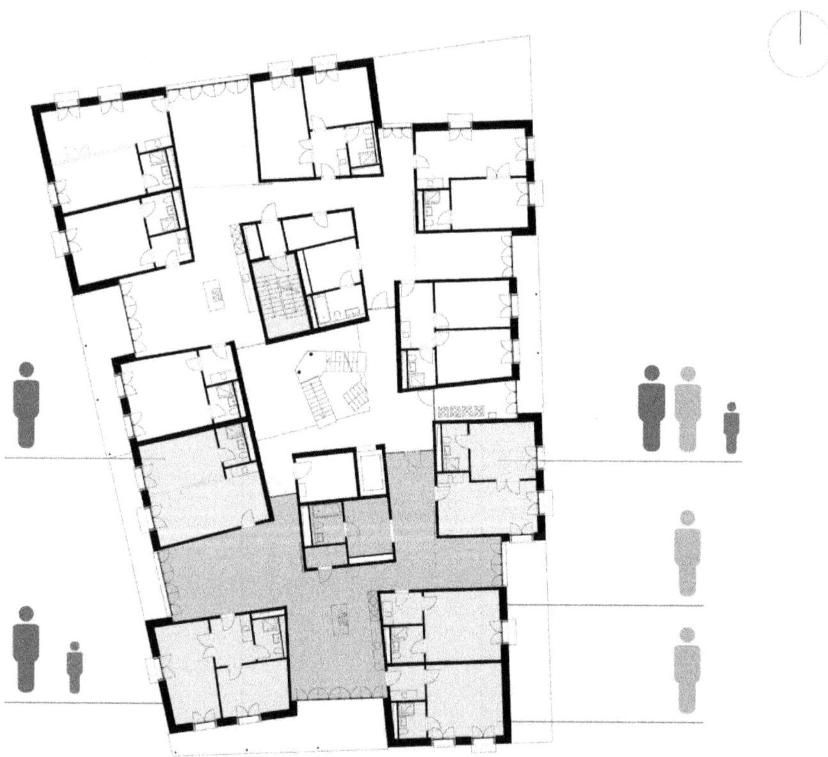

Figure 15.2 Floor plan of cluster apartment; housing cooperative mehr als wohnen, Zurich.

Source: Prytula et al. (2019).

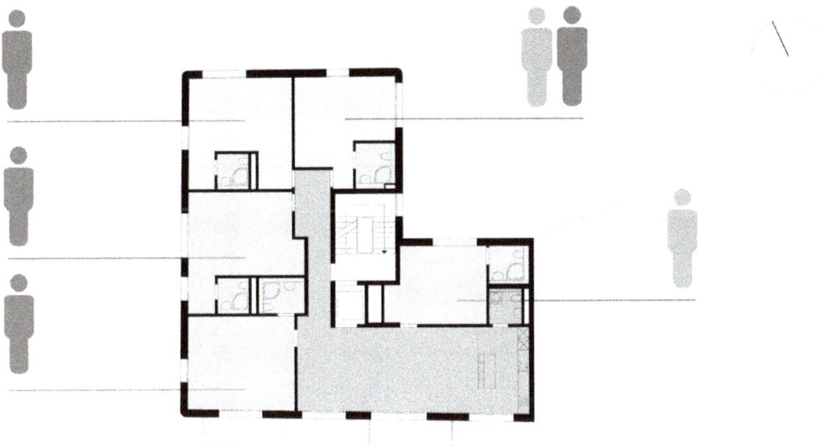

Figure 15.3 Floor plan of cluster apartment; private developer Neufrankengasse, Zurich.

Source: Prytula et al. (2019).

does not seem so small at all (Table 15.2). Yet, compared to the German and Swiss floor space average of 46 m² per person that increases to an average of 67 and 80 m² for the growing number of one-person households (UBA 2019), the cluster apartments indicate a clear deviation from the overall trend of increasing floor space consumption.

This external ecological solidarity is highlighted by the radical shrinking of private units that range from small rooms of 10 m² reminding to cloister cells, to more spacious single rooms to complete mini apartments with 2 or 3 rooms on a total of 51 m². On average, private units have 24,6 m² and are inhabited mostly (60%) by one person. One-third of respondents shares it with another person and only few share it with three or more persons – most often the partner, the child, or a roommate. The small private units, however, are compensated by more or less large common spaces. The average of 14 m² per person translates into large spaces where for instance 8 residents in the cooperative mehr als wohnen can use 171 m² of common space.[1] The comparison shows that floor space in the market case is close to the average and similar to the state case where, however, the common space is much larger resulting in the second largest total floor space. This is higher than the national average and among the case studies trumped only by the cooperative mehr als wohnen. The cooperative cases show the greatest variation

Table 15.2 Floor space analysis for one exemplary cluster apartment in each case study

Case studies	*Total floor space (in m²)*	*Private space per person (in m²)*	*Common space per person (in m²)*	*Total living space per person (in m²)*
Spreefeld	907	31.2	10.0	41.2
mehr als wohnen	357	26.6	24.4	51.0
Neufrankengasse	229	25.3	12.9	38.2
wagnisART	294	19.8	9.6	29.4
Zwicky Süd	320	29.5	16.2	45.7
inklusiv wohnen Köln	426	23.4	23.8	47.2
StadtErle	346	25.4	9.2	34.6
Annagarten	276	15.6	12.0	27.6
Average cluster apartments	394.4	24.6	14.6	39.4
Average Vario apartments	-	24.4	2.4	27.3
Average Germany/Switzerland	-	-	-	46.5/46

with the smallest and the largest private and common spaces per person indicating both the strongest and the weakest commitment to external ecological solidarity.

Practices of Living Together

Lived internal solidarity means individuals interact regularly voluntarily and share the space in ways that respect and enable the use of others. Cluster apartments support such a form of living together that sociologist Törnqvist describes as "individualized collectivism" characterized by a liberty to "not to dwell alone, but rather to decide on *how, when, and with* whom to dwell" (Törnqvist, 2019: 908). This resonates well with most residents describing their shared living as undogmatic where the specific design allows more discretion in choosing the dosage of community life. The user survey confirms across all cases high satisfaction with private and common spaces. Residents explain they have more space available (most lived in 2-bedroom apartments before) and can enjoy what one respondent described as a luxury of space she otherwise could not afford. The survey responses reveal new patterns of space utilization that rearrange locations of core residential functions. Residents thus use the special design options for living together. They do not retreat to their private spaces leaving the common spaces under-used as some project developers worried. The main shared activity is cooking and eating which residents do regularly together but they also use common spaces for meeting friends, work, and leisure activities. Interestingly, cooking together remains a regular activity irrespective of the private units entailing a small kitchen or not. Typical for shared living, the shared kitchen is simultaneously highly appreciated and identified as the main site of conflict.

In contrast, the survey reveals a significant decrease of conflict potential attributed to the private bathrooms. This suggests that not having to discuss the shared use and cleaning of this intimate space makes living together in cluster apartments more robust and harmonious.

Social Demographics

The survey shows a great mix of age and income across the cases but, overall, residents meet the typical characteristics of educated middle classes living in CH (Jakobsen and Larsen 2018). Typically younger than the national age average, the age bias is explicit for the private and the state case that are inhabited by only young adults. This is explained by their specific target groups where the market case addresses young urban professionals while the state case is a form of assisted living where students and young handicapped persons live together. The cooperative cases show a greater mix of ages but while they identify elderly persons as target group, this age group remains overall underrepresented and seems yet hesitant to try housing experiments. On the other hand, cluster apartments appear as a attractive option for single parents whose share is almost twice as high as in the German population (Statistisches Bundesamt 2018).

These demographics and the finding that on average residents have a higher income than the national median income suggest limited external solidarity where only some groups have the social and financial capital to choose living in cluster apartments. Yet, the data also shows a trend towards more social inclusion suggesting that this choice is not only an exclusive luxury. In contrast to a previous survey of Swiss cluster apartments (Grossenbacher 2015), residents with low incomes are now represented in four cooperatives – wagnisART, mehr als wohnen, Zwicky-Süd, StadtErle, and in the state case.

Affordability

Housing costs are an important measure for internal and external solidarity and all interviewed developers confirmed the aim to make cluster apartments affordable for different incomes. Comparative analysis of housing affordability, however, is challenging: affordable to who, where, and for which time, in relation to what kind of housing qualities, other expenses of households, and of course, in relation to local housing alternatives (Haffner 2018).

The research shows a wide range of rents for cluster apartments ranging between 5,65 and 13,00 Euro per m^2 in the German projects, and between 16,42 and 21,57 Swiss Franc per m^2 in the Swiss projects. These rents are affordable for the large majority of current residents, that is, below 30% of their indicated income.[2] It is noteworthy that although they are newly built (except for the case Annagarten), in all cities these rents are below average market rents for small apartments – a reference used by all developers to set the rents for their cluster apartments. Thus relatively affordable, cluster apartments are not truly affordable. Only two cooperative cases achieve rents that are affordable for an income at or below the official poverty line. This is difficult also for cooperatives (Sinning 2017: 310) as it requires to either ask their members to shrink their living space (Annagarten) or to use state funding for social housing (wagnisART) that create tensions for internal solidarity (see below).

Discussion of Strategies for Solidarity-Based Living

The outcomes show that cluster apartments are not the most space efficient and not the most affordable housing but they offer a relatively affordable housing option especially for singles from diverse social groups. Rather than a model for squeezing they show how living on small space together works well especially for individuals who easily could afford to use more space.[3] The following discusses how the socio-material conditions for this choice are shaped. The similarities and differences in outcomes are result of strategic decisions by developers and residents to realize their aims. Each strategy entails specific compromises and trade-offs that then enable collaborative practices for more or less solidarity-based living.

Reducing Size to Lower Cost While Promoting Shared Living

All cases apply the strategy of reducing floor space to reduce the ecological footprint and to lower costs. This is most explicit in the cooperative cases StadtErle and Annagarten that feature the smallest private units, the smallest floor space per person, and the lowest rents. Overall, the size of private units reveals a noticeable similarity to contemporary super-efficient micro apartments like the so-called Vario apartments developed with support of the German Ministry of Building as model for shared student or senior accommodation (Zukunftbau 2019). Both Vario and cluster apartments shrink private domestic space to an average of about 25 m^2 (Table 15.2). While this suggests a new acceptable minimum space standard, the cases also reveal specific limits for reducing living space.

Firstly, the interviewed developers attributed limited cost-efficiency potential to reducing living space because building large buildings with smartly designed floor plans and vertical infrastructure proves to be more cost-efficient. Secondly, all developers recognized that space reduction likely reduces acceptance by residents and increases risks for living together well. To solve this problem, they all adhere to a shared design principle where space redundancy trumps cost- and size-efficiency. This similar decision to design for internal solidarity is highlighted when comparing the common space size average of only 2,4 m^2 per person in Vario apartments to the average of 14,6 in cluster apartments. Instead of reducing size at all cost, the common space shall function as living room for the group that is large enough to enable parallel uses by different residents providing differentiated zones not only for cooking and eating but also for recreation, meeting, or working. The extremes of this design principle for internal solidarity are highlightey by the cooperatives: offering the largest but also the smallest common spaces that make living together more demanding. In contrast, the state case features even the second largest common space and also the market case which presumably is most interested in cost-efficiency to maximize rents shows an average-sized common space.

Empowering Group Cooperation and Solidarity

All project developers recognize that living small together requires a functioning social organization. The main strategy for promoting internal solidarity is a special form of tenure. The collective contract is signed by an association formed by the residents. It institutionalizes the various "belonging structure[s] of independent individuals" (Törnqvist 2019: 911) that may self-organize as a kind of chosen family, friendship, or as more distanced arrangement of conviviality, and practice more or less elaborate forms of collective housekeeping often with a shared budget for furniture and daily shopping. Forging collective responsibility, agency, and reliability it is not meant to facilitate "easy exits" – an ambiguous quality as Törnqvist notes (ibid.) – and demands commitment from all members to finance collectively the rent and the deposit or mandatory cooperative shares. Such collective contracts are unusual even within CH (ibid.: 909), wherefore the finding that seven of eight cases choose this tenure indicates a similar learning process to solve similar problems.

The collective reliability makes renting easier for project developers because the group decides on new members and how to allocate rents between members. This poses a challenge but also gives autonomy to the group and provides an opportunity for internal solidarity used by several cluster apartments in the cooperatives which organize income-based rent differentiation. While all cases support the initial group formation, the cooperatives offer more support for self-governance, for example, through a temporary rent subsidy until the group has consolidated. Cognizant of the tension between internal and external solidarity, the cooperatives mehr als wohnen and Zwicky-Süd also decided to exempt cluster groups from the ambitious project goal to achieve social diversity among residents. This partially explains the limited outcome in social mix but recognizes that living so closely together needs to be a collective decision and cannot be burdened by additional obligations of quotas for income, age or, ethnicity. Illustrating this tension further the cooperative wagnisART faces challenges of "welfare cooptation" (Sørvoll and Bengtsson 2019). Their truly affordable social housing units require individual rental contracts which burdens the group formation as selection of new members becomes not only a matter of group preferences but also of eligible income brackets.

Living Small Thrives in Solidarity-Based Contexts

Living small together typically means that functions of housing such as cooking or meeting friends are partially or fully externalized. The cases address this context dependency of internal solidarity differently. The small market case, a four-story building in the downtown of Zurich, offers no common spaces outside the cluster apartments. Located in peripheral locations, the similarly sized state case as well as the smallest cooperative case both seek to foster the house community by providing a common room and garden space shared by all residents. The medium and large cooperative cases offer even more options for sharing and interaction that – next to affordable rents – are the main leverage for more internal and external solidarity. They realize cluster apartments as part of larger housing projects with a wide mix of units that afford a common infrastructure comprising a variety of community spaces, workshops, laundry rooms, or a wellness area (Ledent 2021; Lutz 2019, 2020). This extended structure of belonging increases possibilities for doing things outside the cluster apartments and reduces conflicts inside it. The larger scale increases what residents value as liberating flexibility where they can adapt to changing housing needs by moving to a different apartment within the project. Promoting solidarity on a project level through solidarity funds financed by all rents to support members financially or by assigning entire cluster apartments to groups marginalized on the housing market, these cooperatives thus address the limits for how much external solidarity a single living group can afford to offer.

Participatory Planning for Solidarity

Lastly, I want to discuss how the cases address the strengths and weaknesses of participatory planning that may increase user's acceptance of small space but also tends to be exclusionary and conflictual thus threatening internal and external solidarity. The market and the state case practice no or very limited participation of residents. This results in more standardized units that allow for conversion into regular micro apartments should the experiment fail. Interestingly and likely because the units are of average size, the survey shows that user satisfaction is not significantly lower than in the cooperative cases which plan with and for the users.

The three cooperative cases in Germany show a typical participation process of CH that starts with a group and aims to identify and bind future residents who commit with time and capital and engage in year-long processes of co-design (Czischke 2018). The outcomes are thus user-driven but closely reflect how much these users want to reduce size to lower rents. This can result in the smallest or in more spacious private units like in the case Spreefeld which simultaneously demands the highest mandatory membership shares. The Swiss cooperatives and the case of wagnisART developed a different model of participation to balance the economic necessity for binding users and their capital early on with the aim for an inclusive project beyond the usual middle-class suspects. Creating dialogues where architects, interested experts, and lay persons deliberate desirable uses of the new housing project, this indirect participation aims at developing a perspective for solidarity-based quality of life. The participation process does not entitle participants to live there (mehr als wohnen, Zwicky-Süd) or strategically curtails self-realization by adhering to the simple rule that no one plans his or her own apartment (wagnisART, StadtErle). Amplifying the voice of experts and interested but not invested individual provides a counterweight to individual trade-offs where users may sacrifice common space to maximize private spaces. The outcomes of such indirect participation processes are thus not custom-tailored to individual needs but show more architectural experiments and innovation for cost-efficient design. This results in the greatest diversity of small and large private units that offer more options for a wide range of different user needs and incomes and thus enhances internal and especially external solidarity.

Conclusion: Deepening Experiments for Learning on Solidarity-Based Housing

The focus on solidarity offers a sensitizing concept to assess qualities of small and shared dwellings beyond existing measures such as housing size standards or rates of user satisfaction imbued by hegemonic ideologies of homeownership. Conceptualizing small and shared living in cluster apartments as practices of collaboration to achieve solidarity sharpens comparative analysis and has allowed identification of differences and similarities between state, market, and cooperative providers which offer lessons to criticize and transform the trend of shrinking domesticity.

The discussion shows that all providers solve problems of living small together through specific innovations in architectural design and social organization which allow collaborative practices to balance privacy and community, hedonism and sufficiency, as relations of choice rather than coercion or conflict. Living small together functions well when, firstly, the architecture gives space for both privacy and community which are not antagonists but two sides of the same coin (Dürr and Kuhn 2017). While private units can be reduced in size, the common spaces underline that a degree of spatial redundancy is necessary to make cost- and space-efficiency liveable. Secondly, the social organization has to empower groups to self-organize through suitable forms of tenure and support. And thirdly, living small thrives well in a context that extends the spatial and social opportunities of small living. These necessary conditions for internal solidarity can be realized by state and market providers, too, wherefore all cases offer a valuable inspiration for collective imaginaries on what it means to live small well.

State and market providers, however, struggle to achieve stronger internal and especially external solidarity because they cannot solve the problems of state and market housing such as land speculation, rising rents, or the limits of specialized eligibility criteria for social housing based on standards. Both the market and the state case are exceptional: it took special commitment to reduce profit expectations and to respond to the demands of the users. The private developer strategically lowers rents for cluster apartments in comparison to higher profit-yielding micro apartments in order to establish a new housing segment, whereas the municipal housing association had to be convinced through sustained grassroots lobbying to enable such special group housing. If the innovation of cluster apartments, however, is reduced to a design blueprint for small living to maximize profit without providing for the social conditions, such a mainstreaming of cluster apartments risks lowering the qualities of living small. Exemplary is the commercial project MinMax in Zurich that provides cluster apartments with external common spaces but organizes this with individual rental contracts offering little support and stability for collective self-organization (UTO Real Estate 2021).

The problems of state and market housing are addressed by housing cooperatives. Their specific form of tenure and self-governance combines self-interest and community and offers a solution to rising rents and the exclusive logics of private property that do not support reliable sharing – which explains also why cluster apartments are rarely realized by homeowner collectives (Baugruppe). The cooperative cases build cluster apartments to produce housing as infrastructure by and for users with diverse needs and desires. Extending internal and external solidarity is here more than a political ideology or lofty altruistic ideal but becomes tangible for their housing production and everyday organization. This is illustrated well by the benchmark of 35 m² living space per person set by the Swiss cooperatives (Hoffmann 2019: 25). This orients the planning of all units and it is coupled with a social rule for minimum occupancy. The rule that no one can use more space than the other establishes a measure of fairness that proves helpful to sustain collective learning of new forms of living together. The outcomes show that cluster apartments do not fully accord to this benchmark per person. But they contribute to its realization on the project level by increasing the available and attractive options for all residents, for example, for parents who no longer meet the occupancy requirement once the kids move out.

To conclude, cluster apartments are not the solution to all housing problems. But as this chapter showed, they are living laboratories that expand collective imagination on what housing can be like when individuals do not only realize their own best use but also consider the needs and interests of others. While this discussion highlighted some conditions and strategies for turning small and shared living into an enabling structure where reduction of space does not mean less quality of living, more experiments and research are called for to address issues of adapting social housing programs to enable such solidarity-based living and to examine the lived practices of living small and shared comparatively. Of course, commercial cluster apartments can enable meaningful forms of living on small space, too, but developing and sustaining lived relationships of solidarity requires a framework that gives security, reliability, context, and orientation. Small living should not only allow learning to solve problems of existing housing but also learning to rethink what housing means as use value and as a social process for creating meaningful sustainable ways of living.

Notes

1 This calculation does not include common spaces beyond the cluster apartment which would result into higher figures per person (Schopp 2017).
2 Evaluation of affordability is based on true costs, that is, income after taxes and housing costs including utilities (Holm and Junker 2019: 9). The assessment of relative affordability entails some fuzziness as each survey response on income is treated as one-person household.
3 This success is context dependent not least because in Germany and Switzerland renting is more than a marginal or inferior form of tenure.

References

Bossuyt, Daniël (2021). "Who Owns Collaborative Housing? A Conceptual Typology of Property Regimes." In: *Housing, Theory and Society*. Online publication. https://www.tandfonline.com/doi/full/10.1080/14036096.2021.1888788.
Chiodelli, Francesco (2015). "What Is Really Different between Cohousing and Gated Communities?." In: *European Planning Studies*. 23 (12), 2566–2581.
Czischke, Darinka (2018). "Collaborative Housing and Housing Providers: Towards an Analytical Framework of Multi-stakeholder Collaboration in Housing Co-production." *International Journal of Housing Policy*. 18 (1), 55–81.
Czischke, Darinka, Carriou, Claire, and Lang, Richard (2020). "Collaborative Housing in Europe: Conceptualizing the Field." In: *Housing, Theory and Society*. 37 (1), 1–9.
Dürr, Susanne and Kuhn, Gerd (2017). *Wohnvielfalt. Gemeinschaftlich wohnen – im Quartier vernetzt und sozial orientiert*. Wüstenrot Stiftung, Ludwigsburg.
Grossenbacher, Jürg (2015). "Clusterwohnungen – Herausforderungen und Perspektiven. Eine empirische Untersuchung realisierter Projekte." (MA Thesis) Zurich University.
Haffner, Marietta E. A. (2018). "Housing affordability in the European Union." In: *Informationen zur Raumentwicklung*. 4, 22–34.
Hofer, Andreas (2011). "Von der Familienwohnung zum Cluster-Grundriss." In: *TEC21*. 7, 23–31.
Hoffmann, Marco (2019). *Wohnen, Leben, Arbeiten im Hunziker Areal in Zürich: Strukturen – Prozesse – Erfahrungen*. AGE Stiftung, Zurich.
Holm, Andrej and Junker, Stephan (2019). Die Wohnsituation in Deutschen, Großstädten – 77 Stadtprofile. Research report. https://www.boeckler.de/pdf_fof/100892.pdf
Jaeggi, Rahel (2013). *Kritik von Lebensformen*. Suhrkamp, Frankfurt.

Jakobsen, Peter and Larsen, Henrik Gutzon (2018). "An Alternative for Whom? The Evolution and Socio-economy of Danish Cohousing." In: *Urban Research & Practice*. 12 (4), 1–17.

Kries, Mateo and Ruby, Andreas (eds.) (2017). *Together! Die Neue Architektur der Gemeinschaft*. Vitra Design Museum, Weil am Rhein.

LaFond, Michael, id22: Institut für kreative Nachhaltigkeit, Tsvetkova, Michael LaFond, and Larisa (eds.) (2017). *COHousing Inclusive – Selbstorganisiertes, gemeinschaftliches Wohnen für Alle*. Jovis, Berlin.

Lang, Richard, Carriou, Claire, and Czischke, Darinka (2018). "Collaborative Housing Research (1990–2017): A Systematic Review and Thematic Analysis of the Field." In: *Housing, Theory and Society*. 37. Online publication. https://www.tandfonline.com/doi/abs/10.1080/14036096.2018.1536077.

Ledent, Gérald (2021). "Size Matters. How Does the Number of Dwellings Affect Housing Co-Production?" In: *Journal of Housing and the Built Environment*. Online publication. https://link.springer.com/article/10.1007/s10901-021-09863-8

Lutz, Manuel (2019). "Living Labs for Housing: Co-operatives Reinvented." *Assemble Papers*. https://assemblepapers.com.au/2019/11/20/lived-solidarity-housing-co-operatives/

Lutz, Manuel (2020). "Lived Solidarity: Housing Co-operatives." *Assemble Papers*. https://assemblepapers.com.au/2020/03/16/living-labs-for-housing-co-operatives-reinvented/

Lutz, Manuel (2021). *The New Together: Towards an Analytical Framework for Comparative Analysis of Collaborative Housing*. Paper presented at the European Network for Housing Research Nicosia, Cyprus, September 28th–October 1st 2021.

Prytula, Michael, Rexroth, Susanne, Lutz, Manuel, and May, Friedrich (2019). *Cluster-Wohnungen für baulich und sozial anpassungsfähige Wohnkonzepte einer resilienten Stadtentwicklung* (Research report). Zukunft Bauen, Bonn.

Prytula, Michael, Rexroth, Susanne, Lutz, Manuel, and May, Friedrich (2020). *Clusterwohnungen. Eine neue Wohnungstypologie für eine anpassungsfähige Stadtentwicklung*. Zukunft Bauen, Bonn.

Schopp, Lisa (2017). "Das Potenzial neuer Wohnformen zur Reduzierung der Pro-Kopf-Wohnfläche im urbanen Raum." (Master Thesis) Technical University Munich.

Sinning, Heidi (2017). "Genossenschaftliches Wohnen in Zürich für alle? Strategien zur Inklusion benachteiligter Haushalte am Beispiel der Genossenschaftssiedlung „Hunziker-Areal." In: *Stadterneuerung und Armut*. Edited by Altrock Kunze. Springer, Wiesbaden, 291–314.

Sørvoll, Jardar and Bengtsson, Bo (2019). "Autonomy, democracy and solidarity. The defining principles of collaborative civil society housing and some mechanisms that may challenge them." In: *Urban Research & Practice*. Online publication, 1–21.

Statistisches Bundesamt (2018). "Alleinerziehende in Deutschland 2017." www.destatis.de/DE/Presse/Pressekonferenzen/2018/Alleinerziehende/pressebroschuere-alleinerziehende.pdf?__blob=publicationFile&v=3

STATTBAU (2019). *Gemeinschaftliches Wohnen im Cluster. Ein praktischer Leitfaden zum Planen, Bauen und Wohnen*. Berlin.

Törnqvist, Maria (2019). "Living Alone Together: Individualized Collectivism in Swedish Communal Housing." In: *Sociology*. 53, 900–915.

UBA, 2019. "Wohnflächen in Deutschland. Umweltbundesamt.: https://www.umweltbundesamt.de/daten/private-haushalte-konsum/wohnen/wohnflaeche.

UTO Real Estate Management AG (2021). "MinMax, Glattpark-Opfikon." www.utorem.ch/portfolio/minmax/.

WBGU, Wissenschaftlicher Beirat der Bundesregierung Globale Umweltveränderungen (2016). *Der Umzug der Menschheit: Die transformative Kraft der Städte: Hauptgutachten*. Berlin.

Zukunftbau (2019). "Variowohnungen." www.zukunftbau.de/variowohnungen/

16 Heterotopia

A New Perspective on Female-Led Tiny House Projects

Alice Wilson

Introduction

> ...with my ex-husband you know, I took care of everything...you feel trapped in that kind of traditional housewife role, taking care of everything right; paying the bills, making the money, taking care of the household, taking care of the husband.
>
> I don't need that. I can choose to have my world be whatever I want it to be. I get to be my own independent woman, quite comfortably not needing anything. So, yeah it could open up a lot of doors for women who are not in the best of situations.
>
> (Deena, 41, USA)

Since April 2020 I have been conducting research with women who have built and live in their own tiny houses. In this time, I have carried out 30 semi-structured interviews via Zoom with women from around the world who responded to my call for participation. I initially intended this research to include face-to-face conversations where I could visit women living in tiny houses in the UK, where I also live and work. The coronavirus pandemic put an end to those plans, and so I broadened the scope of the project to include women from all over the world, since we could easily speak via zoom. This research now includes women from the UK, the USA, the Netherlands, Germany, Brazil, and women who live permanently on the road moving from place to place. I have included any person who self-identifies as female, and have included people who live in trailer-based tiny houses, converted vans, narrowboats, sheds, and shipping containers. These women's ages range from 19 to 60, and include single women, women in relationships, lesbians, mothers, students, entrepreneurs, minimalists, hoarders, ferret lovers, data scientists, and psychic mediums. Although these women's lives and stories are very different from one another, there are common strands that bind them.

In one way or another, they all spoke about feeling trapped by and dissatisfied with the status quo. Some were struggling with financial hardship and were excluded from the housing market by stagnating wages and a

DOI: 10.4324/9781003173052-22

ballooning global housing crisis. Others were financially secure but unhappy with the environmental impact of their lifestyles. Some needed to live and work extremely flexibly because of unpaid caring responsibilities. All of them came to tiny houses as a potential solution to these multiple needs; as a way to create a new home and a new life.

Heterotopia is a term which summarises something about the homes and lives that these women were forging. Variously described as "worlds within worlds" (Johnson, 2012, p. 1), or as a site "that represents incompatible spaces and reveals paradoxes" (Sudradjat, 2012, p. 29), heterotopias are above all spaces of pluriformity and possibility. The lens of heterotopia has been used to draw out an analysis of the body (Harvey, 2000), as well as facets of human behaviour and how these are modified by the built environment (Sudradjat, 2012). The application of heterotopia as a mode of problematising the urban environment has been perhaps the most widespread use of the theory (see Dehaene and De Cauter, 2008). Foucault argues that it is arbitrary to theorise on people's behavioural practises of freedom and the "spatial distributions in which they find themselves" (Foucault, 1984, p. 246) unless the two phenomena are considered together in tandem, as mutually constituting. In this Foucauldian tradition then, tiny house residents can only be understood through tiny houses, and tiny houses can only be understood through the people who live in them. Foucault theorises that freedom can be done and experienced when there is a convergence between spatial distribution and human agency. This paper intends to offer a synergy of these approaches by considering how female-led tiny house builds can be considered to be heterotopias, and what the embodied repercussions of this might be for the women who design and build their own heterotopic tiny houses.

Tiny houses are a phenomenon all over the world but have been particularly noted as a growing subculture in geopolitical areas where chronic affordable housing crises intersect with stagnating wages; namely America, Australia, and the UK (Anderson-Dargatz, 2019; Weetman, 2018). Tiny houses are as flexible as the concept of heterotopia; they encompass converted vans and school buses, timber framed structures built on trailer bases, log cabins, shipping containers, horse boxes, sheds, and renovated garages. Tiny houses tend to be approximately 30 m^2 and cost in the region of £40,000 (Bares, et al., 2017; Shearer, 2018; Shearer and Burton, 2019). Compared to the average UK house price (February 2021) of £249,663, this amount is significantly more affordable (UK House Price Index, 2021). If consumer goods had undergone a comparable inflation in price to that seen in the housing market, a chicken would cost more than £50 (Minton, 2017). The UK housing index reveals that house prices increased by 7% between 2019 and 2020, whilst over the same period inflation adjusted wages increased by 0.9% and have still not yet recovered to their pre-2008 global financial crisis level (Office for National Statistics, 2019). To illustrate the lived impact of these figures, if the weekly wage had increased in line with the housing market in the UK the average would be approximately £2000, in reality it is closer to £585 (ibid). The Nationwide House Price Index calculator suggests that property prices may increase by as much as 200% in the next 20 years (Nationwide, 2020).

Emerging data suggests that most tiny house residents are women (Carras, 2019, p. 26). The prevalence of women tiny housers may not be surprising when considering that women as a group are disproportionately disadvantaged by the affordable housing crisis and wage stagnation, as well as being paid on average less than their male counterparts in the workplace and being in control of a minority of global capital (Hardoon, 2017). Illustratively, there is no area of England that can offer affordable housing to women on a median income, whereas every area of England except London and the South East can offer affordable housing to men on a median income (Reiss, 2019). Similarly, in England the average rent takes up 28% of men's income but 43% of women's (ibid.) This discrepancy partly explains why 67% of statutory homeless people are women (Reiss, 2019). Despite progress towards gender equality over the last 50 years, recent statistical data reveals that more than 75% of large UK companies pay women less than men on average, and the gender pay gap is actually increasing in 50% of these businesses (Smith, 2020).

To compound the oppressive forces of these gendered economic constraints, women are also more likely to be assaulted, raped, and murdered by men in their own home than in any other location (Draucker, 2000; McSpedon, 2019). Even where women are not in mortal danger in their homes, the idea of home and what it means for women is complicated by the impact of unpaid domestic labour and care work. In a 2020 report, Oxfam revealed that the total value to the global economy of women's unwaged labour is $10.8 trillion per year (Hardoon, 2017). For context, this amount is three times greater than the total worth of the tech industry (Hardoon, 2017). Women's unpaid labour in the UK alone would account for 56% of GDP, if it were counted (Office for National Statistics, 2016). The amount of time that this labour takes is a significant factor in women's poorer access to opportunities because they have less time and energy to spare than their male counterparts. The Office for National Statistics estimates that for every 16 hours men spend on housework each week in the UK, women spend 26 (ibid.). This amounts to more than 95 extra 8-hour workdays per year, for no pay (Hardoon, 2017).

Tracey This name should read Deena, not Tracey, a massage therapist in her early forties living in the USA explained her own experience of this gendered care-taking and self-effacing dynamic:

> I was the one that took responsibility and did everything so that it kept the peace. And I found that that did transfer into my later years. With my ex-husband you know, I took care of everything plus him and it does get tiring because then you feel trapped in that kind of traditional housewife role, even though it's on the opposite end of the scale because

> i'm technically superwoman taking care of everything right; paying the bills, making the money, taking care of the household, taking care of the husband. So, yeah I think for me anyways it's like I don't need that like I can choose to have my world be whatever I want it to be.

Given the tesselating constraints that women face, understanding more about what women are striving for when they build their own tiny houses as well as gaining insight into what changed qualities their lives might take on after this housing transition is an important and under-researched topic.

The concept of heterotopia offers an interesting theoretical lens through which to view tiny houses. Flexibility is a key concept which arises in the existing scholarly literature on the tiny house movement and on heterotopia (Sacco, et al., 2019; Weetman, 2018). Residents of tiny houses discuss the physical moveability of the homes as a benefit which brings new forms of adaptability to their lives, as well as the alternative working arrangements that can be undertaken when living costs are dramatically reduced (Boeckermann, Kaczynski, and King, 2019). Since women undertake a majority of care work within families, the moveability of a tiny house can enable them to take their home to the cities which their family members live in, for example whilst they are caring for elderly parents. These findings mirror academic work in the area of critical geography and low impact developments more generally, where a similar emphasis on the importance of flexibility, interdependence, and holism is evident; qualities which would also generally be described as more feminine than masculine (Hechavarria, et al., 2013; Pickerill and Maxey, 2009).

One woman in her thirties living in South Africa spoke of the flexibility that their low cost of living allowed her and her partner to adopt in the co-parenting of their three young children:

> The biggest thing that we have gained from living in a tiny house comes back to time, because when [my partner] got a job he intentionally got didn't get a full-time job because he didn't need to get a full-time job. And we have small children and it was really important to us that we co-parent and that it not just be all on me looking after the kids, so I was working part-time and he was working kind of three-quarter time… so just having that flexibility in the job space to negotiate more has been great.

In this example, the financial flexibility offered by the tiny house enabled a flexible approach to caring responsibilities. The egalitarian sharing of childcare that this couple were able to negotiate since neither of them had to work full time speaks to a flexibilising of otherwise rigid gender norms surrounding motherhood and unpaid care work.

Childcare is not the only example of how tiny houses permit a flexibilisation of gendered social norms. Construction is a masculinised industry, and participants in my research have described the overt and covert sexism they have encountered in the timber yard or the DIY shop by men who undermine their choice of timber or decision to build their roofs themselves rather than hiring a 'professional'. April, a woman in her late twenties living in the USA told this story: "I get into that fight quite a bit at the hardware store. Like, they'll just try to mansplain something and say 'well the guy who's doing this will know', and I'm like *I'm* the guy. Like I'm, *I'm doing it*" (italics added for emphasis).

Rachel, a researcher in her mid-forties living in Portugal expands on some of the nuances of being a female in a traditionally masculinised environment:

> You know, as a woman stepping into a masculine world it's hard, and trying to learn these skills and modify and adapt to work in that environment. But with a very non-traditional building like a tiny house then there's something about making that transition and being that person which is kind of challenging but extremely rewarding. So, the more people that seem to be able to recognize that there's value not just living in a tiny house, but getting involved in its construction and being part of that world is more than just a lifestyle, it feels like more of a bigger identity shift.

Saldanha (2008), drawing from Hetherington (1997), writes on how heterotopias can induce alternative social orderings, in this case, the knowledgeable construction worker is female and the shop assistant serving her is male. Likewise, Wilks and Quinn (2016) use two examples of music festivals to analyse how heterotopias can invert the mundane or taken for granted social order of the world outside. What women building tiny houses shows is that "Architecture is more than a representation; it is a lived, evolving space that is shaped (and made meaningful) through the everyday practices of those using it" (Pickerill, 2016, p. 20).

The critical lens of heterotopia permits a consideration of women-built tiny houses as working to transform interconnections between people, space, and culture. Wilks and Quinn write on the ways in which this triumvirate approach of considering social and cultural capital alongside heterotopia enables a "deeper understanding of the nature of celebration" in their examples of music festivals (2016, p. 23). Wilks and Quinn go on to analyse festivals as "other spaces" (2016, p. 24) and point out how one of the principal functions of a heterotopia is to subvert the spaces around them, specifically the relational modes normalised in the non-heterotopic sites. The tiny house tessellates into this rubric in interesting ways because, on the one hand, they can be assessed as a space which represents the normalised imaginings of the home as a discrete four walled dwelling, compartmentalised by how each area is used, for example, sleeping, cooking, washing. In other words, tiny houses reflect the dominant ideal of a free-standing owner-occupied home surrounded by a garden. At the same time, tiny houses contest hegemonic beliefs about what a home is and could be. Their diminutive size casts aspersions on how much space a person needs to live in and be comfortable and fulfilled. Their relative inexpense inverts the typical self-build story by questioning the 'Grand Designs' white middle-class ownership of the self-build narrative. The affordability of tiny houses and their ease of construction suggests that in comparison to traditional routes to home ownership, tiny houses may provide a more democratic option which opens the possibility of home ownership to more people.

Fiona, a young black single-mother in Florida explained to me that her living costs had reduced from $1,500 to $550 per month. She was able to use inheritance from the passing of her mother to buy and own her tiny home outright, an option which would not be possible for traditional dwellings in Florida because of how expensive they are. The reduction in her cost of living had a cascade of benefits in the rest of her life, including allowing her to leave her full-time job in order to care for her daughter:

> I quit my job. I found it really hard to work full-time and I really wanted to raise my kid because my mom had to support four kids and my dad was there, but he didn't work. So I watched her just like work like a dog, and we didn't get that family feeling growing up and I really wanted to give my daughter that. And I was seeing her maybe an hour a day when I was working full time, and I was like this is not it, so I quit. And because my cost of living is so low I can live off my savings.

One significant way in which tiny houses can be seen to perform heterotopic functions is via a simultaneous confirmation and refutation of neoliberal ideals about self-sufficiency and the dominant social messaging about the supremacy of owner-occupation (Colombini, 2019; Hoolachan, et al., 2017). On the one hand, the tiny house model appears to champion the individualisation of social life and social problems that is one of the hallmarks of neoliberal ideology. The tiny house movement showcases and celebrates individuals who have wrought an individual solution to a structural problem, and in so doing, some argue, leave the structural forces of neoliberalism unchallenged. On the other hand, many tiny house residents openly reject the 'rat race' of hustle culture and state their intention to work less and to consume less; both outcomes which undermine and disempower the neoliberal regime by deprioritising transactional market interactions.

The women I have spoken to in my research often describe their experience of building and/or living in their tiny houses as expanding their sense of freedom and agency. Distancing themselves from the financial obligations and risks associated with rent and mortgage payments opens new realms of possibility for them that were not viable previously. Such freedoms include the freedom to change jobs for something more meaningful but less well-paid, being able to change their geographical location easily due to their tiny homes being built on a moveable trailer base, and being able to choose to live without a partner. The link between tiny houses and a sense of freedom has been echoed in existing literature although it has not focussed specifically on women (Boeckermann, Kaczynski, and King, 2019; Shearer and Burton, 2019). Despite the commonly reported link between tiny houses and an expanded sense of agency for their inhabitants, Foucault (1984) argues that nothing material can be described as functionally liberatory because liberation only exists in the form of action. In other words, tiny houses cannot themselves be emancipatory, but how people use them can be.

Jade, a teacher in her early thirties living in South Carolina pointed out that whilst tiny houses are sustainable and emancipatory in some ways, they also bring with them specific constraints:

> My partner and I have talked about if we ever want to foster or adopt, that's not possible with a tiny house. You can't foster a kid who doesn't have a room of their own. So, if we're talking about true sustainability and actually giving back to our community, I don't know if tiny houses are necessarily the solution.

As Jade's example highlights, tiny housing in and of itself cannot be described as liberatory because its abilities in this regard depend on the parameters surrounding it; how is it used? Who has access to it? What are the barriers to living in this way and who enforces these barriers? Despite this, the frequent references to freedom in the literature on tiny houses suggests that liberty is something which is important to the tiny house community and is something that is associated with tiny houses (Foreman, 2019; Williams, 2014).

The most fitting assessment of how heterotopias can work to create the experience of freedom, just as tiny houses can, is found in the following passage: "[architecture] can and does produce positive effects when the liberating intentions of the architect coincide with the real practise of people in the exercise of their freedom" (Foucault, 1984, pp. 245–6). In this case, the categories presented as separate by Foucault of 'architect' and 'people' here elide into one; the female builder–owner–occupant. Women-led self-build tiny houses, then, present an interesting example of the synergy of intentions that Foucault (1984) describes, by building and then using the tiny house as an expression of a desire for greater freedom, which leads to a lived experience of greater freedom. Julia, a software developer in her mid-thirties living in Alabama described the freedom she experienced in choosing to leave an abusive relationship to live in her car and then in a camper van:

> It was such a sense of freedom and relief. I would much rather struggle to find somewhere to sleep than be in a bad situation, a stable bed and

> stable environment and then just not be mentally okay and worry about my physical safety. So that was it, a big sense of freedom emotionally and physically.

Securing physical safety is a very basic form of freedom, and yet is one that many women do not enjoy. In a less desperate situation is Georgia, a 26-year-old artist in the Netherlands, who described how her tiny house allowed her the agency to pursue her creative process which was not possible before when she had to be in an office for long, regular hours: "A very big big plus is the freedom I get. Sort of time that I have to settle in my creativity, and nature like being able to live by the rhythm of the day." Carla, a business student in her early twenties lives in a van with her partner. Originally from Dublin, she explained to me their plans to drive from Ireland up through Europe to Milan. She described how, because they were living with their families before, they are not saving much money in comparison, but they do have a lot more agency:

> I think we haven't saved money because we weren't spending it to begin with. But what we want is to have as much freedom as possible. You know it's literally like we just can drive anywhere that we want. It's again that flexibility it's just gives you so many options.

One of the most interesting principles of heterotopias is that they can juxtapose in one place several spaces which seem incompatible. Tiny houses can be interpreted as being emblematic of both freedom and constraint. There is an inherent contradiction in the fact that a physically confined space can be a vehicle for greater freedom, and that shrinking one aspect of a person's life can expand another part. A fluxing compromise between the private domestic realm and public or communal domain underpins much of the juxtapositions to be encountered in a tiny house. Women are structurally penalised by the wage gap, the burden of unpaid labour, and the unaffordability of both renting and buying around the world. These forces arguably inform at least in part many women's choice to build and live tiny (McGinnity & Russell, 2008; Reiss, 2019). In this sense, the notion of choice is problematised, since it is only due to constrictive cultural forces of discrimination that women might be viewing the opportunity to live in a 30-m^2 trailer as a positive 'choice'. The following examples illustrate this tension.

Carla and her partner explained that because property in Dublin is so unaffordable, they never considered the option of renting, and certainly not of buying. Whilst they enjoy their lifestyle now, living in their van as young students, when they get to Milan they will be looking for a flat to stay in. Tamsin, a software developer in Minnesota described how she started considering tiny houses when her flatmates moved out and she could no longer afford her rent:

> Getting a one-bedroom apartment here rent is really expensive it's probably like twelve hundred to sixteen hundred dollars, so it just like wasn't gonna fit in my budget at all. And so I was like, well I just wanna be able to afford my life, you know? Everyone was talking about just how this is a way to afford your life. I didn't want to be in massive debt, and if I moved into an apartment that was twelve hundred dollars I was just gonna continuously get into credit card debt because 450 dollars was a struggle for me too some months as well you know.

These examples illustrate how using the concept of 'choice' in the life histories of women living in tiny houses could be construed as misleading, since viable alternatives were scarce. This critique returns us to the tension between structural and individual forces in the tiny house movement. It is better that tiny houses are available to women in housing need, but it would be better still if the housing need was addressed at the source. It is this mixing of several disquieting qualities that identify women's tiny houses as heterotopic sites; tiny houses allow a level of material comfort which would not otherwise be achievable for these women. However, tiny houses also do little to disrupt the cycles of entrenched power that sustain systems of harmful relational models which cause the housing crisis, wage stagnation, and ecocide.

The final principle we will explore is that heterotopias are spaces of illusion that draw attention to the illusory nature of all other spaces. Heterotopias are said to simultaneously reflect and disrupt the world surrounding them. It has been observed that "heterotopias allow us to both confront our illusions and to create new illusions of the utopias we cannot have" (Sudradjat, 2012, p. 30). It is possible that in female-led tiny houses, a space is created where inhabitants can confront the illusion that the modern woman can 'have it all'. To be more specific, tiny houses may facilitate a troubling of the neoliberal ideology that if a person is passionate enough, driven enough, then they can achieve their dreams regardless of the structural barriers in their way.

To pursue the theory offered by Sudradjat (2012), it may be possible that in creating these new spaces, a fresh illusion of a safe and creative agency away from male violence and financial oppression is forged. This assessment fits with those encountered in the literature on tiny houses which demonstrate consistent references to ideas of utopia, freedom and self-direction (Foreman, 2019; Williams, 2014). Difference to and interruption of the mundane status quo is common in heterotopic spaces, in other words heterotopias are places where "change and hybridisation are facilitated." (Sudradjat, 2012, p. 32). Further, they are locations which "interrupt the apparent continuity and normality of ordinary everyday space" (Dehaene and De Cauter, 2008, p. 3–4). Heterotopias are characterised above all as a space of possibility. Foucault's work has been interpreted as offering a liberating "means of escape from authoritarianism and repression." (Sudradjat, 2012, p. 32). This is perhaps exemplified in the case of the female-led self-build tiny house because heterotopias, like tiny houses, capacitate the affirmation of difference.

Tamsin described how although her father was initially sceptical about her decision to live in a tiny house, the quality of life that it offered her was so high that she went against his advice. In the end, he supported the project because he could see how happy Tamsin was:

My dad took it the hardest for sure. He's logical and I'm kind of a dreamer, you know? I'm jumping off the cliff, I'm full into my dreams and he's logical you know, he's an economics guy. And he first said "I'm not gonna help you", and I was like "well, that's okay."

Expanding on the theme of enlarging a sense of self-direction and capability through the build process, Alex, a 28-year-old in Missouri recalled a story about when her sister came to help out on the build and commented on her higher self-esteem:

> I was talking to myself out loud, and I just said something like "oh, that looks so good. I'm so awesome!" And my sister laughed. And she was like "wow, you just talk yourself up all the time now." And I was like "what do you mean?" And she was like "you're just over here telling yourself how capable you are, how good that looks, like look what you just did that's so awesome." And I was like oh yeah I guess I do do that now.

These changes in family dynamics and images of the self, as well as in financial situations and work life sum up to potentially significant examples of change and hybridisation being facilitated by the tiny house project (Sudradjat, 2012).

This chapter has outlined the core criteria that constitute both heterotopias and tiny houses, and has marshalled evidence to support the view that female-led tiny houses can be usefully understood through the lens of heterotopia. Expanding the legal availability of tiny houses has implications for social justice and human rights matters regarding ending gender-based violence, the elimination of poverty, and the reduction of reliance on fossil fuels. Whilst tiny houses are not the right solution for everyone, the speed and inexpense with which they can be built is worthy of consideration. In the context of a global 'shadow pandemic' of male violence against women, increasing gender inequality around the world, and a decrease in life expectancy for the poorest 10% of women in the UK, any spaces which provide an inversion of these appalling but entrenched social norms and patterns of relating warrants attention (UN Women, 2021; Reiss, 2019).

It is my hope that this chapter might lay the groundwork for further research into the life outcomes of women who are able to live in their own tiny homes. Collective agitation for the expansion of access to land, updated planning policy, and enhanced provision of financial products to support women in the construction or purchase of their tiny houses would benefit from the availability of quantitative and longitudinal data on the consequences for women's health, safety, wealth, education, and so on. Feminist urban planner Legacy et al. (2013) points out that city planning has been dominated by whiteness and maleness since its inception. The popularity of tiny houses among women speaks to the democratising potential they possess in enabling some reclamation of power. In her book *The Feminist City*, Leslie Kern points out that "traditional heteropatriarchal households are less common now than ever before and their numbers continue to decline" (Kern, 2020, p. 82). The analysis presented in this chapter of women-led tiny house builds as heterotopias can enhance our understanding of these patterns and help us to gain insight into why household dynamics are changing and how we might best support these metamorphoses.

References

Anderson-Dargatz, G., 2019. *Tiny House, Big Fix*, Orca Book Publishers.

Bares, V. et al., 2017. A Place for Tiny Houses. Exploring the Possibilities: Tiny House Planning Resource for Australia, 2017. Brisbane. www.tinyhousecompany.com.au/s/20170531-tiny-house-planning-resource_v1-0sml.pdf

Boeckermann, L.M., Kaczynski, A.T. & King, S.B., 2019. Dreaming big and living small: examining motivations and satisfaction in tiny house living. *Journal of Housing and the Built Environment*, 34(1), pp. 61–71.

Carras, M. 2019. PhD thesis. Available at: https://research-repository.st-andrews.ac.uk/bitstream/handle/10023/17821/MeganCarrasPhDThesis.pdf?sequence=3&isAllowed=y

Colombini, C., 2019. The rhetorical resistance of tiny homes: Downsizing neoliberal capitalism. *Rhetoric Society quarterly*, 49(5), pp. 447–469.

Dehaene, M. & De Cauter, L., 2008. *Heterotopia and the City: Public Space in a Postcivil Society*, Taylor & Francis Group.

Draucker, C.B., 2000. What is the meaning of sexual violence in the lives of women who have been sexually assaulted by men they knew well? *Western Journal of Medicine*, 173(1), pp. 41–41. http://dx.doi.org/10.1136/ewjm.173.1.41

Foreman, P., 2019. *A Tiny Home to Call Your Own: Living Well in Just-Right Houses*, New Society Publishers.

Foucault, M., 1984. Of other spaces: Utopias and heterotopias, architecture. *Mouvement/Continuité*, 1(9).

Hardoon, D., 2017. *An Economy for the 99%: It's time to build a human economy that benefits everyone, not just the privileged few*, Oxfam. Available at: http://hdl.handle.net/10546/620170

Harvey, D. & David Harvey, F., 2000. *Spaces of Hope*, University of California Press.

Harvey, David. 2000. *Spaces of Hope*. Edinburgh University Press. Available at: http://www.jstor.org/stable/10.3366/j.ctvxcrcz8.

Hechavarria, D.M. et al., 2013. Are women more likely to pursue social and environmental entrepreneurship? *Global Women's Entrepreneurship Research*. Available at: www.elgaronline.com/view/9781849804622.00016.xml

Hetherington, K., 1997. *The Badlands of Modernity: Heterotopia and Social Ordering*, Psychology Press.

Hoolachan, J. et al., 2017. "Generation rent" and the ability to "settle down": Economic and geographical variation in young people's housing transitions. *Journal of Youth Studies*, 20(1), pp. 63–78.

Johnson, P. 2012, Ways-Forward.pdf. *Heterotopian Studies.* Available at: www.heterotopiastudies.com/wp-content/uploads/2012/05/3.3-Ways-Forward.pdf

Kern, L., 2020. *Feminist City: Claiming Space in a Man-Made World*, Verso Books.

Legacy, C., Whitzman, C., Andrew, C., Klodawsky, F., Shaw, M. & Viswanath, K., 2013. *Building Inclusive Cities: Women's Safety and the Right to the City*, Routledge.

McGinnity, F. & Russell, H., 2008. *Gender Inequalities in Time Use: The Distribution of Caring, Housework and Employment among Women and Men in Ireland.* Economic and Social Research Institute.

McSpedon, C., 2019. Keeping count of women and girls killed by men. *AJN, American Journal of Nursing*, 119(10), pp. 65–67. http://dx.doi.org/10.1097/01.naj.0000586208.38831.46

Minton, A., 2017. *Big Capital: Who Is London For?*, Penguin.

Nationwide, 2020, House Price Calculator. Available at: www.nationwide.co.uk/about/house-price-index/house-price-calculator [Accessed February 15, 2021].

Office for National Statistics, 2016. Women Shoulder the Responsibility of "Unpaid Work." Available at: www.ons.gov.uk/employmentandlabourmarket/peopleinwork/earningsandworkinghours/articles/womenshouldertheresponsibilityofunpaidwork/2016-11-10 [Accessed March 29, 2021].

———. 2019. Earnings and Working Hours – Office for National Statistics. Available at: www.ons.gov.uk/employmentandlabourmarket/peopleinwork/earningsandworkinghours [Accessed January 29, 2020].

Pickerill, D.J., 2016. *Eco-Homes: People, Place and Politics*, Zed Books.

Pickerill, J. & Maxey, L., 2009. Geographies of sustainability: Low impact developments and radical spaces of innovation. *Geography Compass*, 3(4), pp. 1515–1539.

Reiss, S. 2019. A Home of Her Own, Housing and Women. Available at: https://wbg.org.uk/analysis/reports/a-home-of-her-own-housing-and-women/ [Accessed August 20, 2020].

Sacco, P.L. et al., 2019. Two versions of heterotopia: The role of art practices in participative urban renewal processes. *Cities*, 89, pp. 199–208.

Saldanha, A., 2008. Heterotopia and structuralism. *Environment & Planning A*, 40(9), pp. 2080–2096.

Shearer, H., 2018. *Tiny Houses: Planning for Affordability and Inclusion*. Academic Advisory Board, p. 7.

Shearer, H. & Burton, P., 2019. Towards a typology of tiny houses. *Housing, Theory and Society*, 36(3), pp. 298–318.

Smith, R., 2020. Gender Pay Gap in the UK – Office for National Statistics. Available at: www.ons.gov.uk/employmentandlabourmarket/peopleinwork/earningsandworkinghours/bulletins/genderpaygapintheuk/2020 [Accessed February 11, 2021].

Sudradjat, I., 2012. Foucault, the other spaces, and human behaviour. *Procedia – Social and Behavioral Sciences*, 36, pp. 28–34.

UK House Price Index. Available at: https://landregistry.data.gov.uk/app/ukhpi [Accessed February 15, 2021].

UN Women, 2021, The Shadow Pandemic: Violence against Women during COVID-19. Available at: www.unwomen.org/en/news/in-focus/in-focus-gender-equality-in-covid-19-response/violence-against-women-during-covid-19 [Accessed March 26, 2021]

Weetman, V.M., 2018. Resistance is fertile: Exploring tiny house practices in Australia. *Australian Planner*, 55(3–4), pp. 232–240.

Wilks, L. & Quinn, B., Linking Social Capital, Cultural Capital and Heterotopia at the Folk Festival. Available at: http://compaso.eu/wpd/wp-content/uploads/2016/07/Compaso2016-71-WilksQuinn.pdf

Williams, D., 2014. *The Big Tiny: A Built-It-Myself Memoir*, Penguin.

Conclusion

Summary and Core Arguments

This collection has examined the rise of shrinking living space across a wide set of contexts and typologies, and engaged with a range of concepts that seek to explain the intensification of these forms of housing and home. The book has taken a critical lens to the growing trend of living small – situating it within contemporary housing crisis conditions and questions of inequality and injustice. Although varied in their conceptual and empirical approaches to shrinking domesticities, the contributors convey four key interrelated observations:

Firstly, shrinking domesticities should be understood as embedded within contemporary practices and discourses that emphasise housing as a financial asset. Contributions such as Bergan and Dufty-Jones' and Kruth's chapters highlight that reducing domestic living space is often not a pragmatic decision based on heightened housing costs, reduced land availability and so on, nor an expression of freedom from neoliberal constraints, but rather a means for housing developers and investors to extrapolate even greater levels of capital, often at the expense of those who reside in these micro-homes. This can be the case even in regions where the public sector is still a major housebuilder, as Lilius, Friesenecker and Krankl emphasise in relation to Vienna and Helsinki. Indeed, we see in the above contributions how increasingly the interests of cities are aligned with those of capital, with many authorities adopting policies to encourage these new housing models. In short, we need to be mindful that micro-living functions as much within existing neoliberal housing markets and frameworks as it does outside of them.

Secondly, the collection asks us to pay attention to the ways in which shrinking domestic space is narrativised, and how this is crucial to understanding its growing influence. In particular, the promotion of shrinking domesticities as an aspirational lifestyle choice warrants more careful analysis by both academics and policymakers. Contributions by Durrant and Brill, Owen, and Meissner examine and challenge the ways in which micro-living is often positioned in relation to minimalism, degrowth, sufficiency

DOI: 10.4324/9781003173052-23

and the prioritisation of experiences over material things. Relatedly, in our chapter on *Nomadland*, we the editors question the predominantly positive portrayals of micro-living in relation to freedom. Together these contributions argue that such narratives threaten to obscure the structural causes of increased reliance on shrinking living space, such as the financialisation of housing, austerity policies and the decimation of public housebuilding. This is particularly pertinent given the emphasis placed on the relationship between reducing domestic space and environmentalism. Whilst Alexander and Shearer, Lütke and Elbracht, and Meissner's contributions note the truly sustainable potential of shrinking domestic space, in particular through the tiny house movement, they also ask us to critically examine the proposition that such lifestyle decisions are (a) often the product of diminished choice, and (b) often at odds with arguments around degrowth as consumption of tiny housing and its associated lifestyles continues to grow.

Thirdly, the collection emphasises the need for greater engagement with arguably the true experts on shrinking domesticities – the people living in these spaces. Despite being such a rapidly growing phenomenon, academic and policy engagement has tended to sideline the lived experiences of micro-living residents, and the ways in which they adapt to reduced domestic space. Chapters by Winther, Carras, and Wagner and Driessen in particular bring to light the need for greater understanding of the long-term implications of shrinking living space for everyday domestic practices and household life.

Finally, contributors map out the potential of shrinking domestic space to be truly radical. Through chapters such as Wilson's that explore the empowering qualities of women-led tiny housing, Lutz's investigation of cluster apartments accommodating non-normative household structures, and Pickerill, Barker and Wang's examination of tiny houses as conduits for social and environmental justice, the collection asks readers to critically consider the ways in which reduced living space might genuinely contribute to a better world through social, economic and environmental lenses.

Towards a Future Research Agenda

This collection has brought together cutting-edge research that critically examines the rise of shrinking domesticities. Together, the chapters present a range of empirical and conceptual contributions to the growing trend of living small, and provide a springboard for future areas of inquiry. Whilst it must be acknowledged that the collection does not provide a complete account of shrinking domesticities, it posits important questions that warrant greater attention in housing studies and social sciences scholarship. Here, we map out a future research agenda via three developing areas of scholarly interest that warrant further investigation.

Shrinking Domesticities beyond the Global North Context

Notable in their absence in this collection are examples and experiences of shrinking domestic space beyond the European, North American and Australasian context. We have observed a significant gap in academic literature that critically explores the issue of shrinking domestic space outside of the West. While there is a strong and growing body of critical scholarship on urban density in South and South-East Asia (see for example Chowdhury, 2020; Rao, 2007), focus tends to be mostly on topics such as transport infrastructure (e.g., Zhao, 2020) and maintenance (e.g., Tripathy and Carrière, 2020) rather than domestic density. Existing literature on micro-living outside of Western cities is often promotional in tone (see for example Pretorius, 2019), either neglecting to explore, or indeed celebrating, how shrinking domesticities can be co-opted by, complicit with, or a result of neoliberal housing priorities. In particular, there is little to no research focusing on the ways in which micro-living is being rebranded in the Majority World. This absence is particularly pertinent in the context of regions such as urban sub-Saharan Africa, South Asia and South America where growing interest in formally branded, glamourised forms of shrinking living space coexist with long histories of large-scale informal housing. In cities such as Johannesburg and Buenos Aires, new real estate concepts framing micro-apartments as aspirational are emerging while nearby informal iterations are being systematically disinvested, de-legitimised and marginalised (Scheba and Turok, 2020). Equally, the increasing rebranding of micro-living as aspirational rather than functional is important to consider in hyper-dense cities with long traditions of living small, such as Tokyo and Hong Kong.

While the largely Western focus here provides commonality and comparability across contributions and sections, this remit is not unproblematic. It arguably reinforces the colonising power of particular 'Global North' imaginaries of home, and deprives fruitful examinations of similarities and differences – socially, culturally and economically – between regions. A major future research agenda therefore centres on examination of the social, political, cultural and economic role of branded micro-living in non-Western contexts. There is a clear need to understand the shrinking of domestic space and its rebranding as an international phenomenon. Whilst that is a task beyond the scope of this book, it is something that we, the editors, seek to contribute to in future work through a series of seminars (funded by the Urban Studies Foundation) with colleagues at the Universities of Witwatersrand (Johannesburg), Tokyo and Buenos Aires in 2023.

Shrinking Domesticities and the Global Covid-19 Pandemic

Shrinking domestic space has inevitably taken on increased pertinence in the context of the Covid-19 pandemic and will undoubtedly be an integral area for future research. Important policy and academic research has highlighted the role of insufficient domestic space in increasing risk of transmission and severe illness from the virus (Butler, 2020; Tinson and Clair, 2020; Varshney and Adalbert, 2021). In such instances it is no exaggeration to argue that shrinking living space has contributed to the pervasiveness of the global pandemic. Alongside this, the impact of overcrowded and small living spaces on both physical and mental health has further revealed itself in the context of lives led increasingly at home. It will be important to expand this avenue of research, particularly in terms of the relationship between overcrowded housing, the pandemic and the growth of branded forms of micro-living.

The size of living space and comfort of possessions has also attained new value. As we have noted in other work, homes during periods of lockdown have had to expand in terms of their functionality, acting as offices, schools and leisure facilities at times when there has been literally nowhere else to go (Harris and Nowicki, 2020).The pandemic was initially characterised by mass exodus from urban areas, particularly among those with the financial privilege to access larger accommodation outside of the city. However, at the time of writing this appears to have been a somewhat temporary phenomenon. In fact, branded micro-living in some instances has become more popular than ever before. This is especially the case with tiny housing. For example, as part of research conducted with producers, sellers and managers of tiny housing in Austin, Texas, we found that demand had skyrocketed in the city and surrounding region by the end of 2020. Reasons for this appeared to be twofold. Firstly, and related to urban flight, participants' clients expressed a desire to leave the city for the surrounding countryside. Secondly, many cited financial difficulties resulting from job losses and other financial concerns due to the pandemic as the predominant reason behind their decision to 'go tiny'. These varied motives again elucidate the at times paradoxical relationship between shrinking domestic space and choice – a relationship complicated all the more by the pandemic. This is particularly prevalent in the urban context. On the one hand, the city has long been seen as a space where people are freer from the constraints of prescriptive societal ideals such as the nuclear family and heterosexual domesticity, and freer to engage in countercultural expression. On the other, the pandemic has foregrounded how other kinds of freedom are hindered by big cities; freedom to have more space and time for oneself and freedom from the financial pressures of small, expensive housing and high costs of living. Future research agendas are likely to examine how these second kinds of freedom in particular have been appreciated more during the pandemic and explore whether this has instigated long-lasting changes in imaginaries of what constitutes freedom and how it relates to urban micro-living.

Alongside this, we also posit that the relationship between shrinking domestic space, the pandemic and the digitisation of the home warrants exploration. This will build on a growing body of work that examines the home as a site of surveillance and control. Scholars such as Sophia Maalsen, Jathan Sadowski, Desiree Fields and Anna Jackman have explored the infiltration of digital surveillance, from smart appliances (Maalsen and Sadowski, 2019) to drone technologies (Jackman and Brickell, 2021) into our everyday domestic lives, and the growing role of digital platforms in the financialisation of housing (Fields, 2019). As our virtual and non-virtual worlds become increasingly enmeshed – a process catalysed by pandemic social distancing requirements – this line of inquiry is set to become an important site of expansion in studies of shrinking domestic space, and will be the focus of an upcoming special issue edited by Tim White, Sophia Maalsen and Dallas Rogers.

In sum, the impact of the pandemic on the future of shrinking domestic space, and the forms it will take, remain multifaceted and ultimately unclear. At the time of writing, the term 'post-pandemic' remains one relating to the future, as many parts of the world experience their worst outbreak of cases since the pandemic began. This constantly changing picture only strengthens the need for research that traces emerging patterns of shrinking domestic space in the long aftermath of Covid-19.

Shrinking Domesticities and Societal Structures

Finally, this collection has laid the groundwork for a future research agenda that forefronts the relationship between shrinking domesticities and societal structures across a wide range of scales, from transnational housing markets to individual decisions regarding home and family life. Collectively, the chapters in this volume have asked us to consider lived experience and political economy together in order to better understand the long-term political, social, cultural and economic implications of shrinking domestic space. Going forward, then, we invite scholars to further explore what the growing trend of living small might mean for society more widely. This is especially important in relation to particular demographic groups, for example families, retirees and comparisons of low-income and middle-class interpretations of shrinking domesticities. For many decades, if not centuries, narratives of housing and home have centred on nuclear family and Fordist labour models. Increasingly, these ways of living are changing, and housing and domestic life with it, but in ways that are fragmented and where the range of genuine choice is limited. One of these key changes, shrinking domestic space, is not just responding to, but also reshaping people's life choices, and life courses – for example how and when they have families, their expectations of what constitutes reasonable living standards and what retirement will look like.

At its worst, the promotion of shrinking domestic space reinforces injustice and normalises precarity. It is a compensatory tactic that, rather than addressing crises, simply repackages what we expect from our domestic lives (Harris, 2020a, 2020b). This rebrands a global economic system that profits from reduced living standards as an exercise in freedom from housing norms. And yet, at its best, shrinking domesticity can present us with genuine alternatives to failing housing markets and exploitative neoliberal systems, reworking our expectations of domestic life in ways that incorporate the reduction of household carbon footprints, subvert normative expectations of the lifecourse (i.e. celebrating options beyond the heteronormative nuclear family) and encourage us, particularly in the Global North context, to challenge our reliance on hyper-consumption.

In sum, then, the growing trend of living small has big implications for the future of housing, and societal structures more widely. It is the outcomes of those implications that remain to be seen, and we argue should be central to future social sciences scholarship on housing and home.

References

Butler, P. (2020). Poor Housing Linked to High Covid-19 Death Rate in London Borough. *The Guardian*. Available online: www.theguardian.com/world/2020/aug/17/poor-housing-linked-high-covid-19-death-rate-london-boroughbrent

Chowdhury, R. (2020). Density as urban affect: The enchantment of Tokyo's crowds, *Urban Geography*, 41(10): 1277–1283.

Fields, D. (2019). Automated landlord: Digital technologies and post-crisis financial accumulation. *Environment and Planning A: Economy and Space*, 0308518X19846514.

Harris, E. (2020a). "The Compensatory Mechanism: Cultures for Crisis Times" *New Formations*, 99: 66–87,

Harris, E. (2020b). *Rebranding Precarity: Pop-Up Culture as the Seductive New Normal*. London: Zed Books.

Harris, E. & Nowicki, M. (2020). "GET SMALLER?" Micro-Living in the age of Covid-19, *Geography Directions*. Available online: https://blog.geographydirections.com/2020/06/01/get-smaller-micro-living-in-the-age-of-covid-19/

Jackman, A. & Brickell, K. (2021). Everyday droning: towards a feminist geopolitics of the drone-home, *Progress in Human Geography*. Online first.

Maalsen, S. & Sadowski, J. (2019). The smart home on FIRE: amplifying and accelerating domestic surveillance, *Surveillance & Society*, 17(1/2): 118–124.

Pretorius, S. (2019). Market demand for micro-apartments among small families in Gauteng (Doctoral dissertation).

Rao, V. (2007). Proximate distances: the phenomenology of density in Mumbai. *Built Environment*, 33(2): 227–48.

Scheba, A. & Turok, I. (2020). Informal rental housing in the south: dynamic but neglected. *Environment and Urbanization*, 32(1): 109–132.

Tinson, A. & Clair, A. (2020). Better housing is crucial for our health and the COVID-19 recovery, *Health Foundation*. Available online: https://www.health.org.uk/publications/long-reads/better-housing-is-crucial-for-our-health-and-the-covid-19-recovery

Tripathy, P. & Carrière, D. (2020). Filtering density and doing the maintenance work. *Urban Geography*, 41(10): 1–9.

Varshney, K. & Adalbert, J. (2021). Overcrowded housing increases risk for COVID-19 mortality: an ecological study, *Health Services Research* 56(2): 75–76.

Zhao, Y. (2020). Folding Beijing in Houchangcun Road, or, the topology of power density. *Urban Geography*, 41(10): 1–13.

Index

Note: Tables are shown in **bold type** and figures are in *italics*. Endnotes consist of the page number followed by "n" and the note number i.e. 251n1 refers to note number 1 on page 251.

For Product Safety Concerns and Information please contact our EU
representative GPSR@taylorandfrancis.com
Taylor & Francis Verlag GmbH, Kaufingerstraße 24, 80331 München, Germany

www.ingramcontent.com/pod-product-compliance
Ingram Content Group UK Ltd.
Pitfield, Milton Keynes, MK11 3LW, UK
UKHW022317250926
475702UK00046B/904

* 9 7 8 0 3 6 7 7 6 4 4 6 3 *